Productive Software
Test Management

Productive Software Test Management

Michael W. Evans

A Wiley-Interscience Publication

JOHN WILEY & SONS
New York   Chichester   Brisbane   Toronto   Singapore

Library of Congress Cataloging in Publication Data:

Evans, Michael W.
    Productive software test management.

    "A Wiley-Interscience publication."
    Bibliography: p.
    Includes index.
    1. Computer programs—Testing. 2. Electronic data
processing departments—Management. I. Title.
QA76.6.E9784 1984   001.64′2   84-3585
ISBN O-471-88311-5

Printed in the United States of America

10 9 8 7 6 5 4 3 2 1

Preface

The trend in data processing application is toward distributed systems composed of modular elements linked through hardware and software to provide unified functional support. While such system organization provides economies in software development and maintenance, there are significant penalties in both productivity and overall project effectiveness for poorly managed, unplanned software testing. Though these penalties can be paid in any project area, the project costs are especially excessive for problems encountered during software test.

Costs include:

1. Inefficient manpower utilization.
2. Unreliable systems.
3. Redundant testing.
4. Poor phasing of resources and responsibility.
5. Increasing confusion during testing over time.

As systems become more complex and the complexity of interactions between components increases, the testing issues become acute, often impacting or precluding overall project success.

This book guides the software manager through the software testing morass. The book will identify the individual components and test levels that must be integrated into a cohesive structure, and outline how the testing program is to be planned and managed. It will identify tools, techniques, and methodologies that must be incorporated if testing is to succeed.

The book offers solutions to the recurring management problems characteristic of software testing, which invariably turn into crises during the later stages of a software project. Problems all center around a single theme: The project planners have not adequately estimated what will occur during the testing period and cannot control resources and activities during this critical implementation stage.

This book provides the software manager with an integrated approach to managing software and controlling the project during test. Using our previous book, *Principles of Productive Software Management,* as a basis, this book expands the management planning and control disciplines into the areas required by software testing and removes much of the uncertainty associated with this phase of the program.

MICHAEL W. EVANS

Morgan Hill, California
April 1984

Acknowledgments

This book is based on the experiences of the author gathered through a variety of technical and management test situations. The experience gained during these years has proved invaluable and, hopefully, is portrayed in the chapters that follow.

There are too many individuals who contributed ideas which have been used in project situations and have indirectly contributed to the book to mention singly. However, several corporations and individuals deserve a special thanks.

I would like to thank the Expertware Corporation for its patience, understanding, and support without which this book would not have been possible.

Also, I would like to acknowledge and thank Michael A. Blackledge and Walter G. Murch, each of whom worked for more than 20 years in the U.S. Air Force and now, as retired officers, are employed as software and command and control specialists by Sandia National Laboratories and Science Applications, Inc., respectively. Many of their ideas have been incorporated into the manuscript.

I would like to provide special recognition to Lieutenant Colonel Howard Wendt of the U.S. Air Force, who had the fortitude to review the final manuscript. I would also like to thank Gil Levean of the Defense Communications Agency, whose professional review greatly enhanced the quality of the manuscript.

Two sources deserve special recognition: Louis Picinich of Expertware, who reviewed the manuscript at length, and Jack Bond of the National Security Agency, whose encouragement and review of the manuscript was invaluable.

I would like to thank Pam Piazza of the Mellonics Division of Litton Industries and Jack Munson of the Systems Development Corporation who encouraged me during development of the manuscript.

I would finally like to thank those whose support in production of the manuscript made the generation of text possible. My wife, Charlotte, who typed the manuscript from my chicken scratch, my sons Michael Jr., and Robert, who performed small tasks essential to the production of the book, and Scott, who helped with the art.

I would like to also give thanks to Jim Gaughan of John Wiley & Sons, without whose encouragement there would be no book.

M.W.E.

Contents

1 Introduction

Testing, the backend of the project, must be planned for from the beginning of the development effort in parallel with the design and implementation tasks, and it must be the focus of all project activities.

The software manager glumly walks into the conference room to face the assembled staff of supervisors and senior technical personnel. The state of the group is universal fatigue and clearly evident general depression— brought about by overwork and frustration. As the manager faces the group, their eyes turn to him for guidance. What has happened? Despite all the work and staff commitment, the system that has been so laboriously developed through the sacrifices of so many has failed because of an inability on the part of the project team to integrate the various software components into an operational configuration and to demonstrate its functional integrity. The money has been spent, the schedule has been exhausted, and the project is far from complete. People working on the project are at the breaking point. Everyone in the room asks the same questions: What happened? What could we have done differently? Where do we go from here?

THE TESTING CRISIS—RECOGNIZING THE CAUSE

This all-too-common scenario has been replayed on both small and large software projects, for simple applications as well as for complex applications. The project problems leading to this dilemma are many. They are rooted in the manager's inability to deal effectively with the many small crises that plague the early stages of the software project.

A poor project start causes a manager to lose control of the project during the grueling middle stages of design and code, which significantly affects productivity during the later stages of test and integration. The allocation and commitment of resources to the various test levels is confused and ineffective, and the flow of data and responsibility becomes confused throughout.

1

During initial periods of the project, the software manager had been too concerned with critical short-term milestones, forgetting that if the project was to succeed in the long term then a structure for testing had to be laid out from the beginning. The manager should never be too busy to support essential technical and management test planning, even though this planning had no apparent short-term payoff. By not planning early, the manager sowed the seeds of disaster because he had not recognized the long lead times required to plan, implement, and structure an effective test and integration program or to develop the assortment of tools, techniques, and methodologies essential for integration and test success.

What happened in this hypothetical project that prevented the manager from recognizing and dealing with the problems of the project?

Initially the problem symptoms were subtle; creeping schedule milestones and poor productivity early in the project. As the project entered the early testing stages, the results of the inadequate early planning became evident. The manager had failed to define the means by which qualified software units were to be controlled and integrated into software builds, and had not defined the environment essential for success. The further the project went into testing without correcting the problems of management, the less productive the project became.

As a result, the process of test and integration became increasingly inefficient. As more and more software became available, the problems became increasingly acute, ultimately affecting all areas of the project and precluding meaningful progress.

As the test problem reached crisis proportions, management efforts to deal with the problems of poor testing became more intense. The symptoms of poor test planning—unacceptable schedule performance, cost overruns, technical shortfalls, and inadequate resource availability—necessitated unplanned responses. Crisis management became the rule within the project, totally supplanting the sense of order and project structure. Meaningful project progress and focus was lost, resulting in a testing environment, project structure, and data and technical flow unable to sustain even the simplest project tasks. Software schedule progress slowed, reaching a point where no progress was made toward achieving the basic objective of the project: development of an operational software capability responsive to the needs and expectations of the user.

Avoiding the Problem—What Could Have Been Done

The software manager could have avoided this scenario by early project emphasis on testing. The correct emphasis would have resulted in plans, schedules, and budgets for the implementation of the project test. Integration requirements properly implemented could have established a smooth, controlled flow of data and responsibility, clear, baselined requirements, controls over resources, data, and the accomplishment of work, and a sustained project focus toward test milestones. This preplanned and controlled application of resources, technical methodologies, and tools and techniques would have assured that the testing structure was consistent with other project areas and was tailored to the characteristics of the project.

The software manager could have established the basic test and integration and structure criteria as part of the initial software project planning. The manager could have defined the basic test environment in sufficient detail to support all test levels; he or she could have defined data products and project review requirements.

From this initial planning, the manager could detail the project testing requirements to be satisfied in the context of the overall project structure; the various testing activities to be phased, scheduled, controlled, and supported; the resource requirements for each level of testing, and a plan for resource application and monitoring. From this secondary level of test planning the software manager could then schedule and budget for the application of resources required for software testing and implement a project structure consistent with the needs, technical characteristics, and requirements of the project. The manager could have then initiated a series of parallel project activities to implement the test environment and structure.

This early planning approach would have accomplished four essentials for project success:

1. The activities of the project would be focused from the outset on the most critical and complex stage of the project, software test, and integration.

2. Sufficient project time and resources would be scheduled to facilitate development of the long lead-time requirements of testing.

3. Resources and project controls would be planned for and applied to the project in accordance with the testing requirements and anticipated needs of the project.

4. Common project crises occurring during the test phases would be identified and anticipated, and the associated productivity impacts would be avoided.

In our hypothetical project the manager should have planned for testing. He should have rigorously implemented the planned testing environment. Had this been done the project would have experienced a smooth flow of data, an effective application of resources, and a testing structure consistent with the needs and requirements of the application. Instead, testing was an uncontrolled, confused attempt at meeting project milestones. The manager was beset by general unwarranted optimism not justified by project realities, continuous resource shortfalls, and a lack of project understanding concerning the importance of early test planning. These all resulting in poor test development productivity. This requirement for early planning seems obvious; however, it proves to be a common and catastrophic cause of software project problems and poor productivity.

Test and integration milestones must be the focus of all project planning and support. The early project planning specifications and controls must detail the most demanding period of the project, test, and integration.

Resource requirements for testing must be assigned early to allow for the identification and specification of critical testing parameters and definition of long lead-time items essential for testing success. These long lead test requirements—tool and test case development, hardware and simulation development, personnel acquisition, and so forth—must be translated into a project environment which assures the smooth flow of project data and responsibility and facilitates the effective transition of project effort into the test phases of the program. Finally, test plans must be developed and published early and then maintained as project requirements change.

Throughout the period of software development, the software manager must assure that the project testing focus is maintained. The test planning and test development requirements must be integrated fully into the project structure in accordance with documented plans and requirements of the project.

Finally, the software manager must ensure that the individual test levels which are required for development of an operational system configuration are defined, the relationships between them clearly identified, and the data interfaces and controls specified, implemented, and enforced.

This book provides an ordered set of steps for planning, managing, and controlling test. The software project environment used as a model for the book, although representative of a large segment of the medium- to large-scale software development is certainly not a universal model. The testing environment described in the book, when tailored to other models, will prove equally effective. This book addresses the software test problem from the aspect of management as well as providing a description of the "how to's" of software testing. It serves as a guidebook for the software test manager.

The remaining chapters deal with the problems of testing management. The book has been written for managers responsible for the test and integration of software; software personnel concerned with planning, controlling, or working within a software project having a test component; and customer, quality assurance, technical and management personnel, who must interface with software test management in a project situation.

2 Test Requirements Identification

Software test and integration is the period of the project when poorly defined project requirements, inadequate systems engineering and support, and ineffective project management and control practices must be addressed and resolved if the project is to succeed.

As illustrated in Figure 2.1, a typical software development project has five primary segments. These project segments are a blending of management, technical, and support activities which occur in parallel throughout the life of the project. They give focus to the project and ensure that project requirements are anticipated and reflected in the design, code, and test requirements of the project. Early planning and implementation of tools, techniques, and project methodologies facilitate the coordination, implementation, and monitoring activities which are components of the project environment. This early planning will ensure that predictable crises and adverse productivity impacts are anticipated and avoided.

The development and implementation of test plans and test support activities are major elements of the development process. They span all development phases and are primary determinants of productivity and ultimate project success.

The initial test activities must be accomplished very early in the project, prior to specification of the technical and support requirements. During these early project stages, the specific levels of testing are defined. Project plans for managing and controlling each level must be determined, documented, and implemented. Completion of these early test activities results in an integrated set of plans and specifications that serve as the basis for defining the specific tools, techniques, and methodologies to be applied to the test implementations. These are documented in the Software Development Plan.

5

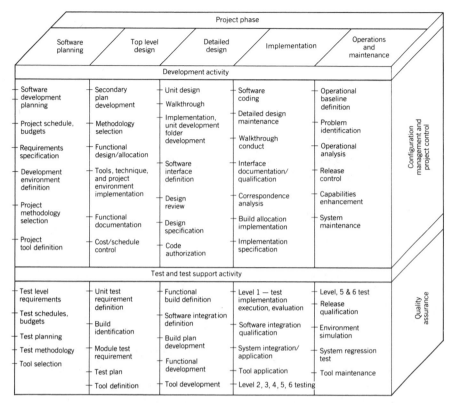

Figure 2.1   Software project segments

The second phase of test planning occurs in parallel with the derivation of the functional design of the software. During this phase of test planning the generic testing requirements defined in the early planning stages are translated into specific requirements at each test level; detailing how the test is to be accomplished, controlled, and supported. Completion of the second phase of test planning results in a specification of requirements for each level of test.

As illustrated in Figure 2.2, implementation of the test plan should result in a structured flow of data and responsibility through all levels of test and integration. At the first level, the module level, the implementation of the smallest element of development, normally the module, is evaluated. This testing level is usually conducted by the development staff and verifies that the module compiles without error. This test level is the first check that the module has been developed in accordance with project standards and conventions. The results of module testing are documented in the Programmer's Notebook component of the Unit Development Folder (UDF). In project environments not using UDFs as a project tool, an analogous documentation component is needed to define module and unit test re-

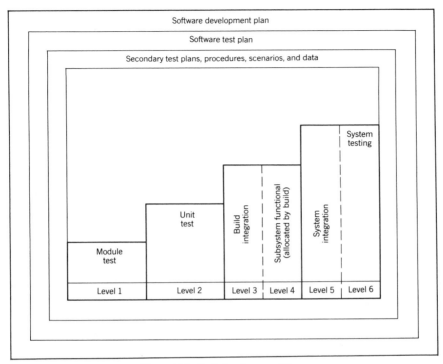

Figure 2.2 Test structure and flow

quirements. Even at the lowest levels, unplanned and undocumented testing is a waste of critical project resources.

At the second level of software testing, unit level testing, individually qualified modules are integrated into a unit configuration. A unit is a logical grouping of modules, normally one to ten, which support an identifiable, traceable software function or group of related functions. At the unit level, modules are integrated in a hierarchical fashion tracking the execution sequence of the software within the unit. Units are qualified in two aspects. The first verifies that the implementation of the unit is in accordance with the design and that all execution paths through the software execute reliably. This testing is extremely critical since it is the only time in the test program where this detailed analysis is possible. The second component of unit testing validates that the unit, as implemented, satisfies its allocated functional, performance, specified interface, and performance requirements. Unit tests are conducted by the development staff and are planned and documented in the UDF. At the completion of unit testing and approval at a walkthrough, the unit is released for software integration.

It is at this point that software is placed under project level configuration management and control. The unit design, code, and test information as defined in the UDF is baselined after successful completion of the various levels of software walkthroughs. After control procedures are instituted, the development organization may only make changes to controlled software after project level approval of the proposed modification. The quality assurance organization may serve as the "gatekeeper," reviewing the results of the unit test walkthroughs and authorizing the inclusion of the software into the Program Support Library.

At the third level of testing, software integration testing, qualified units are integrated into software builds for functional and interface testing. Builds are logical subsets of the overall software capability. They are selected because of schedule and functional compatability. Identification of components for individual builds must be consistent with schedule projections and compatible with the functional design of the software. As a prerequisite to this level of testing, early planning of build structures and content is essential. As with unit testing, builds are integrated in a hierarchical fashion, tracking the execution sequence of the software. During this testing, qualified units are integrated into an operational configuration; data relationships and internal execution characteristics, including performance benchmarks, are verified against the software design; and internal execution sequences and support characteristics are verified. Build testing should be conducted by an independent organization or team familiar with the overall software design. Ideally this team has representation from the software system engineers who defined the design initially. Build testing is conducted using versions of the software formally controlled by the project through configuration management. These releases are generated formally by the project library and documented in Version Description Documents (VDD). All problems uncovered are documented and corrections are formally tracked and controlled. Corrections made to controlled software components require qualification at module and unit test levels through informal regression testing prior to use in a level 3 configuration.

Build test requirements are documented in Build Test Plans and Build Test Folders (BTF). The Build Test Plan documents the build test configuration, test methods to be followed, tools to be used, procedures to be executed, criteria for completion, and test results.

The Build Test Folder is analagous to the Unit Development Folder. It is a central place for collecting and documenting the test requirements, procedures, scenarios, and test data for each build, describing the configuration of the build through Version Description Documents (VDDs). The BTF will provide a schedule for development, execution, and completion of each test case in the build, the documented test results, and the notes, action items, and approvals for each Build Test Review. At the Build Test Review the manager certifies that the build was completed in accordance with project requirements and the results are properly documented in the BTF.

The final build is a fully integrated software subsystem executing in a controlled test environment.

At the fourth level of software testing, software subsystem testing, the integrated builds are qualified against functional requirements allocated to software subsystems. A subsystem is a major component of the software system defined by functional completeness, hardware support, testability considerations, and interface characteristics. Where the previous test levels were concerned with evaluating internal aspects of the software subsystem execution, this test level looks at the software from an external perspective. This test level is planned, executed, and evaluated by an independent test team that has not participated in the software design or implementation. The test team should develop all test plans and specifications exclusively from system functional, performance, and interface specifications.

This independent test team is concerned with software functional qualification. The team should report to the software manager at the same level as the development and software systems engineering organizations. The team should have responsibility for functional test budgets, schedules and performance of all level 4 testing. This team should be independent from the development and integration teams to provide an independent and objective look at the functional integrity of the software.

When problems are found at this level, or at level 3 test levels, the problem should be documented on a Software Problem Report (SPR) and processed through software configuration management. Before being used in a level 3 or 4 test configuration, software must undergo a regression test at level 2, selected previously run level 3 and 4 test cases (depending the level at which the problem was found), and must be qualified using tests specifically designed to integrate and demonstrate the integrity of the fix.

The tests are driven, to the maximum extent possible, from data external to the system provided from a controlled, reproduceable data source. The status of the functional tests is retained in the BTF; however the details of the testing requirements are not. As with build integration testing, functional testing uses formally controlled and documented software configurations. Completion of the final functional build is a full qualification of the software subsystem.

The fifth level of software testing integrates qualified software subsystems into an operational system configuration. These tests are in two parts. The first is to qualify the internal software system characteristics against design specifications, data requirements, control interactions between the executing subsystems and the internal integrity of the integrated software system. These tests should be conducted in a simulated system environment. They are planned, executed, and evaluated by system engineering personnel familiar with system design and the role of software in the system configuration. The tests are documented in a system level test plan and use controlled, documented software configurations. Completion of these tests qualify the software for the second part of the level 5 integration. This initial stage of level 5 testing is an extremely critical stage of integration. Most often the problems uncovered through this testing occur due to interface errors—misunderstandings, inaccurate specifications, incomplete design, and inaccurate implementation for specifications. At the previous test levels the interfaces between internal software components are exercised and qualified. If the previous test levels are properly conducted these level 5 tests focus on the intersubsystem software interfaces.

The second part of level 5 testing takes an integrated software configuration and integrates it with the system hardware. These tests should exercise each of the major hardware and software interfaces using a predefined test set. If properly planned, the system integration tests conducted at level 5 should be incremental, phased to the level 3 and 4 build test schedules. This allows the incremental addition of system capability over a long period of time rather than a single, one-shot integration of a full system configuration.

At system testing, or level 6, the software is operationally qualified both from a system requirements standpoint and with the actual system hardware. The tests are executed using qualified, controlled, and documented software and hardware configurations and live, reproduceable, and controlled data sources. All problems are formally documented and tracked. Corrections are made by the software organization and regression tested and qualified prior to integration into the test configuration. The amount and type of regression testing is determined by the project level review of the problem and recommended correction. The test requirements are documented in the system level test plan.

Under this test structure, three fundamental rules of software testing should be adhered to:

1. There is never any more than one unqualified test object in a test configuration at the current level.
2. The hierarchical levels of the software are sufficiently limited to allow the controlled execution of software at the lowest levels in the hierarchy.
3. All simulated or actual data, software, and test materials used during testing are preplanned, controlled, documented, and reproduceable to ensure that testing results are valid and repeatable.

THE TESTING PROBLEM

During the test and integration stages the software project is hostage to the quality and effectiveness of the previous project activities. Problems which would have seemed small if encountered earlier in the development cycle may have major impact on the project in terms of project success, technical, cost, and schedule performance, and the reliability and quality of the software system if encountered during the software test.

How many software managers have been told late in the project, when budgets, schedules, and resources have been depleted, that problems have been found requiring significant time and resources to correct?

The software manager finds himself or herself on the horns of an unresolvable dilemma. On the one hand, the manager has to maintain schedules and budgets while, on the other, he or she has no control over the magnitude or complexity of the technical problems being found or the resources required to correct them. The manager has lost control over the technical commitments required to satisfy project goals and objectives.

In order to minimize project exposure during test and integration, and to lessen technical, cost, and schedule impacts, early project emphasis must center on the technical and administrative tasks required during testing. Project planning, technical and project support facilities, and technical activities must be consistent with the rigorous demands of testing.

As illustrated in Figure 2.3, this requirement for early project focus towards testing is required because of the nature of the data explosion in the software project environment.

Early in the development, the project is required to control a small, manageable quantity of data expressed as requirements and interface specifications. These requirements are reasonably static, not undergoing frequent or substantial modification. The software manager and staff may have found

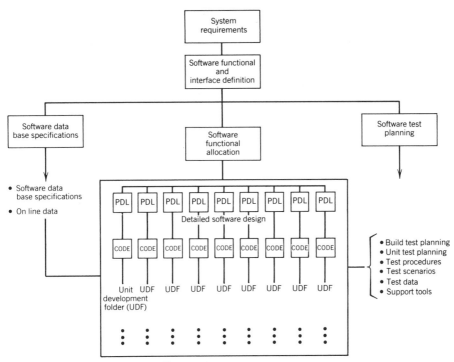

Figure 2.3   Data explosion

that even with poor, almost ineffective configuration control procedures the integrity of the data may be maintained.

From these basic requirements, the software project will define a set of software functional, interface, and operational requirements upon which the software design is to be based. The amount and complexity of the data to be controlled by the project has increased substantially, causing the manual and ineffective control practices to be cumbersome and ineffective. This data, once defined, is reasonably static, not requiring frequent or significant change.

There is, however, an explosion of information as the project moves through the design, code, and test phases of development. In a short period of time the amount of data that must be produced and controlled by the project increases by an order of magnitude. Unless planned for, this data explosion can catch the project without sufficient controls, discipline, and support facilities to manage the process of development. The data explosion continues throughout the remainder of the development and, unless dealt with effectively, results in project chaos.

A second problem that must be dealt with early is the long lead time associated with planning, implementation, and application of tools, test data, and project controls essential to testing success. The development of these essential components of the test environment must be accomplished in parallel with the technical aspects of design and coding. They must be available when needed by the project if project productivity is to be maintained. A late development start of these items virtually assures that the components will not be available in time to avoid test and development impacts.

Planning for Integration and Test

The process of software testing should be a structured flow of data and responsibility through all six levels of test and integration.

In a software project environment, the period of test and integration should be the most productive and technically challenging segment of the development cycle. During this period, a well-run project is characterized by high staff motivation, clearly defined project goals and objectives, a rigorous application of project controls, and a structured flow of data and responsibility as the software transitions through the six levels of testing. In this project environment, the atmosphere is electric. Adequate resources are available when needed, personnel vie for access to test facilities at all hours of the day and night, and individual convenience is secondary to the needs of the project. System releases are well documented and rigorously qualified, outstanding problems clearly identified and corrections made and tracked in accordance with project procedures. Documentation is current with the system releases. Budgets, schedules, and project performance are the primary motivators of the technical, management, and support segments of the project staff. And the productivity and success of the project is the concern of all project personnel.

Contrast this with a project experiencing difficulty during testing. In this project environment the flow of data is inefficient and unclear, project responsibility for the planning and implementation of each test level is unclear or overlapping, and resources required for test support are not available as needed. These features result in project delays and development stoppages until adequate support is found. The staff has no clear understanding of what is expected and required of them. The offices do not fill until late in the morning and they empty early in the afternoon. Schedules, budgets, milestones, and project goals and objectives are secondary motivators, less important to project personnel than personal convenience and short-term avoidance of project commitment or conflict. Software releases are loosely defined and poorly qualified and problems found in the software are ignored, lost, or forgotten.

The differences between these two scenarios lie in the ability of the software manager to effectively plan for all phases of testing and to translate these plans into a productive test structure within the project environment. In a productive project environment these plans were defined early when sufficient time was available to develop essential tools, techniques, methodologies, and project procedures. The activities which coordinated and controlled each level of the test program were preplanned and orchestrated through the software manager. The flow of data throughout each test level and between organizational boundaries was clearly defined. There was a clear delineation of specific technical and management responsibility for each testing data product, level of test, and support function. There was a rigorously enforced structure of project reviews and audits which qualified software and project data for test application. Through planning, the project technical and support functions were integrated with the testing activities. The thrust of the project was focused and channeled towards the test and integration of software. The test and integration environment was tailored to the size, complexity, and project characteristics intrinsic to the software application.

In order to fully establish this test environment, the software development environment must be tailored to the project and include:

1. A structure of software management and project controls which orchestrate, coordinate, and monitor the many tasks associated with development while not impeding progress or overly restricting development prerogatives.

2. A project support environment which is tailored to the needs of the project, provides essential support when required, and effectively blends automated, procedural, and administrative components and project elements into a cohesive project structure.

3. A planned application of essential project resources derived through rigorous analytical procedures and applied to the project through a multilevel scheduling technique.

4. An effective set of project reviews, audits, and quality assurance practices embedded in the project structure to monitor project integrity and software quality.

5. Independent project analyses to validate the integrity of the software product and maintain traceability between evolving project products during development.

6. A linked set of project methodologies which support each of the areas of development.

7. A controlled flow of data and responsibility as data and technical development proceeds from requirements design to code and ultimately software maintenance.

8. Rigorous configuration management and control practices which are applied from the beginning of the project through delivery of the system to the customer.

9. Early planning and development of testing requirements, which produces a smooth and orderly implementation into a test environment consistent with project needs. The controlled, traceable, and reproduceable execution of test cases which effectively exercise predefined segments of code result in a qualified software configuration.

10. Rigorously enforced project standards and conventions which assure the uniform development of software products and consistency of design, code, and documentation.

Each of the components of the software engineering environment provides a critical segment of project support extending throughout the development period. As previously described, the true test of the effectiveness of the project is how well all the various components of the project support the test and integration period. This engineering effectiveness must be planned into the project from the outset and provide the project with a structured environment which supports each development phase.

Problem of Early Test Planning

The planning of a software project requires that the software manager have an early understanding of what is to be accomplished. Without this understanding it will be difficult to project how the development process is to be managed and controlled; to estimate resources needed to specify, design, implement, and test the product; to plan for applying the resources and doing the work; or to develop and hold to a realistic project schedule.

Initial software planning is often an imprecise process based on incomplete information, poorly specified and misunderstood requirements. During the early planning there are undefined project development and technical requirements. Productivity and project success projections are often not consistent with the realities of the project or the historical performance of the company. For this reason a prudent manager should plan the project in a hierarchical fashion, first defining in a top level plan the basic requirements for developing the software (what is to be done) and a structure for the development process (how it is to be managed and controlled).

TYPICAL PROJECT ORGANIZATION AND WORK ALLOCATION

As illustrated in Figure 2.4, the manager should define the project structure by planning the final system demonstration first. The test manager or planner should work backwards through the various levels of testing and finally through the front end of implementation, design, and requirements specification.

This planning process will define a software project environment which will simultaneously support three categories of testing: system testing, software testing, and development testing. The testing categories are:

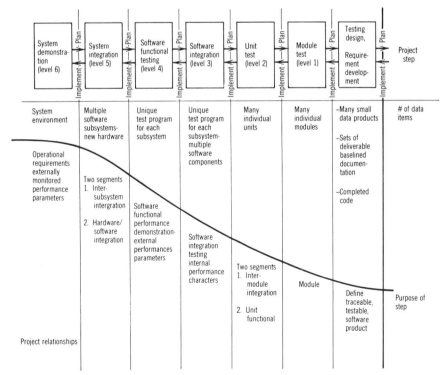

Figure 2.4   Reverse planning

1. **Systems Testing.** The level 5 and 6 testing requirements which integrate qualified software subsystems into an executable system configuration and demonstrate performance against contractual and approved user requirements.

2. **Software Testing.** The level 3 and 4 testing requirements which integrate qualified software units into individual executable subsystems and qualifies subsystem performance and interface integrity in relation to approved allocated functional requirements.

3. **Development Testing.** The level 1 and 2 testing requirements which initially evaluate the implementation of software and assess the integrity of modules and units before use in an integrated environment.

If planned for, these testing categories may be concurrent. This concurrency, although efficient, must be supported by the software organization during the latter stages of the program. As a result, project controls and flexibility must be planned into the project environment from the beginning to support this requirement.

SOFTWARE ORGANIZATIONAL STRUCTURE

As illustrated in Figure 2.5, when discussing the role of the software manager and staff the assumed project organizational structure is a centralized software project. The manager has responsibility for software requirements specification, design, code, integration, and test of multiple software subsystems. These subsystems are loadable, executable entities and may be software or firmware.

Delegating Test Responsibility Through the Work Breakdown Structure

As illustrated in Figure 2.6, the delegation of testing responsibility is hierarchal, treeing down from the program, through the software project, and finally to the test organization. The vehicle for this work assignment is the Work Breakdown Structure (WBS). The WBS is a product-orientated division of hardware, software, services, and other work required to develop a system capability.

Program definition begins well before the start of the software development. During this period the basic program cost parameters are developed, the technical, administrative, and programmatic requirements defined, the WBS developed, and the initial schedules, personnel, and resource commitments are made.

The WBS is the means by which the program office allocates work throughout the organization. At the top level, the WBS is an identification of the program requirements. Treeing down from these is a hierarchy of end items to be developed. These then decompose downward into the

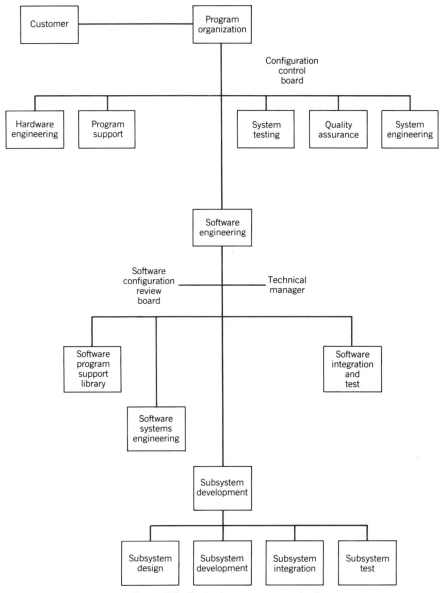

Figure 2.5 Typical program organization

smaller components of the product which are essential to the development of the system. This decomposition continues, eventually reaching the lowest level over which the program manager will retain direct management control. At this level the program should define a set of cost accounts for collecting, monitoring, and evaluating expenditures by task category and work packages for allocating work to the functional organizations. The work

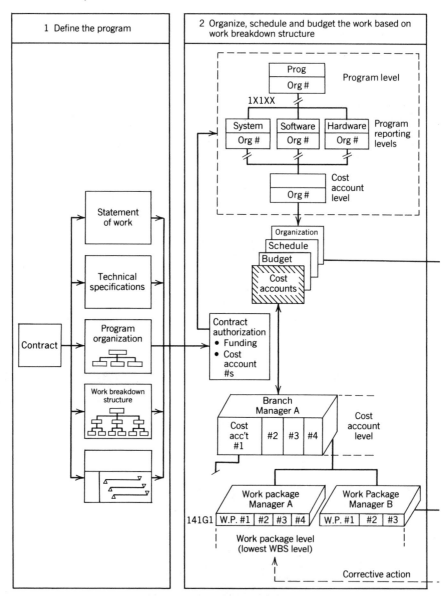

Figure 2.6   WBS Relationships

packages are the means by which specific tasks are delegated to the functional organizations and work is allocated, progress is monitored, and success evaluated.

Work packages are detailed descriptions of work to be accomplished. They are job-specific, and result in a set of products or services which can be assignable to a single organizational entity. Work packages plan what

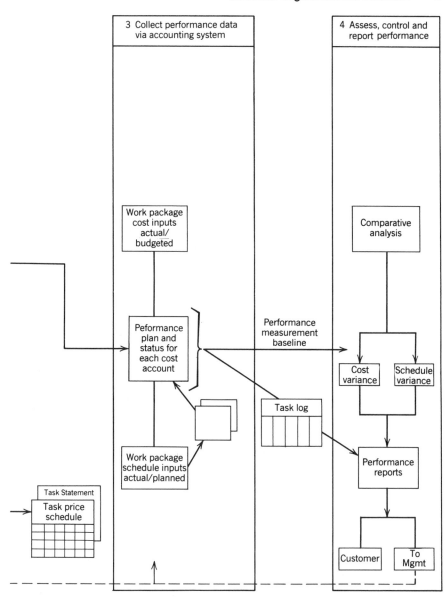

must be accomplished, by whom and under whose responsibility. They provide an estimate of the resources and schedules required to develop the products assigned.

Organizing, Scheduling, and Controlling the Work

From the WBS, organizational responsibility, schedules, and budgets are allocated through three levels.

1. **The Program Level.** The WBS documents the program task framework and includes all tasks on the WBS which have not been delegated to functional managers and are the direct responsibility of the program.

2. **Cost Account Level.** The program manager assigns organizational responsibility, schedule, and budget for each of the lowest level WBS tasks to the functional managers.

3. **Work Package Level.** The work packages defined as a result of the cost accounts are scheduled and budgeted. Each work package is assigned a manager who is responsible for work package performance, definition of tasks, allocation of resources assigned to the work package, and the production of quality products. The work package manager will suballocate the work package to various segments of the organization.

The responsibility for software test is a major segment of the software work packages.

Software Project Organization

In the overall program environment, the software project is one segment of a larger system development managed and controlled by a program staff. This program organization typically has hardware, system engineering, system test, and other program functions which support the development and test of an operational system configuration.

As one of the program organizational components, software development is assigned to a software manager. All software-related work packages identified and tracked by the program Work Breakdown Structure are assigned to the software manager who has responsibility and accountability for project performance within the cost and schedule parameters.

The manager has overall responsibility for all software activities identified in the software work package(s). Directly supporting the manager are the Software Configuration Review Board (SCRB), which provides the software configuration control functions. Software quality assurance (SQA) functions monitor the health, status, quality, and integrity of the software. Although reporting to the program, they provide the manager visibility into the development and test process. Reporting to the manager in a line capacity are several organizational elements responsible to the manager for development of the software data products.

The software configuration management organization manages and controls the the flow of approved data within the project, provides a focal point within the project for all data management functions and documentation development.

Software systems engineering has responsibility for interpretation of allocated system requirements, derivation and documentation of the software subsystem design, and support to each of the subsystem development groups during level 3 integration.

The subsystem development groups are responsible for the software design, code, detailed documentation of software units and modules, as well as unit and module testing.

A final group will integrate and functionally qualify the software subsystems. This group is the independent test organization and it has responsibility for the functional qualification of each subsystem (level 4) and the integration of the subsystems into an executable software configuration (level 5A).

EARLY PROJECT FOCUS TOWARDS DELIVERY REQUIREMENTS

As illustrated in Figure 2.7 and discussed previously, the preliminary project requirements for system testing should be defined first. This testing category is normally the responsibility of the program organization. This organization plans, develops, executes, and controls this level of test. This test level will demonstrate system validity in relation to contractual performance, operational, and programmatic requirements. Based on the requirements for system testing, requirements should also be defined for integrating the system into an operational configuration. From these, software subsystem functional demonstration requirements should be defined, and the process continues until the requirements for the lowest test level (module test) are identified. All these test requirements are then detailed through secondary test planning activities and implemented in the order of the software development. In the project environment, the implementation of the test requirements is in the reverse order to which the requirements were defined.

Preliminary Definition of the System Test Segment

Through an analysis of the contract, basic program, and system documentation, four categories of project support should be identified by the program organization before any system test planning is initiated.

1. What are the end test requirements which, when satisfied, will result in customer acceptance of the system?
2. What are the software reliability and performance requirements which must be satisfied if the software is to be operationally acceptable?
3. What are the operational characteristics of the system and what is the essential support environment of the software application?
4. How complex is the system application and how does this complexity translate into hardware, software, operational, and support requirements?

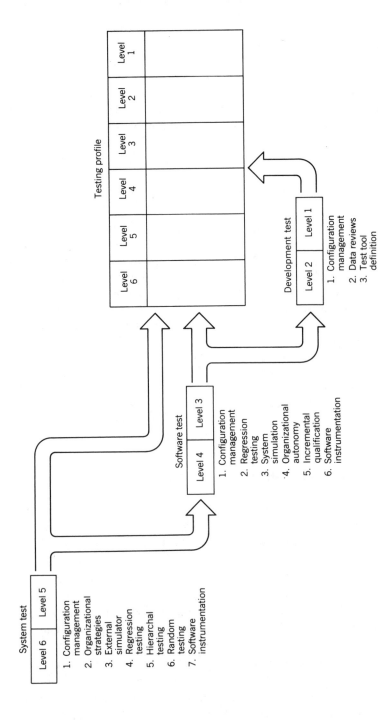

Figure 2.7 System test definition

The program and software managers must understand that the project environment, technical and development complexities, and development and test methodologies must result in a product which will be accepted at the end of the development. Advancing the state of the art is unimportant if not required by the project, increasing the expertise of personnel at the expense of the project is not critical, and using test rigor to build more reliability in the software than required by the contract is unnecessary. In order to succeed in the development, the software manager must develop, within cost and schedule, a system which passes a predefined test set and is accepted for operational deployment by the customer.

From an analysis of the program requirements, high-level test requirements identify a system test environment which will satisfy the contractually required categories of project support. The purpose of system testing is to demonstrate that the integrated hardware and software system satisfies the contractually agreed to operational and system performance requirements. The requirements for these tests are normally documented in formally approved test plans and procedures developed by a program-level organization.

The effectiveness of the system test environment is very visible to the customer as well as impacting the success or failure of the program. This environment should be based on:

1. The degree to which hardware and software must be demonstrated separately and as an integrated system(s).
2. The requirements traceability which must be demonstrated before the software is accepted for operational use.
3. The duration and complexity of the specified system test.
4. The test documentation and customer approval requirements which are essential development milestones.
5. Test milestones which are essential customer interface points.
6. Test procedures, tools, techniques, and methodologies which are essential components of the system test program.
7. Reliability demonstrations which must be completed before the system is considered acceptable.

These basic system parameters significantly affect the way that the program and software project is structured during the latter stages of system testing. To a large measure they establish the essential controls which expedite and ensure the effectiveness of the system testing environment. The system testing required by the contract significantly affects how extensively the program and software managers incorporate control and discipline into the program and software project structure. The parameters should define how much emphasis each of these areas is given when determining the specific requirements for the project during the system test period.

Software Subsystem Testing

After defining the requirements for the system test category, the requirements for software subsystem testing may be developed.

These tests are at an individual software subsystem level. They are preferably developed, executed, and evaluated by an independent test team and are usually subject to customer review and approval. These tests qualify the software against approved software functional specifications. Unlike the system test levels, there are multiple subsystems qualified through individual, separately specified test segments. System integration tests verify the internal execution characteristics of the system, while software functional tests (level 4) qualify software subsystem from an external, functional perspective. Software integration tests (level 3) evaluate internal execution characteristics of individual software subsystems.

The test levels are built from the approved functional specifications for each subsystem and must be consistent with the system level 5 integration requirements.

Early specification of requirements for each software test demands that the manager answer several critical questions.

1. What are the technical characteristics of the functional requirements to be demonstrated?
2. Do the software subsystems execution characteristics allow external monitoring of performance and execution integrity?
3. Do the relationships between individual subsystems allow a valid functional demonstration in a stand-alone environment?
4. Is sufficient qualified hardware available to establish a valid software test configuration?
5. Is the software divisible into testable, functionally compatible builds?
6. What resources have been projected, budgeted, and allocated to the functional qualification activities?

Answers to these questions determine, to a large measure, the basis for identifying basic project requirements for the software functional demonstration for each subsystem?

Development Testing

After software subsystem testing requirements are identified, the requirements for the development tests may be defined. Development tests qualify the smallest, divisible component of the software architecture, the unit for integration into a subsystem configuration.

The tests are designed from the detailed software design specifications. They are informal, conducted by the development organization and do not use data or software controlled by the project.

It is necessary to define a general set of requirements for unit testing and ensure that the requirements correspond to the size, complexity, and technical characteristics of the software unit. The software manager must know the answers to the following:

1. What manual and automated support facilities will be available for use during the period of unit testing?
2. How complex is the software application, how dynamic are the execution characteristics of the operational environment, and how testable are individual units in a stand-alone test environment?
3. What are the reliability requirements for the software and how much of this requirement may be demonstrated at the development test levels?

Answers to these questions are major determinants in the definition of the requirements for the development test levels.

	Development test		Software test		System test	
Test level Project requirement	1	2	3	4	5	6
1. Configuration management (formal control of end items)	X	X	X	X	X	X
2. Configuration management (informal non end item control)			X	X	X	X
3. Organizational structures						
a. Independent			X		X	
b. Autonomous				X		X
c. Integrated	X	X				
4. Simulation			X	X	X	
5. Hierarchal test			X		X	
6. Random test				X		X
7. Instrumentation		X	X		X	
8. Regression test		X	X	X	X	X
9. Incremental qualification			X	X	X	X
10. Incremental reviews		X	X	X	X	X

Figure 2.8   Test Linkage

TESTING RELATIONSHIPS—LINKING THE TEST LEVELS

As illustrated in Figure 2.8, the individual requirements for each test level should be summarized by test level. This summary should identify which components of the project environment must be integrated into the project environment to:

Ensure a smooth flow of data, effective control of testing data integrity, and a clear transition of responsibility as the test program moves from level to level.

Ensure that the project is adequately structured to support each individual test level, considering the technical characteristics, the administrative and support characteristics of the project.

This early definition of project requirements based on testing is an essential, albeit preliminary, step in the planning process in that it forces a top-down look at the basic project structure before detailed plans for the project or projections of required resources are made. The parameters presented previously are representative of those which should be considered when analyzing the project versus testing requirements. Other parameters, such as test case design, organizational requirements, iterative formal test result reviews, and prototyping, should be considered when evaluating the requirements. These parameters have a large impact on resource and facility requirements, schedules, budgets, and project complexity. They should be extracted from contract and customer requirements, company and program practices, standards, and requirements, proven industry techniques, and theoretical methodologies and practices not proven in actual project situations. If done properly, the testing profile defined for the program should show a clear application of techniques, methodologies, and testing requirements as the testing proceeds through each level.

3 Laying the Groundwork for Testing

Software test and integration planning is solving predictable project crises before they impact productivity.

EARLY SOFTWARE PROJECT PLANNING

As illustrated in Figure 3.1, the initial specification of project requirements provides the basis upon which the structure of the test program may be based and meaningful projections of cost, schedule, and resource requirements may be developed. This planning will identify requirements which the software project must address if each of the test levels are to be adequately supported. Early analysis is essential if the flow of work between levels is to be smooth and productive. As described in the previous chapter, once these project requirements are defined, three parallel project activities should be initiated. These activities translate these basic requirements into a plan upon which the project environment may be based. These activities are:

1. Generation of a software development plan. This plan is based on development and contractual requirements of the project, and describes what is to be done during each project phase and how the process of software development is to be managed and controlled.
2. Specification to project methodologies that result in a traceable, testable set of system and software requirements, which provide a firm technical basis upon which the development may proceed.
3. Preliminary software budget and schedule development that will document resources to be applied to the project, and provide a plan for application and preliminary budgets to allocate resources to specific functional areas and organizational segments.

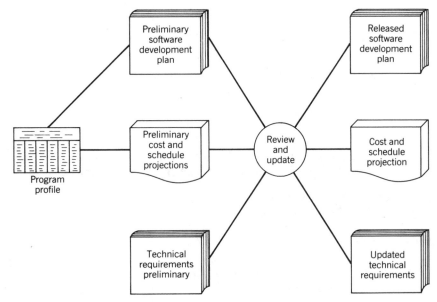

Figure 3.1   Requirements relationships

In order to develop these initial plans, the project characteristics identified for each test level should be analyzed using a structure that represents the most stringent application of the requirement or project discipline as a basis. This definition should be the basis for the specification of the project environment and should be documented in the software development and second-level project planning documentation. As previously defined, this phasing of resources, project disciplines, organization elements, and technical and management controls serves as the basis for the allocation of resources, as well as projecting costs and schedule requirements for each test level.

The phasing of project requirements to the schedule and the basing of project and plans on predefined test requirements should be a precursor to all software planning. This planning is done early in the project, laying the groundwork for all development of software subsystems.

This period of the project is the most critical from a manager's standpoint since this is when the structure of the project as well as development, management, and project control procedures and techniques are defined. Also, during this period the technical requirements and characteristics of the project are developed, and the cost, schedule, and resource constraints which limit the perogatives of the software manager are identified. In short, it is during this period that the software manager decides what he or she is going to do maximize probability of project success.

Despite the importance of this early planning to the ultimate success of the project, it is often difficult for a manager to find time or resources early in the project to perform these functions. The normal project is front-loaded with a myriad of essential short-term tasks that require the direct participation of the software manager and the staff to complete. Early customer reviews, program planning meetings, project staffing, budget negotiations, and project organization development all compete for the software manager's time and sap the limited resources available to the software project early in the implementation. Longer-term problems, such as software project planning, meaningful cost and schedule projections, critical early test planning activities, as well as planning and development of a productive project environment, are often deferred in lieu of these short-term requirements in the hopes that, "After these crises are over, time will be available to address the pressing long-term issues of the project." Unfortunately, the reality is that there are always new crises in a project situation.

Once the manager falls into the trap of trading short-term project requirements for long-term planning requirements, he or she has sown the seeds of poor productivity. The commitments on the manager and staff increase, requiring more rather than less time to complete. As the development proceeds through the design and development stages, the time that the manager hoped would be available for planning evaporates. The situation is compounded since the early project planning, which would have brought order to these later project phases, has not been accomplished, resulting in, at best, an inefficient project environment and, at worst, development chaos.

The software manager must recognize the importance of this early planning to the long-term health of the project. This planning, and the specific requirements for it, should be integrated into the project environment, sharing equally in importance with the short-term and early technical activities and milestones. These early activities should be under the direct supervision of the software manager. In the case of the Software Development Plan, the manager should have primary responsibility for defining the plans content and in determining the requirements for the tools, techniques, methodologies, and project management procedures and controls.

The Software Development Plan—The Essential Starting Point

Generation of the Software Development Plan, as illustrated in Figure 3.2, is the first step in laying out the requirements for software test and integration. This level of planning should be based on the test requirements profile, which was described in the previous chapter.

The Software Development Plan is a definition of what will be done during each step in the development, what resources will be applied to the project, a plan for applying them to the project, and controls to monitor the project in the context of the development environment.

Practices and procedures for managing and controlling the development are also defined. The Software Development Plan is the direct responsibility

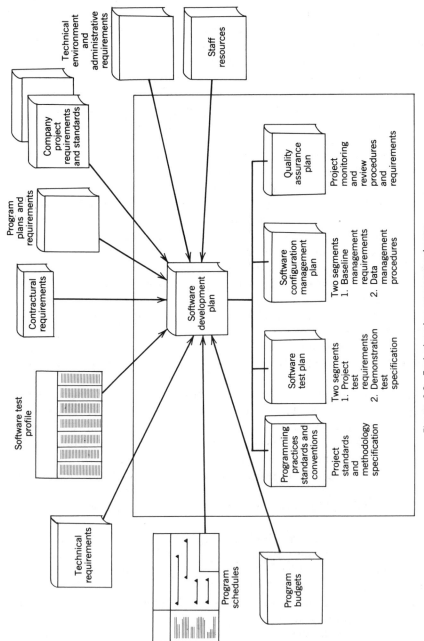

Figure 3.2 Test planning correspondence

of the software manager, although segments of the plan may be delegated to other areas of the project, provided the manager is committed to the resultant plan and to implementation of the project requirements specified within.

The purpose of the Software Development Plan is to create and document a project structure which will support the predictable, orderly development of the software within cost and schedule constraints. The SDP lays the foundation for the test program. The project structure must be tailored to the test requirements profile, customer, company, technical, and contract characteristics and requirements. The tailoring process is the means by which the software manager assures that the selection and implementation of the development, support, and control methodologies are consistent with the needs and characteristics of the particular software application.

As the primary software management document, the Software Development Plan should be maintained throughout the development period by the software manager. The manager should provide all updates to higher management, customer agencies, and the project staff.

The nature of the software development process demands that this early planning be rigorous, complete, and tailored to the development requirements of the project. The complexity of the disciplines essential for development, the nontangible nature of the early data products, and the essential relationship between requirements, design, code, and testing data require that a carefully planned and orchestrated set of technical and administrative tasks be accomplished.

The early specification of methodologies is a critical part of the generation of the Software Development Plan. By basing the plan on the inter-test profile, a testing focus is maintained. The phasing of responsibility, sizing of project resource requirements and planning of work is focused toward the project acceptance. By emphasizing test and integration as the basic planning task, the various technical, management, and support methodologies may be scaled to the actual delivery requirements under the contract. Software planning should define the flow of data between each project organizational segment and the data relationships between each individual project methodology. This planned flow of data, with the corresponding requirements for review, audits, and project support significantly augments productivity and programmer effectiveness. Time is not wasted reworking information to meet a specific project format requirement, to make the data usable to other areas of the program, or to make it acceptable to the customer. Caution should be applied to the interpretation of what is in the contract. Good development and management disciplines and practices are prerequisites to development of an acceptable software product irrespective of what the customer or contract demand. Adequate technical requirements and design specifications, complete and effective testing, rigorous management controls, and frequent informal and formal reviews of the project and data are essential whether or not they are required by the contract.

The basic requirement of any contract is to deliver a product and it is the responsibility of management to develop and implement a project structure to ensure this.

Initial project plans must be modified and tailored to the specific characteristics of the project through an update that factors in cost and schedule requirements and the technical requirements of the project.

In the Software Development Plan, the software manager describes the criteria to be followed in the technical areas of the project as well as general requirements for planning and implementing this criteria in the context of the project structure. These general criteria must be translated into project standards and conventions which, when implemented, will define the technical and support requirements of the project and establish the specific methodologies to be followed in development of the software.

The plan contains ten primary categories of information:

1. **Introduction and Scope.** Documents the purpose and scope of the development and test segments of the software project.

2. **Project Goals and Objectives.** Documents the goals and objectives of the software project as defined in this segment of the Software Development Plan. The specification of the goals and objectives provides the basic development criteria for the project and define the framework from which the project environment is to be defined and developed. The goals and objectives should be developed from the contractual requirements of the project, the requirements of the program as well as the commitments and development objectives of the software manager.

3. **Organization and Organizational Controls.** Documents the organizational structure for the project, the flow of data and responsibility as the project transitions through the various development phases, and defines the charter and roles of each organizational element.

4. **Management and Technical Controls.** Defines what procedures and criteria are to be used by the project to monitor the cost and technical aspects of the software project data, and the requirements for test and integration of the software as required by the contract and company standards.

This section should also provide an overview of the measures and controls which will be applied to the software development process to assure that the project is on schedule, within budget, and technically successful. It is in this section that the basic philosophy of managing the software project is documented.

The methodology chosen for controlling and statusing schedules/budgets should be described in detail in this section. The project requirements for software design/implementation, configuration management, verification, and validation (test), and the quality assurance methodologies should be provided in second-level planning documents.

5. **Work Definition and Flow.** In this section, the software development process is described in terms of the major work phases. A diagram showing

the major phases and the major products for each phase should be included to introduce overall work flow and should identify project baselines. For each phase, a narrative should be included to describe the products generated to mark the end of the phase, and the flow of work within each phase.

6. **Development Environment Definition.** The environment in which the software will be developed and tested is defined in this section. It includes discussion of the computer system on which the software is to be developed, its detailed configuration specifications, its location and method of program access, the test configuration (if different from the development configuration), and security access requirements. Requirements for overlapping development, test preparation and test execution as well as library control, reviews and audits, and project support requirements should be discussed.

7. **Software Development Methodology.** The methodologies selected for software designs and implementation should be identified and briefly described in this section. If any special software tools are to be employed as part of the methodology, such as design languages, they should be identified and described. If the methodology is described in the literature, reference should be made to the specific authors and titles. For example, it is not enough to state that a "top-down" methodology will be used, rather a specific, documented methodology must be identified. The particular methodologies, standards for development, and detailed procedures for their use should be described in a separate document, which should be referenced in this section of the Software Development Plan (SDP).

8. **Configuration Management.** This section should describe the general method by which the software products will be controlled throughout the project. It should describe the storage format for the version of the products, how access to the products is achieved by the staff, what approval is necessary for accepting a product as "official," and what control and general tracking procedures will be applied to changes in official products. The reader should be referred to the Configuration Management Plan for detailed procedures by which these controls will be implemented.

9. **Software Test and Integration.** This segment of the plan should introduce the overall testing structure, identify the test phases and levels, and describe the testing requirements by level. It should describe the philosophy of building and testing the system and make reference to the documents which will be produced by the test organization. The reader would be referred to separate Test and Integration Plans and procedures for a detailed description of the test program.

10. **Quality Assurance Provisions.** This section should enumerate and describe checkpoints at which the quality of the development process will be evaluated. The section should include a description of all customer-scheduled reviews as well as internal reviews, such as design and code walk-throughs and documentation reviews. For each review, the method for re-

porting the findings and correcting problem areas found should be detailed. If necessary due to length or customer requirement, a separate Quality Assurance Plan may be generated to describe all the methods by which the software manager intends to assure the soundness of the software products being developed.

The plan is the basic documentation of the software organization and control structure and describes what will be accomplished by each segment of the project and how the process will be orchestrated, managed, and controlled.

The Software Development Plan should be treated as the basic project management guidebook and, as such, should be rigorously maintained and updated as project conditions change.

This early project planning is the means by which the software manager may give early form and structure to the project. It is through this plan that the myriad of development tools, techniques, and methodologies are selected and applied to the project. The development and application of the plan will provide a documented structure for the project and will communicate the roles, resources, responsibilities, and development requirements upward through the customer and program organizations and downward through the software organization.

The segments of the plan which most affect the test and integration environment (and which must be scaled to reflect project requirements) are: the project standards and methodologies for software requirements specification, and design and development methodologies defined in the Software Development Plan and Programming Practices Standards and Conventions (PPS&C). The Software Development Plan should identify plans for implementing and controlling each level of testing, plans for implementation of the two segments of software configuration management, and project review and monitoring procedures to be expanded in the Quality Assurance Plan.

Methodology Definition—Linking the Segments of the Project

As illustrated in Figure 3.3, the various project methodologies used by a software project determines how the development will transition through the various phases of the development cycle, and the integrity and acceptability of the software product.

Five factors must be considered by a software manager when selecting or reviewing the selection of a methodology set for application to the project.

1. Have the proposed technical techniques been proven in development applications of similar size and complexity with similar environments and characteristics?

2. Do the techniques produce data products consistent with the documentation and review requirements of the contract, and can these

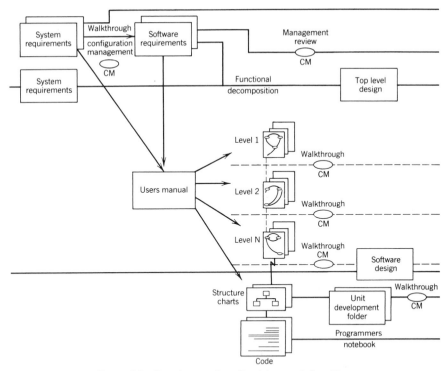

Figure 3.3   Development methodology relationships

products be used, without modification in other phases of the development?

3. Is there clear traceability between requirements specified by the methodology and those needed by related methodology, and are the individual requirements definable, testable, and demonstrable in the context of overall project requirements?

4. Is it possible to plan the overall flow of the project, interfaces, and relationships between project segments, and define a schedule which integrates specific requirements of the selected methodologies into a consistent and effective project structure?

5. Are the project resources and proposed methodologies consistent with project budget and schedule constraints? Is it possible to tailor or configure the application of the methodology to the characteristics of the project?

REQUIREMENTS DEFINITION

Decomposition of the baselined user requirements for use in the system design proceeds is a two-step process:

1. **Specification Analysis.** The requirements specification includes system requirements, environmental considerations, performance requirements, interface requirements, support requirements, and narrative. Requirements defined in the specification become the basis for design, implementation, and test activities.

2. **Requirements Amplification.** The requirements set is ideally an ordered set of user requirements. These requirements must be allocated to the software and hardware and extended to include: derived requirements which adapt the software to the applications configuration; performance constraints; software control requirements which control and schedule system execution; reliability; fault isolation; and recovery requirements which assure acceptable system performance in anomalous environments.

These requirements provide the technical basis for development of the system as well as providing the ultimate criteria for customer acceptance. The requirements are extracted from the contract specifications, interface documentation, user and operational requirements, and basic technical and tradeoff analyses which analyze and allocate the requirements to hardware and software components of the system. These requirements are defined at the program level rather than being the sole responsibility of the software organization. The results of the requirements definition should result in a clear, nonambiguous, traceable, and testable set of requirements which, when completed, will represent the technical contract between program and software project organizations responsible for developing the subsystems. These specifications should be reviewed by the software organizations prior to acceptance for implementation. Acceptance through these reviews, whether conducted as formal program or project reviews or internal software structured walkthroughs, should serve as the basis for placing requirements under both program and software project configuration management and control. This early control is essential to ensure the ultimate integrity of the system and software test levels.

Technical Requirements—The Basis for Success

The process of software engineering is a means by which a set of specified operational requirements is translated into an operational plan to achieve the needs, goals, and objectives of the user.

Derivation of the system requirements is a precursor to all development and test planning as well as providing the basic criteria by which the customer will accept the system from the contractor. For this reason the buyer of the system should provide a major input to the definition of the requirements as well as approving the final requirements before system and software design is initiated. The configuration management and control of these requirements is essential after approval if the integrity of the requirements are to be used as the basis for definition of the system.

Many factors limit the success of the engineering process in the software development environment. The process is difficult to manage and control, the technology difficult to plan, implement, and support. Often the most difficult of all problems is the specification, management, and control of the system requirements which provide the basis for the development effort.

Managers often attempt to apply project management and control techniques, technologies, support methodologies, project standards, conventions, and development procedures which worked on small systems to the development of large systems or vice versa. The simple fact is that these applications generally do not work. The software project management environment must be scaled to the technical and administrative requirement of the project. Requirements must be clearly specified, tightly controlled, traceable throughout the functional decomposition, software design, code, integration, and test. The software development process must result in requirements that are testable and demonstrable in a clear, nonambiguous manner.

SYSTEM REQUIREMENTS CHARACTERISTICS

Before investigating what constitutes a valid system requirement, the program or software project manager must understand system application to include the overall purpose, technical, operational, and user needs for the system, and the overall environment and support characteristics of the system. Understanding the system application is the essential first step in the hierarchical definition of the system requirements. These requirements provide the basis for the user acceptance of the system.

The requirements are the basic definition of what the user needs and support that must be provided if the system is to satisfy its operational expectations. They are:

1. **Operational Needs.** A nonambiguous, traceable, and testable definition of the specific operational needs to be satisfied by the system. Each individual requirement must be clearly defined, expressing in a traceable, testable fashion what the system must do to be acceptable to a user.

2. **Interface Requirements.** A clear, technically complete and approved specification of the operational interfaces to be satisfied by the system. These interfaces describe the operational concept for the new machine interfaces and the technical specifications for the external system interface.

3. **Performance Budget Requirements.** An early identification of critical system performance budgets which are essential components of system acceptability.

Specification of these three categories of requirements is an identification of what the integrated system must do.

In order to be usable for test definition, the user's needs must be translated into a statement of individual requirements. The statement of needs describes, in an operational sense, what the system must do to satisfy the user. These user needs must be translated into a set of "shall statements" that identify clearly testable requirements for the system that may be traced through the various levels of hardware and software design, implementation, and test. These requirements then serve as the basis for level 6 testing. Several problems inhibit the clear definition of this level of requirements. First, and probably most importantly, the user does not always know what he or she is buying or what he or she needs the system for. The interfaces are not well known or understood, and the performance criteria and the operational requirements for the system are not understood or clearly defined. The requirements become detailed and clarified as the user refines his or her needs and understanding of the system. Unless the basic requirements are clearly specified and controlled by the project from the outset of the system development, these frequent, uncontrolled changes disrupt an orderly process and will inhibit or, in many cases, preclude project success. Early control is essential to success!

In addition, at this stage of the project it is difficult to scale the technical requirements of the system to the constraints and limitations imposed by program budgets and schedules. The specified system is often too ambitious to be developed within the constraints and, as a result, the test and integration program will be shortened as schedule and resources run out. This problem may be minimized by iterating the requirements specifications after completion of the initial budget and schedule definition, scaling and tailoring the system specification to the development realities. This requires customer negotiation. The customer must be aware that, although he may not get the grand and glorious system he expects, at least he will get a system.

SOFTWARE REQUIREMENTS CHARACTERISTICS

These requirements are the basis for all software project activities. The initial software requirements set defined early in the program is used to update and modify both cost and schedule projections and is the basis for software project plans.

Before the plans for the project are solidified, the technical, interface, and performance requirements for the software must be allocated by the program systems engineering organization. These requirements should define clearly, in a nonambiguous, traceable, and testable fashion, what the software must do to satisfy system requirements.

Specification of the software requirements is the first technical task of the software development activity. The requirements are the basic specification of what the integrated software system must do to satisfy the allocated requirements of the system. As with the methodologies used to specify system requirements, those used to specify the software requirements should provide clearly testable and traceable requirements, controlled at an individual software subsystem level. These requirements are the common link between software test planning and the technical development.

The methodologies used to define and document the software requirements must interface with those used to specify the system level requirements. These methodologies result in an allocated set of software requirements upon which the functional design process may be initiated. These requirements are the basic functional criteria for software acceptance testing. When allocated to software subsystems they should be reviewed at the project level through internal project reviews and, if required, at a customer review. After review, they should be placed under the baseline and data management segments of software configuration management.

The linking of these requirements to lower and higher level requirements is an ongoing task which must be an integral part of the methodologies selected and used by the project.

Functional Design

Functional design is an orderly process which decomposes the functional definition of the system into lower and lower levels until the final level is reached and the software systems design process can proceed. There are several key elements which must be considered in the definition and allocation of functional requirements to system design components. These are:

1. **Requirements Traceability.** By decomposing software functional requirements from the system requirements and interface definitions, complete and clear traceability is maintained back to the specified needs of the user.

2. **Functional Allocation.** By defining a top-level flow of systems support, and vigorously decomposing each of the elements which comprise this support to lower functional levels, a systems designer assures that what he specifies as functional system requirements accurately reflects the top-level design of the system as well as the needs and requirements of the user.

3. **Data Collection and Control.** By vigorously maintaining a dictionary of system data elements, keyed to the functional allocation and decomposition process, a complete definition of internal system data requirements is maintained as the design progresses.

The purpose of the functional decomposition process is to successively break the individual software subsystems into successively lower levels of detail, adding essential derived and functional requirements as the decomposition proceeds. The lowest level of abstraction represents the basic division of the subsystem into separate, loadable components which may then be described in program design language or some other form of design representation. This decomposition process ensures that a system perspective is retained throughout the functional definition of the software and that requirements traceability is maintained throughout all levels of functional design. The functional specifications should be reviewed by the project as each level of decomposition is completed. After project approval functional decomposition should be placed under configuration management.

The functional decomposition provides the basic criteria for specification of level 3 test requirements and will be reviewed with the customer.

Detailed Software Design

The specific software functional, interface, and software support requirements establish the basis for the detailed design of each of the software subsystems and the units which comprise them. Upon completion of the top level design, the subsystem requirements are specified and described in a manner consistent with the operational and support requirements of the project, the requirements of other segments of the development, and the requirements for the software and system testing levels. At this point, detailed software design begins. This means that the top level design is expanded to a level that enables code to be generated as the next development activity.

Routines within each module are designed with all outputs and the processing stages defined. Timing and memory budgets are allocated to each routine, sources and destinations for data are defined, the hierarchy of interfaces among modules is defined down to the routine level, and restrictions on each routine are specified.

Internal and external data inputs and outputs are specified. The minimum and maximum data values are determined precisely, and the type and location of each data field is prescribed. Factors such as the protocol between software and communications hardware are described in detail before the definition of functional interfaces during preliminary design.

Functional requirements must be translated into design parameters from which software coding may proceed. The design process starts with requirements ordered and structured in accordance with the hierarchical functional architecture. These requirements are decomposed and documented in functional specifications which summarize the functional requirements. Completion and early approval of these specifications will resolve design issues prior to the start of code.

The data developed during this design phase is the basis for two levels of test planning.

1.   The software architecture, interface specifications, and unit design provide the basis to complete the level 3 test planning. From the detailed design parameters the integration plans may be complete, subsystem builds may be specified, detailed, and scheduled, and criteria for successful completion defined.

2. The detailed allocation of functions to units and the specification of the unit and module design provide the basis for defining level 1 and 2 development testing requirements.

Coding Development

The methodologies to be followed in developing and testing code may be less rigorous than those used during the decomposition and design process.

There is a tight coupling between the software development environment, specified project and contract standards and conventions for code readability, and in process reviews of the coding process conducted through project walkthroughs. The code represents a physical and tangible commodity which may be reviewed and evaluated, unlike the design process which deals with nontangible data products that are difficult to evaluate. The coding methodology must satisfy several basic software development requirements.

1. The implemented code must be readable, understandable, and traceable to the requirements of the software design.
2. The code must be traceable to the software architecture, data base components, and the requirements for coding specified in the coding standards and conventions used by the project and documented in the Programming Practices, Standards and Conventions (PPS&C).
3. The code must be sufficiently modular to facilitate the development and testing of several software segments while providing elements for execution in an integrated configuration.

Testing Methodologies

There are separate and distinct methodologies for each test level which must be defined and linked to the design methodologies and to each other through the software development planning process. The system test levels (5 and 6), although normally a program requirement, significantly affect the software planning process. Software subsystems must be tested in accordance with requirements allocated through the system design methodologies; interface integrity must be demonstrated before the subsystems are integrated into an operational configuration; and the software test levels and system test levels must be tightly coupled to permit the concurrent qualification of integrated system and software subsystem releases.

The methodologies selected and used by the program should make use of the tools, techniques, and methodologies applied to the software test levels and provide a smooth, controlled transition of data and responsibility between the test categories and organizational boundaries.

The methodologies applied to the software test category should be consistent with the design and implementation methodologies used. There should be clear correspondence and traceability between the test specifications and the design specifications which result from the design process. If hierarchical design methodologies were used, and the development proceeds in a hierarchical fashion, hierarchical testing methodologies which integrate the system from the top down are most appropriate. If, on the other hand, the development does not rigorously follow a hierarchical pattern due to functional, schedule, or resource requirements, a blending of testing methodologies for software integration is most effective.

The development testing methodologies should be consistent with the requirements of the software test levels and result in functionally qualified and complete software units being integrated into a software build configuration. The methodologies used for unit and module testing are, by their nature, less rigorous than those applied to the software and system categories. The methodologies application is heavily influenced by the unit and module technical and development requirements, the interface and execution characteristics of the unit and module, and project available support facilities, tools, and resources to be applied during these test levels. The methodologies defined for software testing in the software development plan must control the development products used to develop the design, the code, and the unit and software testing plans, procedures, and data products.

Configuration Management

The configuration management methodology selected is the means by which all the products of software development are to be identified, stored, and controlled with regard to changes. Configuration management is the heart of the project, for no matter how rigorously the requirement for documentation of plans and specifications is enforced, no matter how traceable or testable the requirements, or how effectively the design is derived, if these products are not made available to the staff, if the list of existing products is not known, and if changes to these products are not controlled and communicated to the staff, interface problems within the project will exist. Tests will fail and the test configuration will not be reproduceable. Configurations will be lost, requirements will not be traceable to design and then to code. Project disaster will be a real possibility.

The methodology selected for configuration management should espouse the following principles:

1. **Configuration Identification.** All products, both documentation and software, must be uniquely identified and an inventory maintained so that at all times the products which exist are known.

2. **Configuration Description and Location.** The form in which each product exists must be known as well as where it is physically located.

3. **Configuration Product Approval.** Each software product should undergo official approval channels before acceptance into the system configuration.

4. **Configuration Change Control.** A method must be devised by which the changes to the official system configuration are documented, reviewed, and formally approved before application, and a method for keeping track of the different versions of changed products must be addressed.

During the earlier project planning stages, a general profile for the application of configuration management to control of data during the testing levels is defined. The software development plan translates these general requirements into a specification of what software configuration management procedures and discipline are to be implemented to support the specification, design, implementation, integration, and qualification of software and supporting data.

In the software development plan the requirements for the tools, techniques, and methodologies to be implemented in the project for both the baseline and data management segments of the configuration management disciplines are defined. In order to avoid the impacts associated with poor control of data within the project, and the ineffective or inefficient flow of data during test and integration, the disciplines associated with configuration management must be tailored to the project characteristics and the requirements for resources and project support clearly identified.

These requirements which should be factored into the plan include:

1. What are the primary data products which are to be controlled by the project, what reviews will ensure their integrity, and how, once control is instituted, is the integrity of data products to be maintained at the project level.

2. How are the relationships between the various project baselines to be maintained at the project level.

3. How are the relationships between the various project baselines to be maintained? Also, how is the correspondence between the test and integration and requirements specification, design, and implementation segments of the project ensured?

4. What automated and manual procedures and practices should be implemented to ensure the controlled flow of data between organizational elements of the project.

The success of the configuration management disciplines in the project has a direct effect on the success of the test program. If the requirement, design, interface, or data base specifications used to develop the test requirements are not controlled, the integrity of the entire test program may be suspect. If not controlled and properly documented, software releases cannot be provided by the project for test. These releases must include a definition of what has been qualified or what changes have been made. If changes to the software requirements, design, or code are not controlled, it is not possible to tell the state of the system at any time and, as a result, not possible to meaningfully test it.

In short, the configuration management disciplines determine the project data environment during test and must ensure the integrity of all data used in planning and developing test requirements.

COSTING AND SCHEDULING SOFTWARE TESTING

The allocation of sufficient resources and schedule to complete software testing is essential to project success. Unfortunately costing and scheduling software is an imprecise activity often resulting in significant shortfalls during testing. These shortfalls result in testing perturbations which jeopardize the success of the project. The accuracy of these projections is impacted not only by difficulty in accurately defining costs but in the methodologies used to cost and schedule software.

Much work has been done within the industry in the areas of software sizing, productivity estimation, cost derivation, and work and resource allocation. Unfortunately, unlike other industries where the costs associated with development correlate to some quantifiable measure such as square feet, software product costs correlate to project development productivity and functional attributes which are difficult to size. The software industry, unlike older and more established industries, has not yet developed standard tools, techniques, and methodologies for projecting or validating software development resource requirements. When estimating software, the typical base unit of measure for the sizing of a software product, and hence the basis for estimating resources required to develop it, is the line of code.

This measurement is not a very good one, and is similar to predicting how long it will take to produce a painting by estimating the number of brushstrokes that will have been applied when the painting is complete.

First of all, there is no obvious relationship between the lines of code produced and what the user really wants to buy. While it means something to a customer buying a house to say that he wants approximately 2,000 square feet, it means nothing to a customer buying a software system to say that he wants 100,000 lines of code. Secondly, most programmers do not know how to estimate lines of code. Most programmers have not done the same work over and over again, and do not have a reference point from which to measure. Finally, there are any number of ways a set of specifications can be coded to achieve the same basic result, even when the input and output formats are fixed. Even if we could estimate lines of code with any accuracy, this quantity would only be clearly useful when the functions to be coded are defined with regard to input, processing, and output. Specifying the job itself is a major part of the work to be done.

The customer seldom provides a detailed software specification, and the cost and schedule projection cannot wait until the specifications are complete. Like it or not, the project must estimate not only how long it will take us to build the product but also how long it will be before it can be determined exactly what the job is to do. A cost relationship must be established between user requirements and the work that must be done to meet these requirements.

In order to ensure the validity of the estimation procedure, a functional approach at software estimation is essential. The technique is based on practical experience. Much promising work has been initiated through a variety of government and industry sources designed to augment the costing methodologies and techniques. In most cases the research is not complete, nor have the results been structured in such a way to make them directly usable by an estimator responsible for sizing a software application and projecting development resources.

An effective technique for software estimation is to measure software size against functional attributes, rather than lines of code, and use functional size standards, analogous to a standard circuit, to derive a size projection.

This size may or may not be expressed in terms of lines of code; however, because of industry convention, the line of code is most convenient. Under the estimation approach described below, the line of code is the unit of measure analogous to square feet, rather than serving as the basis of estimation.

Estimating the Size

As illustrated in Figure 3.4, the estimator works from a basic set of high-level user requirements allocated to the software architecture by system engineering activities. These requirements are user and operationally oriented and do not include derived or support requirements. From this requirement list, the estimator functionally decomposes each requirement at least three levels in accordance with the defined architecture of the software or, if not defined, an assumed architecture. This decomposition is not rigorous, designed to estimate rather than design. It does provide, however, a functional basis upon which the software may be sized.

Each lowest level function is then identified on a software estimation worksheet, illustrated in Figure 3.5, from which the size estimate will be developed.

Each individual function is assigned a size based on expert judgment of the estimator, experience on similar applications, or an estimator's book of standard software functional sizes compiled from industry experience.

Each function is assigned a complexity weight to offset productivity differences resulting from complexity and staff experience and the size is multiplied by the offset to get the weighted size.

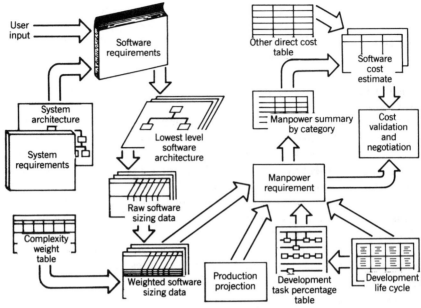

Figure 3.4   Costing techniques

Manpower Projection and Categorization

From this estimate, a determination of the types of manpower required to develop the software application is made. This is done by first projecting the development productivity based on expert opinion, analogous experience, industry statistics for similar applications, direct project experience, management-dictated values, or educated guess.

Accuracy of the productivity projection is critical since a small change in estimated productivity may have a major effect on the size of the final estimate. The estimated productivity used by the author is .6 hours/line of high-order language code for a new application and 1.0 hour/instruction for modified code. This number is for all direct labor required to design, develop, document, and test a software product.

The number of manhours required to produce the software are then defined by dividing the weighted lines of code by the productivity. This then is the basic manpower requirements for the software development.

Categories of manpower are then applied to each task, providing a cross section of manpower for the development by personnel classification. Using average direct labor rates for each manpower category, these manhour estimates are translated into a cost estimate. Nonlabor charges are then applied to derive a final cost figure.

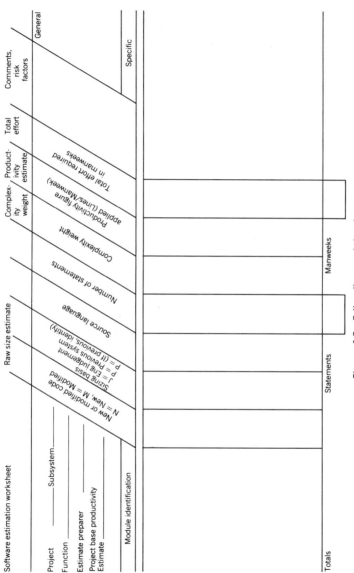

Figure 3.5 Estimation worksheet

47

Validating the Cost

The final step is to validate the cost estimate against a predefined standard. In my experience, two techniques are most effective:

1. **Independent Cost Derivation.** Two or more groups independently derive the costs. The resultant estimates are then compared and discussed in a face-to-face meeting between the teams. Based on this meeting, a consolidated estimate is produced.

2. **Parametric Models—Parametric Costing.** Permit the analysis of costing integrity by comparing the cost parameters against standards contained within the model. It allows the estimator to investigate the effect of project and productivity changes on the overall integrity of the cost estimate. These models normally assume a size estimate as a starting point, limiting their usefulness in initial cost derivation.

These techniques are essential components of the costing methodology. An effective analysis of costing integrity will ensure that the size estimates used to derive the cost have been compared against a second opinion, that the procedures used to develop the costs are valid, and that assumptions and costing parameters are consistent with industry and other development experience within the company.

The software costing methodology described above is a functionally oriented way to develop a cost projection from an initial set of user or operational requirements. The estimates gain validity as the project proceeds and as the technical data used as a basis becomes more detailed and refined. The initial cost estimate is a "best guess" including all manpower support requirements; configuration management, software engineering, test and integration, quality assurance, and support.

The key to validity of an estimate is not as much in how precise the projection is but how accountable the software manager is to producing software against the productivity projections required to meet the cost and schedule commitments.

This management accountability, and the degree to which the manager is willing to commit resources to the project to support it, is the ultimate measure of project success.

Scheduling the Test Process

Monitoring the planning, implementation, and conduct of software testing is a complex process, requiring implementation procedures, effective scheduling, collection of accurate status, and early identification of productivity problems. As illustrated in Figure 3.6, software test scheduling process is a four-part activity, corresponding to the various levels of program planning. At the top level are the system schedules which correspond to the contractual milestones between the customer buying the system and

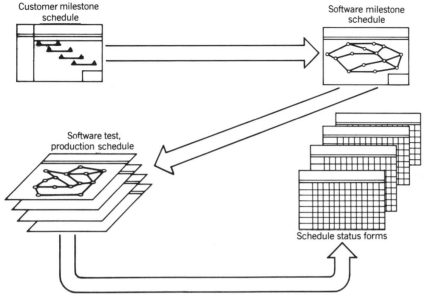

Figure 3.6   Schedule relationship

the contractor designated responsibility for implementation of the system. This "Program Master Schedule" identifies the major program activities which lead to delivery of an operational system capability. The schedule illustrates the individual milestones which must be supported by the program during the system development and the program event which, when completed, satisfies a contractually defined milestone. The Program Master Schedule serves as one of the primary inputs required to develop the program work breakdown structure as well as providing the basic schedule requirement upon which development success is measured.

From this Master Schedule, secondary schedules are developed which correspond to the individual work packages used to assign work from the Work Breakdown Structure. Unlike the Master Schedule, which identifies what must be done by when, these second-level or subordinate schedules provide a plan for doing the work.

These schedules support early program planning which culminate in a Work Breakdown Structure, work packages to be assigned to the functional organizations, implementation activities which are defined through the various work package plans, schedules which will be used to plan and control the individual tasks required under the work package, and the technical work used to satisfy the work package requirements. The subordinate schedules define the sequence of activities expected in the development of the work package, the phasing of these activities, internal and external constraints which will impede, or preclude progress if they are not satisfied, and the sequence of related tasks which will take the longest on the schedule, thereby pacing the other work package schedules. Normally the most effective form for the work package schedule is the PERT network. A PERT network will define, in detail, the overall plan for developing the major milestones required under the work package. This PERT network is developed by the work package manager, monitored on a regular basis to ensure adequate project performance against schedule requirements, and on an "as required basis," to reflect changing project conditions or scheduling realities. This schedule is normally constructed early in the planning effort and lays out the work package from beginning to end.

In the case of software testing tasks, work package schedules are not adequate to plan and monitor the day-to-day activities of the testing staff. When scheduling test and integration activities, several rules must be adhered to if the schedules are to prove valid.

1. A period of time must be included to specify, design, develop, and incorporate the tools, testing techniques, and essential technical parameters which will determine the testing environment. These activities need not be scheduled serially with the normal test planning and development; however, if scheduled in parallel, sufficient resources to support the activities must be budgeted and made available.

2. The software test schedules should include not only formal customer and project milestones but also identify critical internal test milestones. The two activities most frequently overlooked in schedule development are the development of test scenarios and data, and the integration of tools, techniques, and methodologies into the test environment. Scenarios, often proving the most difficult test planning task, are required for each test procedure. Scenarios describe, on a test-step-by-test-step basis, the specific test stimulus and control requirements. From these, data are developed which will cause the system to exercise areas of the software subsystem or system. These areas represent a significant segment of the test schedule and must appear at all scheduling levels. The second internal schedule requirement is the phasing of newly defined tools, techniques, or methodologies into the software test environment. These often do not integrate smoothly into the testing environment and time must be provided to redefine and modify the techniques as needed to ensure an effective project test environment.

3. The software test schedules must be phased to reflect the realities of test execution and portray problems which will be experienced. Whenever the test environment changes; that is, new tools are incorporated, the test level changes, the test cases are changed, or a new software release is installed, there will be a "damping" effect. Immediately after the change is made, the number of test-related problems will increase and productivity will drop to unacceptable levels. During this period problems in the new component are ironed

out, corrections are made to the system and problems are discovered as a result of the new test component. This damping will occur at all test levels and must be considered when laying out the schedule.

Scheduling of software test activities, as with other software development, requires a third level of scheduling. These lower-level, or production schedules, plan the accomplishment of individual milestones identified on the work package schedule. As illustrated in Figure 3.7, these schedules are developed directly from the work package schedule and define at a detailed level the task and task relationships required to get to a specific test milestone.

Production schedules are most effective when scheduling activities less than six weeks in advance. Attempts to schedule at this level of detail any further out than six weeks is difficult to do because of the intricacies of the testing task relationships, the complexity of the test schedule, and the difficulty of projecting how a specific task will be accomplished before firm commitments of resources to the test milestone are made. Each of the individual milestones on the production schedule should be assignable to an individual and not be more than one week long. These schedules are effective motivators in the early stages of test planning when the data products are nonexecutable and difficult to produce. During this stage, the activities

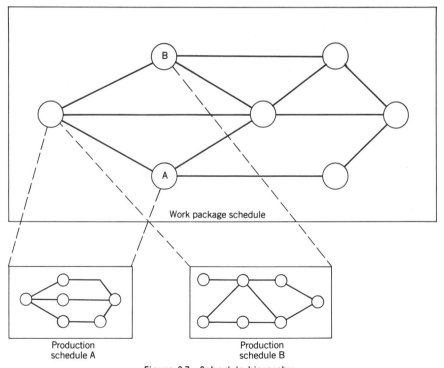

Figure 3.7   Schedule hierarchy

of the test staff must be continually focussed towards a narrow set of near-term goals rather than longer-term, less-defined milestones. Using this type of schedule, the relationship between the early test tasks is retained and the potential for overlap, redundancy, and surprises is minimized.

The development of production schedules is done backwards by the task leader assigned responsibility for the milestone. He or she defines the requirements and criteria for the milestone completion by discussion with the software test manager, interface meetings with task leaders who will use the output of his task, and reviews of contractual and work package requirements. From this list of milestone requirements is developed a list of the specific tasks, activities, and events which must be completed to satisfy the milestone. Each of these individual activities is then expanded to define the tasks, activities, and events required to satisfy each task, and the process continues until all the individual events are defined to produce the milestone.

From this linked list, a secondary analysis is performed which deletes redundant tasks, determines task constraints, defines essential task relationships, and links the individual tasks into a logical flow. At this point, the basic data is normally turned over to a scheduler who will develop the PERT schedule.

Once the basic schedule logic is drawn, the logic is adjusted modifying the projected work flow, the constraints, and the task relationships. This process will continue until the task leader is confident that the logic is correct and properly structured. The next step is for the task leader to time phase the schedule by calling in the individuals who will accomplish the work and having them define how long their particular task will take. Once all the scheduled activities have been time phased, the end date is computed and, if beyond the end date on the work package schedule, the individual task spans are negotiated with the personnel assigned responsibility. This negotiation continues until the milestone schedule is pulled back as far as possible. If the milestone dates are still incompatible with the work package schedule requirements, the task leader and software test manager negotiate the dates. Any unresolvable schedule discrepancies are resolved between the software project manager and software test manager.

This use of production schedules provides the motivation necessary to meet the critical early test milestones as well as providing the detailed planning necessary to coordinate and control the latter test stages. The production schedule will allow the test manager and the task leader sufficient early visibility into problems in the test schedule and early warning to permit correction of problems without major impact on cost, overall test schedules, or productivity.

EARNED VALUE—MEASURING PRODUCTIVITY

Use of the production schedule solves only part of the test scheduling problem: how to project the short-term work to be accomplished. The other part is to project and measure the productivity of individuals working against these schedules and assess their potential for success. An effective technique is to apply an earned value system to the monitoring and evaluation of progress against test schedules.

EVALUATING PROGRESS

As illustrated in Figure 3.8, the implementation of earned value system has three parts. At the top level, the software development activity described on the work package schedule represents 100 percent of the total software development effort. The individual tasks which comprise the development may be categorized into three areas: design tasks which represent 40 percent of the effort, coding tasks which make up 20 percent of the effort, and testing tasks which represent 40 percent of the overall work to be accom-

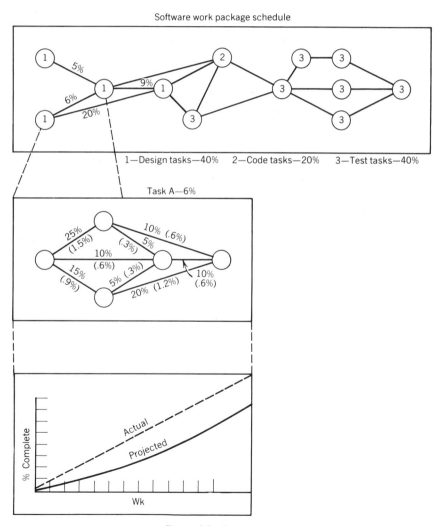

Figure 3.8   Earned value

plished. This categorization is done in two segments. The first segment identifies which category each milestone on the PERT falls into; 1 being design, 2 being code, and 3 being test. The next step is to assign a percentage to each categorized milestone relative to the total category. The percentage is multiplied by the overall percentage for the category to identify what percentage the individual milestone represents of the overall job.

The second level of earned value planning occurs when the production schedule for the milestone is completed. At this point a percentage that represents how much of the overall milestone production is represented by a submilestone on the production schedule. This percentage is multiplied by the overall percentage assigned to the milestone to derive the percentage that the submilestone represents of the overall job. The third step is to add all the completed submilestone percentages from all the production schedules to come up with a cumulative percentage of the job which must be completed if project productivity will be adequate to support the milestone date. This technique is unique in that it measures productivity rather than cost or schedules performance of the project. Rigorous use will provide the software test and project managers with early warning of poor performance and provide sufficient time to allow corrective procedures.

The final step in the use of earned value is the collection of data. The test manager weekly identifies which milestones have been completed and awards the preassigned percentage credit. This credit is only given when the milestone is completed and no partial credit is possible. The percentages are summed for all completed milestones that week and plotted against the projected accomplishment. The trend is projected to show projected overruns or underruns based on current performance.

Integration of the Cost/Schedule Projections

The initial cost and schedule estimates are the means by which the software manager validates the program budget and schedule information included in the software development and support work packages before committing to them. From this initial cost and scheduling, the software manager has a basic idea of the magnitude of the development. Early in the project these projections have not yet been modified to reflect the technical requirements of the project or the project requirements documented in the software development plan. This tailoring will be completed after the three initial, parallel planning tasks are complete.

This estimate represents all costs associated with the area, including project technical, support, management, and project control and quality assurance functions. In order to allocate these resources to the test and integration activities of the project, the resource projections and software schedules must be integrated. This is accomplished by reviewing each development schedule and categorizing each schedule milestone into design, code, or test. Each test milestone should be further broken into test support,

Software test

Test support costs	Module test	Unit test	Integration test	Functional test
7%	2%	3%	16%	12%

Figure 3.9 Test percentages

module test, unit test, integration test, and functional test. Any costs associated with system test (levels 5 and 6) activities are not included in these estimates and, as a result, should be treated as part of the program budgets. The percentages for each milestone should be multiplied by the 40 percent that testing represents of the overall project.

The resultant percentage is the percentage that each test milestone represents of the overall project budget.

Figure 3.9 illustrates representative percentages which may result from this analysis. The management, project control, review, and project level support functions are included in these estimates. The percentages in the figure are designed to illustrate the typical allocation of resources. A further breakdown and allocation of resources is accomplished by determining from the test profile the project parameters which are critical segments of each test phase. The overheads associated with each component identified on the profile are determined and used to suballocate resources to each project test level. The percentage identified for the profile component is multiplied by the percentage identified for the test level to generate a percentage that the profile component represents for the development as a whole.

These percentages, although based on nondocumented technical experience rather than detailed quantitative historical data, nevertheless are representative of the resources to be allocated to each testing area.

Application of the Initial Cost and Schedule Projections

The preliminary cost and schedule projections serve as the initial basis for sizing and allocating resources to the test activities. These initial estimates must be updated to reflect changes resulting from definition of the technical project requirements and the environment and development characteristics specified in the software development plan. The estimates provide preliminary basis for evaluating the allocation of resources to each test level.

PLANNING FOR CRISIS AVOIDANCE

Software development is a complex process requiring the careful integration of diverse disciplines, technical activities, and administrative project controls. Too often software projects are implemented without first defining and implementing firm plans to project how the software will be developed. The true measure of project effectiveness is how well management orchestrates the development activities, the effectiveness of the tools, techniques, and methodologies applied to the project, and the smoothness of the data flow and transition of responsibility as the implementation proceeds. Management controls must be defined and implemented to assure schedule and budget compliance, software quality, and correspondence to user requirements. In short, the software manager must plan and manage the disciplines required of software development and not just monitor their progress.

For the software manager, the pitfalls in software acquisition are numerous. To the uninitiated, the labyrinth of software development is overwhelming. The terminology is unclear, the technology is complex, and the acquisition, administration, and management of technical personnel and development activities seemingly impossible.

The manager too often throws up his or her hands in the midst of the development crisis, failing to recognize that although the form of the software management problems may be unique, the specific management techniques, practices, and procedures required to develop, integrate, and demonstrate software are based on good engineering management principles.

The characteristics of the software product which contribute significantly to the management dilemma are the lack of physical products associated with software development and the complexity of the management program necessary for control of software development.

Through rigorous application of discipline and judicious application of tools, techniques, and methodologies, software development can become an engineering discipline rather than a technological art form.

Too many software development projects experience difficulty because of the occurrence of situations which should have been anticipated, but weren't, resulting in significant productivity loss, a development catastrophe, or both. These crisis situations fall into three major areas.

1. *Project Planning Problems.* These inhibit the manager's effectiveness, limit the amount of time the manager has to commit to the project, or restricts his or her ability to deal with the technical, administrative, or political aspects of the development.

2. *Resource Availability Problems.* These result in the nonavailability of critical resources at key times in the project, an inability to assign or allocate the proper mix of resources to solve a particular project problem, or the loss of critical support at a key point in the development.

3. *Test and Integration Problems.* These are unanticipated, catching the project without sufficient, available resources and project experience, schedule, budget, or technical flexibility.

These crises creep into the project and their symptoms, although difficult to deal with, are unmistakable. These symptoms include:

1. A general lack of motivation on the part of personnel assigned to the project.
2. An inability on the part of the software personnel to meet schedule or cost milestones and to identify specific causes for the slips or over-runs.
3. A lack of general project understanding of how tools, techniques, and methodologies are integrated into the project environment, and the roles, responsibilities, and technical requirements of personnel and organizations within the project.
4. An inability to clearly state project goals, objectives, and technical project plans.
5. An overall lack of clear project organization, little or no communication between organizational elements, and an unclear flow of data within the project.

Early project planning is the means by which the software manager avoids the impacts associated with crises which will befall the project. These plans are what give structure to the project during the early requirements and design phases of the project, and throughout the latter stages of implementation, integration, and test. Unless this planning is done early and maintained and modified as project conditions change, the focus of the project may be lost and productivity reduced.

In order to avoid the crises which will affect the project, the manager should scale all plans to support the most stringent project period, nominally the test and integration period of the project. By not planning for the most stringent and demanding project environment, the manager will find that he or she will continually be reacting to inadequate project support, poor project performance when the complexity and magnitude of the data outstrips the ability of the project to control it, and frequent resource shortfalls not anticipated or budgeted. Proper planning will ensure that project resources will not be overloaded when the project activity or data production reaches a critical point.

Ideally, the manager should structure all project plans to the most complex of all project activities, scaling them to support the needs of the development. In order to ensure that these requirements are properly scaled, it is essential that the planning be accomplished in reverse order. The requirements for software delivery should be defined first, followed by a definition of each of the levels of testing in the opposite order to which they will occur in the project. After the test requirements are defined, the requirements for code, design, and requirements definition should be identified. This reverse planning will result in a project profile which may then serve as the basis for the software development plan, cost and schedule projects, and technical planning.

This early project planning is the means by which the software manager gives early form and structure to the project. It is through this planning that the myriad development tools, techniques, and methodologies are selected and applied to the project. The rigorous development and application of the plan provides a documented structure for the project and communicates the plans for development upward through the customer and program organizations, and communicates the roles, resources, responsibilities, and development requirements of each organizational component downward through the software organization.

Once the plans, schedules, budgets, and project requirements are clearly defined, the manager must take an active and effective role in ensuring their implementation. Technical personnel will threaten to quit, managers at all levels will threaten funding restrictions and career impacts, customer personnel will threaten program impacts if their ideas are not incorporated into the program. A variety of observers outside the program will point out critical shortcomings, and "grave concerns." The manager must, however, keep his or her focus changing only the project environment when it makes sense in the context of the approved, implemented, and documented project environment. Unless the manager retains his or her focus, rigorously implementing the project plans despite external pressures, he or she will find the project quickly bogging down in the morass of poor requirements, missed milestones, or overrun budgets. In this situation, there is a tendency to monitor project performance rather than manage the project and direct its progress; there is a disastrous temptation for the manager to retreat to the safety of management reports and projections and away from the unpleasant day-to-day management and decision-making process essential for success.

The effective software manager must realize that he or she is responsible and accountable for the project, that he or she must focus, direct, and control the activities of the project, and that he or she will only succeed to the degree that he or she can organize and motivate others.

The manager must pay close attention to all project areas at all times and must be able to recognize when procedures are not working well. There should be no crisis or reactive management, but rather a smooth, controlled flow of data and responsibility as the project transitions through each stage of development.

Resource Availability—The Right Ones When Needed

The nonavailability of critical resources when needed is a common cause of software productivity impacts, often limiting or precluding implementation success. Consider the project problems resulting from slippage in a critical hardware schedule, the unanticipated termination of a key employee, or the removal or redirection of a key resource in the midst of the development. Unless anticipated, these situations can be devastating, undermining the ability of the project to develop the software in accordance with predefined budgets and schedules. Because of the nature of the software development process these crises most often become critical during the integration of the software into an executable configuration.

These project crises can be avoided, but only if they are anticipated, solutions planned, and the planned solutions rigorously implemented.

As illustrated in Figure 3.10, the common resource-related problems which may be anticipated fall into three categories.

1. Hardware facilities essential to the project but not available when needed.
2. Personnel resources required at a given point in the project but, due to conditions outside the control of the software manager, not available when needed.
3. Resource shortfalls in key areas resulting from poor early planning, changing project conditions, or both.

Each of these problems has a significant potential for occurrence. The software manager should recognize their potential and develop a crisis matrix similar to that in the figure. The matrix should be maintained as project conditions warrant and identify each key resource on the project that constrains the development, its commitment to the project, the risks associated with loss, and an alternate optional source for the support.

When dealing with resource crisis planning, the primary options available to a manager involve the continual prioritizing of key resources, the backing up of all resources, and the planning of alternatives early when sources are easy to find.

Potential Technical Test and Integration Crises

The majority of the critical project crises occur during software test and integration. It is during this period that all deferred project problems, all poorly defined interfaces and hardware support, all poorly executed systems engineering, and all ineffective or poorly conceived management or technical controls must be dealt with and resolved if the project is to succeed.

As illustrated in Figure 3.11, the potential for catastrophe associated with testing, may be best dealt with through early planning.

The early project planning provides a vehicle for the software manager to document plans, procedures, and practices which will be followed during the test and integration period of the software project. The early planning critical to the long-term success of the project effectiveness is a component of project health and development productivity. Through this planning the manager anticipates predictable crises which will, in all likelihood, occur

Crisis area	Affected phase	Impact	Early symptoms	Planning option
1. Schedule difficulty due to extended development and code time	Requirements definition, design, code integration, and test	Software not ready when tests ready for execution	Insufficient time to test software resulting in schedule slop	Phase software testing into build testing software when available
2. An inability to translate requirements and design to test procedures	Test and integration	Nonfunctional software test procedures	Delivery of a system not responsive to user needs	Conduct customer user reviews of test data iterating requirements and specifications when needed
3. An inability to develop executable test cases from procedures	Test and integration	Test personnel cannot specify test script from procedures	Test scripts not adequate representation of software execution characteristic	Phase development personnel into test planning activities
5. Insufficient interface definition and inability to duplicate exact test conditions	Test and integration	Nonpredictability of test results	Software systems with known problems delivered to customer	Hard code test scripts readable through simulator
6. Ambiguous user specifications or system operator instructions	Test and integration	Insufficient data to develop procedures	Procedures which do not match system support requirements	Plan tests early and iterate details as system detail increases

7. An unavoidable schedule delay between system releases when new software configurations stabilize	Test and integration	Repeated delays in qualifying system release	Significant schedule impacts due to poor initial performance of software releases	Schedule informal software burn-in period with each release
9. Delays associated with corrections of problems	Test and integration	Repeated slips due to problem correction delays	Poorly qualified systems	Plan for software configuration management and overlap system releases
10. Insufficient internal data available to diagnose and correct problems	Test and integration	Necessity to retest repeatedly to diagnose problems	Poorly qualified releases	Plan simulation and instrumentation development, installation, use, and removal
11. Baselines lost during development and corrections lost during test	Test and integration	System releases not controlled or of unknown content	Frequent test and development restarts	Plan, implement and integrate strong, effective software

Figure 3.10 Predictable resource problems

Crisis area	Affected phase	Impact	Early symptoms	Planning option
Hardware				
a. Non availability of hardware or key test support equipment	Test and integration	Schedule delays due to hardware slips	Software schedules keyed to hardware availability	Plan to simulate critical hardware interfaces and support
b. Inadequate hardware availability or reliability	Test and integration	Frequent impacts due to hardware failures	Significant hardware-caused delays on the software schedule	Find alternate hardware source or simulation facility from beginning of project
c. Inadequate hardware facilities to support needs	Requirements definition, design, code, integration, and test	Difficulty scheduling resources, early unnecessary overtime to support availability	Poor productivity, low morale	Find adequate alternate facilities, keep project files organized so they may be split by facility
Personnel				
a. Insufficient manpower available	Requirements definition, design, code, integration, and test	Excessive overtime required	Employee demotivation and turnover	Provide for manpower pool, sharing resources between test, development, and support

b. Loss of key individual	Requirements definition, design, code, integration, and test	Obvious dissatisfaction, poor mouthing project, bad attitude	Project delay, poor productivity, inadequate support	Find and train key man backups early in project
Resource a. Delays in promised resources	Requirements definition, design, code, integration, and test	Early excuses from person providing resource—poor early schedule performance	Resource nonavailability project delay	Continually check availability—back up all plans
b. Diversion of key resource	Requirements definition, design, code, integration, and test	Failure of program or company to commit resource through project period	Scheduling impacts and project delays	Back up all planned resources

Figure 3.11 Predictable test and integration problems

during the testing period. These crises, summarized in Figure 6.2, will occur during the testing period unless addressed during the planning period when solutions may be integrated into the project plan. If not effectively dealt with, these crises can cause the software project to stop during the most critical period of the development: integration, test and system qualification.

Because of the pressures on the software manager during the planning period, there is a tendency to defer verification and validation planning until "we can get to it." On the surface it appears that there is plenty of time to resolve testing issues since there is no immediate pressing need for answers to the verification and validation problem. There is a temptation to look on it as a problem whose "time will come."

Deferring test planning is a trap which the software manager may fall into early in the project. The test problem is the most stringent of all project requirements, necessitating the effective implementation, integration, and application of a variety of project disciplines to succeed. These disciplines must be initially defined and implemented in accordance with the requirements for testing in order to ensure a smooth project transition from software implementation to test and integration. Adequate project control over technical products and project resources during this period is essential. The software manager must, from the outset, plan for the worst and assume from the beginning that software verification and validation will not go well and will continue to be difficult until the last customer acceptance test has been run. There is no room for optimism in test planning!

INTEGRATING SCHEDULES, BUDGETS, THE INITIAL PLAN, AND THE TECHNICAL REQUIREMENTS

At this point in the software project planning process, four separate data items have been developed.

1. **The System Requirements.** These have been defined, documented, and placed under program configuration management. In addition, a preliminary allocation of these requirements to software and hardware has been made and, in the case of software requirements, been placed under software configuration management.

2. **A Preliminary Software Development Plan.** This has been developed to describe what will be done by the project to support implementation of the software and how the process will be managed and controlled.

3. **Schedules, budgets, and project performance monitoring.** These have been developed based on a preliminary analysis of the software requirements, the allocation of work assigned through the work packages, and the percentages allocated throughout the software project by the software manager.

4. **Project Crises Matrices.** These have been created to identify the specific project areas that the software manager feels require emphasis, the early project symptoms that indicate problems in the area, and planning options which can minimize the effects of crises on the project if they occur.

These four areas must be integrated if the planning is to be complete, consistent between planning areas, and relevant in the context of the project environment.

This integration step in the planning process entails reviewing the software development plan a section at a time against the complexity and technical characteristics of the software requirements, the constraints imposed by budget and schedules, and the planning requirements defined in the Crises Matrices. Through this review the manager ensures the initial plans are properly scaled to the requirements of the application and essential planning requirements are included and adequately covered in the Software Development Plan. As a result of this review, three actions may result.

1. Schedules, budgets, and technical resource requirements are augmented to provide sufficient support to the project.
2. The Software Development Plan is modified to scale the support to the budgets, schedules, or technical constraints of the project.
3. The technical requirements of the project are modified, scaling them to the development environment and to the cost schedule and technical constraints of the project.

The updated software plans and technical requirements must be reviewed with the program to ensure that they are consistent with the requirements of the work breakdown structure. This review should balance technical requirements of the program against development, organizational, and program support and management requirements of the software project. The requirements and plans should also be reviewed with the technical personnel assigned responsibility for the technical development. The review is essential to ensure that the technical personnel who will program the work understand the requirements and plans and are committed to the modifications. This review is essential to ensure that the technical personnel understand the development requirement and are committed to the development plans, budgets, and schedules.

4 The Software Test Environment

If the test environment and data development is not initiated early, there will be insufficient time to develop them and still maintain project test schedules.

As illustrated in Figure 4.1, the software project environment establishes the basic structure within which the software test and integration segments of the project are tailored, scaled, organized, and applied.

From early in the project emphasis should be tailored to support the later phases of testing: test execution, analysis, and problem correction. The integration and application of tools, techniques, and methodologies should be phased into the project in a preordered sequence which ensures a controlled and effective flow of project data and a smooth transition of responsibility. The project environment during testing should address the following questions.

1. What data products are required for development of each of the test products, where are they located, how do I get the latest version, and how do I change it?

2. How can I get a complete version of the latest software, who will develop it, how will it be documented, and how am I assured that I am using the same version as other areas of the project?

3. Where are the project support facilities provided, how are they provided to the using organizations, how are they supported through automated facilities, and how are they integrated into the project environment?

4. Organizationally, how are the data management project support and control aspects of the project integrated with the test and integration segments of the project?

The software test process uses and develops several categories of project data. Library control will establish, control, and monitor the status of soft-

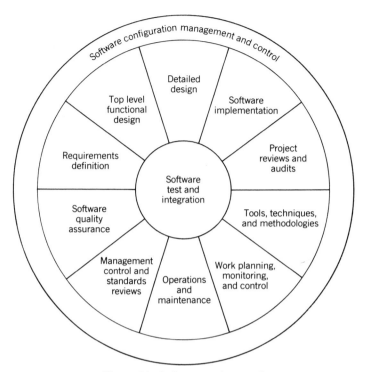

Figure 4.1   Software environment

ware requirements and design baselines and, later, the programming products. Library control will be closely coupled with development, test, and integration activities.

The type, form, and organization of the data developed by the project changes as development milestones are crossed. In order to assure that software development is controlled and built upon a firm, documented basis, the technical data should be placed under control as early in the project as feasible. This is normally within the first several months of the project.

The following sections detail how changes to software products are controlled, as well as the record-keeping activities, which must take place in order to provide detailed project status information throughout the software development cycle.

THE PROGRAM SUPPORT LIBRARY—CONTROLLING THE PRODUCTS OF SOFTWARE DEVELOPMENT

The Program Support Library (PSL) is the means for managing and controlling the flow of data inside the software project. The PSL should be centralized in the project, integrating manual, automated, and procedural techniques to the problems of software configuration management and control. The automated segments of the PSL consist of a multi-directory data base containing various versions of the software, a set of tools such as text and word processors, file management tools, problem-reporting and electronic mail facilities, and management and support tools that monitor and control the data resident in the PSL. In programming projects of even moderate dimensions, this automated PSL support is essential to maintaining data integrity and keeping pace with the testing phases of the project.

The PSL is organized into four logical areas. The working area is the segment of the library where the uncontrolled developing data products reside. This area, although controlled by the technical personnel on the project, is allocated, structured, and supported through the PSL.

The controlled segment of the library is controlled at a software project level. All data resident in this area can only be entered or changed after a project review or formal approval of a change.

The configuration management portion of the library is the work area for the PSL. The area is administered by the librarian and contains working PSL files, PSL data, and information which is transitioning between areas of the library.

The documentation area of the library has two components. The first is the program baseline component, which contains copies of all data reviewed and approved by the customer and a working area where project documentation is developed. The baseline area is controlled by the program manager through the Configuration Control Board. The document development area is the responsibility of the document coordinator assigned responsibility by the software project for producing a particular deliverable project.

These areas are logical groupings of information, each having different project control and support requirements. Access to the information, control of all data contained within the library, the flow of information throughout the project, and the integrity of all information within the PSL is the responsibility of the PSL librarian. The librarian provides:

1. Technical control and project monitoring of the integrity and consistency of all PSL data in relation to project standards. In this role the PSL, quality assurance, the review and audit activities of the project and the technical review boards all work closely towards a common end.

2. Organizational facilities and support for controlling and administering the flow of information throughout the software project, between the project and other segments of the program, and all data released to the customer.

3. Reporting procedures, processing and support for the standardized reporting and documentation of software requirements and interface

issues, design or implementation questions or problems, and coding or testing discrepancies.

4. Documentation and controlled dissemination of library contents and data products.

5. Control of software data products, including documentation, source code, executable software configurations, and status records for all software elements.

Two forms of control should be integral to the approach and are provided for configuration management control.

1. Informal development control and code, build and test parameters should be maintained and controlled by each project area.

2. Formal configuration management files under project library control should contain the released version of all software documentation, software and test results.

This project component is the responsibility of the PSL librarian. The Program Librarian controls the major release level of all baseline and other controlled documents and assures that all releases are carried out in a timely manner. He or she implements and enforces software and firmware configuration management and control procedures as well as reviewing library submittals for proper approvals and adherence to project standards. He or she assures that backup procedures are maintained and that the controlled material is properly secured. Finally, the librarian transfers code from user files to controlled files, providing official code and data for use during problem investigation and to carry out official testing.

Standard File Organization

In order to keep up with the demands of the project the PSL should use an integrated configuration management file control structure. Specifications and other controlled documents should be on the PSL files as well as all source code. Through the project librarian control of each software data product should be ensured.

Text editors and file formatters available on the automated facility should be used to support document and source code entry and modification of configuration management procedures.

The file structure to be used to support software development and configuration management should reflect the hierarchical structure of the program code development process. The file structure illustrated in Figure 4.2, provides a hierarchical architecture to track the development process.

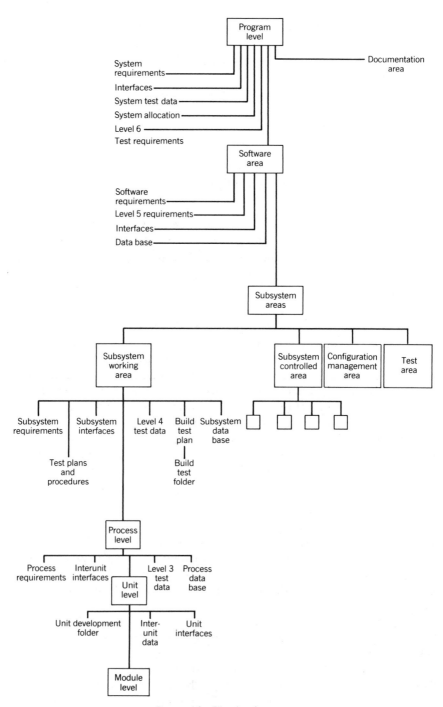

Figure 4.2   File structure

WORKING PSL AREA

The working area, allocated by the librarian, supports the following.

1. Transfer files for building systems for test.
2. Source files of software not released to the librarian.
3. Source files of test data structure.
4. Test data, tools, and simulation facilities.
5. Executable test versions of the software and preliminary versions of requirements, design and test data.

The structure of the PSL working areas tracks the format of the controlled area. At the subsystem level, the PSL working area provides for storage of system functional requirements allocated to the function; system and intersystem interfaces supported by the subsystem; software testing information unique to the subsystem; and subsystem design and transaction flows that, when implemented, support the funtional requirements of the subsystem. The next hierarchical level of the working area of the PSL provides an area for the storage and control of programmer-controlled implementation and test data. Within this level, the software designer stores working versions of the data base for the software systems design, interprocess interface information, and data dictionary information required for development, test, or integration of the process. The lowest level of the hierarchy, the unit and module level, should provide for the storage and control of Unit Development Folders and programmer notebook information. The working area also provides for storage of working copies of data base elements. The area contains a copy of the controlled data base for working modification and update. The working area provides for the storage of various project utility software developed during the implementation. These utilities are treated as tools, not maintained or supported by the project but available through the PSL for programmer application.

The final component is the build segment, which is an area within the working area for storing working copies of software builds and build records for informal versions testing.

The working area is the domain of the individual programmer and not subject to project control. All items contained in the working area may be modified by the programmer responsible, directly, without PSL approval or cognizance.

Transfer of Data

All software should undergo three basic walkthroughs: unit design walkthrough, unit code review, and unit test walkthrough. Successful completion of these walkthroughs should be required to accomplish schedule milestones and authorize transfer of data from the working area of the PSL to the controlled area.

The second method of transferring software from informal to controlled status is through Software Configuration Review Board (SCRB) action. These actions result from the processing of approved Software Problem Reports (SPR). This board should review and evaluate all software reports, authorize appropriate corrective actions to be taken, and track the status of all changes made. If it is determined that the recommended change affects approved specifications, cost, or schedule parameters, the SPRs are forwarded to the project for resolution.

When the SCRB tasks the Software Development Organization to implement an approved change, the individual assigned responsibility for the correction obtains the correct version of the affected software and the related documentation from the librarian. The data is copied from the controlled library area to the working area. The software development staff does all work in the working area. When it is completed, the software and/or documentation is ready for release to the controlled library through SCRB approval. When an SPR is reported closed by the software organization, the SCRB examines the corrected package for adequacy and completeness. Upon approval of this package, the SCRB notifies the librarian to accept the changed software, it is necessary to complete a Version Description Document (VDD) to log the SPRs closed, and to incorporate the changes into the controlled software library.

When data is approved for transfer, either through SCRB action or project reviews or walkthroughs, the librarian should transfer the information from the working area to the hold segment of the configuration management area. The librarian generates either a new or interim system release, documenting the configuration in a Version Description Document.

When processed, the data should be transferred from the user area of the PSL to the controlled area, where it should be released for use within the project.

A third method for transferring information into the controlled segment of the PSL is the acquisition or reuse of software in a software system or subsystem configuration. Before recommending a software product for use in a system or subsystem configuration, the project should evaluate the software against the following criteria.

1. **Compatability.** Are the language, interfaces, operational compatability, size, and software documentation compatible with the technical and development requirements of the project.

2. **Traceability and Testability.** Is the software component testable and traceable when integrated into the subsystem configuration.

3. **Completeness.** Does the software component satisfy the technical, interface, and support requirements of the application without significant modification.

4.   **Cost and Schedule.** Can the component be integrated into the configuration without a major commitment of cost or schedule.

5.   **Usability.** When integrated, will the software perform within the operational and reliability requirements of the system application.

These parameters should be evaluated at a review conducted by the software project before the decision is made to use the software. The review should evaluate the software against the project requirements, identifying modifications required to make it usable by the system. Specific changes to documentation, the technical configuration of the software, or changes required to make it compatible with the needs of the project are identified. The results of these analyses and the real costs of acquiring and integrating the software are identified before a commitment is made to use it in the configuration. If approved, the software should be acquired by the PSL and a specific plan for integrating it and validating the component should be developed.

CONTROLLED PSL AREA

The controlled area of the PSL is the center of all project configuration management and control. This library segment is the repository for three categories of data.

1.   **Requirements and Functional Allocation.** Contains the agreed to operational, functional, and interface baselines upon which the software development is based.

2.   **Design and Implementation Information.** Contains controlled software and data base design and coding data which has been approved through a project walkthrough or review.

3.   **Software Test and Support Data.** Contains controlled test data, tools, and supporting utility software used by more than one segment of the project in developing, integrating, or demonstrating the software.

The structure of the controlled PSL segment should be hierarchical, tracking the way that data will be produced by the project during the development, the phasing of data production, and the organization of the working areas.

Definition and control of the system requirements and interfaces is at the top of the hierarchy. At this level the basic development specifications and criteria for the software system are defined. These are the basis for all development activities as well as being the technical base for the software to software integration phase of level 5 testing. The system requirements should establish a structured and traceable definition of system requirements allocated to specific software subsystems controlled by PSL. Designers of the system define system flow and processing as well as test requirements linked to the system requirements. This definition should be controlled through the PSL.

Implementation and integration data require PSL production and modification of software systems to support integration activities from baselined software data resident in the controlled area of the library. This data is provided to the project through the PSL and documented in release specific Version Description Documents. These document the specific contents of each software release as well as the status of system and software discrepancies.

Controlled source builds are generated through the PSL to support software system testing. These builds utilize the automated facilities of the PSL, selecting the latest version (or selected versions) of each module required in the build from the controlled area. Modules that are not available in the controlled area are flagged and the librarian has the option of selecting replacements from the working area. These software versions are assigned unique version numbers and the contents are formally maintained as the current supported sofware system.

All library builds should be documented through a Version Description Document. The VDD is generated through the PSL. The VDD documents specific requirements of the system builds, each module by release level included in the system release, all SPRs closed by this release, and discrepancies that remain open. VDDs should be automatically provided by the PSL system. In addition, the PSL releases interim versions of the system software based on current controlled versions.

CONFIGURATION MANAGEMENT AREA OF THE PSL

The configuration management area of the PSL is the configuration management working area accessible by PSL personnel. The function of this segment is to allow storage of configuration management data essential for PSL functioning as well as storage and control of user-supplied data that describes documentation production requirements. It also serves as a holding area for transitioning software project information from the working area of the PSL to PSL-controlled files.

This PSL segment is controlled by the PSL librarian. PSL-supported configuration management tools and data are stored in this area and the librarian may approve modification without additional review or approval.

THE DOCUMENTATION AREA

The documentation area of the PSL has two segments: one controlled by the program through the Configuration Control Board (CCB), and the second used to develop deliverable data products from information contained in other areas of the PSL. Documentation, application programs, and support software that have been signed (bought) off by the Program Office go under control of the Program Office. Changes to be made to any of these are subject to Configuration Control Board review and approval. CCB procedures that are implemented during the program will be adhered to by the software development teams for all programs and documents under CCB control. The CCB should work closely with the SCRB, and the PSL to control released code and documentation that are under investigation and/or being redone. This joint responsibility should continue until the initiating Software Performance report, problem report, or change request is officially closed.

If a discrepancy is determined by the CCB to require contract change, this should be negotiated with the customer. Once a change has been approved by the customer, it is returned to the CCB and logged as approved by the CCB secretary. The CCB should make the determination as to how the software and hardware are affected. They then update the scope of the software effort and the software project should increase or decrease its effort.

The second segment of the documentation area is controlled by the individuals assigned responsibility for the production of project deliverables.

The specific outline for each document development and the section-by-section content requirements of each is stored in the documentation area by the document coordinator. This serves as the basis for the development, production, and evaluation of all format project documents, as well as the identification of data control and format requirements collected as the development proceeds.

TEST AREA

The test area is one segment of the PSL which most likely will not reside on the file structure. The reason for this is that configuration management and the file structure as described above is an effective control mechanism for textual and source data, but does not lend itself well to control of object code.

The PSL releases controlled source code and documentation to the test organization along with a VDD documenting the contents.

The test group compiles this source on the target machine, link editing an executable test version of the software system. All problems identified on the system are documented on the SPR form, and updates to the controlled library will be through approved source code updates.

Software Performance Reports/Software Configuration Review Board Processing

During testing, problems are discovered with controlled software result in preparation of a SPR which is prepared and sent to the Project Librarian. The originator indicates the type of problem. If this person performed the analysis, he or she may propose a solution. If possible, the originator should also indicate the impact on cost, performance, and schedule and the consequence if the problem is not corrected. The Project Librarian sends a copy to the SCRB (Software Configuration Review Board) and places the SPR on the agenda for the SCRB meeting.

The Software Configuration Review Board is established to evaluate all proposed changes to the software and for processing/disposition of Software Performance Reports, authorize appropriate corrective action to be taken, track status of all changes in progress, and close the Software Performance Reports after the changes have been made.

When the SCRB convenes, it decides if the SPR is outside the scope of the software baselines or review board responsibility. Out-of-scope changes require concurrence on classification by the project CCB and increased tasking by the program manager. Otherwise the SPR is processed. It can be rejected, approved for study, or approved for implementation. If rejected, the SCRB chairman signs the SPR as rejected, the SPR is closed, and the Project Librarian will give a copy to the originator. If the SCRB determines that an SPR originated from the CCB is not software related, the SPR will be returned to the CCB.

If the SCRB is tasked by the CCB for the software change under a contract change, a determination will be made by the SCRB as to the extent of modification, and a draft task statement will be prepared as an estimate of the required effort, for CCB approval. Once the task is approved, the SCRB will direct the required changes with the same controls as discussed above.

The composition of the SCRB will vary from activity to activity. For example, during the Define and Design Activities, members of the design team will be represented. During later activity, members of the integration and verification team will be represented.

The software project environment described above provides a structure which supports the smooth and controlled flow of data from the beginning of the project through integration and test. Centralizing the software configuration management functions in a Program Support Library provides an effective means within the project of ensuring the integrity of all data used throughout the project. Integration of manual, automated, and project review procedures into the PSL environment provides project environment capable of dealing with the explosion of data which will occur during the detailed design, code, integration, and test segments of the project.

Control and Release of Software During Test

As illustrated in Figure 4.3, the control and release of software during testing is a complex project requirement. The PSL must have the capability to generate and document multiple system releases concurrently to support the various test levels, and generate various maintenance versions for each controlled system release.

Each of these releases has included a different set of functional requirements, is described through different releases of the project documentation,

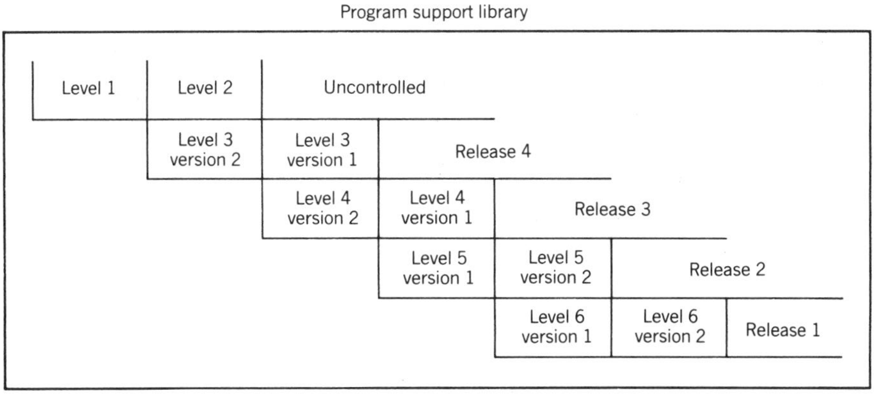

Program support library

Figure 4.3   Software control and release

and is used at different test levels. Each system release may also have different maintenance versions outstanding, each with different configurations and with different problems outstanding and corrected.

All software released by the PSL, whether it be a formal software release or an informal version under a release, should be formally documented by the PSL. All builds should be primarily generated from the controlled files with data being included from working files only.

Basic Library Tool Set

In order to automate the library functions, a set of tools tailor standard system support functions to the library support requirements. These tools assume a standard file structure as described above.

Status accounting and support tools control the inventory of software maintained by the library as well as provide automated facilities for documenting baselined application software configuration. Six primary tool categories support the status accounting and support functions of the library:

1. **Library Inventory.** Facilitates entering individual components into each of the segments of the library file structure, documenting the complete contents of all library segments by version; generates hard-copy library reports, summarizing the contents of the controlled and documentation segments of the library.

2. **Version Description Document (VDD) Production.** Uses statistics maintained by the library to automatically generate version description documentation, which describes each baselined configuration by release level of each component of the software and documentation, problems, and reports that have been closed by this software release, and problem reports that remain open.

3. **File Support.** Maintains the file structure, facilitating the entry and removal of components, compressing files when needed, and monitoring file usage to assure space availability.

4. **Release Control.** Collects data from the controlled and documentation segments of the library; configures the data into a release configuration; and generates a package for distribution.

5. **Library Cross Reference.** Correlates the contents of all library segments of the file structure; provides the linkage between components; provides facilities for the librarian to modify linkages; and generates hardcopy cross-reference reports.

6. **Schedule Control.** Defines and monitors production schedules in response to requests for application software from qualified subscribers.

These tools, when implemented, will provide an efficient means for utilizing automated facilities in generating and documenting software releases for distribution. These tools also establish the environment by which the librarian maintains the file structure and documents library contents and status.

Separate categories of configuration control tools support documentation of operational problems experienced in field application, control of baselined software configuration, and documentation and control of software updates. The configuration control tool categories are:

1. **Automated Problem Reporting.** Facilitates the on-line reporting of operational software discrepancies either by the librarian or by contractor personnel; prompts the user, formats the input, summarizes the problem reports, and categorizes problems according to application area.

2. **Audit Checklist.** Supports evaluation of software submittals and documentation of the audit ranking.

3. **Status Change.** Allows the librarian to categorize the software submittal, identify and change the submitted status, and work with other tools to move software between library segments as the status of the software changes.

4. **Support.** Allows approved subscribers to interact with the library through interfaced terminals.

5. **Problem Summary Report.** Generates a hard-copy, ordered report of outstanding problems keyed to specific application tools.

6. **Problem Alerts.** Flags critical problems of application software components.

7. **Library Segment Move.** Moves software, documentation, and data elements between file segments of the library, maintaining traceability as the data is moved.

These tools should be implemented to minimize required development resources.

SOFTWARE QUALITY ASSURANCE DURING TEST

During test planning, development, execution, and analysis the software quality assurance activities fall into two major categories.

1. Internal, program, and customer project reviews, walkthroughs, and audits which monitor the integrity of software data while it is under development and assure that when the data is used by the test areas of the project it will be of consistent quality.
2. External evaluations of the health, status, and integrity of the software project, ensuring that any problems are uncovered early enough to avoid test impacts.

These reviews and external monitoring activities are the eyes management has into the development process. They are the means to maintain visibility into the development activities and provide the data a manager needs to make accurate, meaningful decisions.

These reviews and audits span the entire period of development validating the integrity of the technical baselines and evaluating the integrity of the project. If rigorously enforced and used as the configuration management status monitoring points, these reviews ensure that the data placed under project control meets project requirements, standards, and conventions and is of sufficient quality and integrity to provide a basis for test planning and development.

Program, Customer, and Internal Reviews

All system and subsystem software should undergo five major customer reviews. These reviews, often known as "dog and pony shows," are formal presentations describing the results of project analysis, design, or test activities. The five reviews are:

1. **Systems Requirements Review.** Presents the understanding of the user's requirements, the plans for developing, testing, and integrating the system, and the tools, techniques and methodologies to be used.

2. **System Design Review.** Presents the evaluations of the proposed system application, the interfaces and data requirements, the specific techniques to be used for developing the software and the schedule and cost for development.

3. **Preliminary Design Review.** Describes all functional requirements and interfaces, the functional design, and the development environment.

4. **Critical Design Review.** Determines if the integrity of the program logical design is adequate to start coding and test that the design materials are complete, adequately specified, and properly controlled. The final plans for development should be presented and reviewed.

5. **Acceptance Test Review.** Evaluates the completeness of the test procedures, the adequacy of the test scenarios which detail the requirements of the procedures, the test data, the test tools used, and the level 2–5 test results.

These reviews maintain visibility into the process of software development; however, these reviews are "after-the-fact" evaluation of end item and milestone development. Problems found during these reviews have already impacted the program and many require a significant commitment to correct. For this reason, the project should apply internal walkthroughs to evaluate application requirements, developing design, code, and level 2–6 data products. Customer participation is encouraged at these walkthroughs. All data product reviewed and approved at these walkthroughs should be baselined through the PSL and released for use by the next phase of development. The ten walkthroughs are:

1. **Requirements Walkthrough (RW).** Evaluates the requirements received from the customer for completeness, consistentcy with related software systems, and for testability, traceability, and technical integrity. A "what of" analysis of the requirements should be performed at the walkthrough. The walkthrough should be chaired by the technical manager and supported by the software systems engineering staff.

2. **Operation Concept Walkthrough (OCW).** The operational concept should be reviewed at the OCW. The Operational Concept for the software should be reviewed prior to formal presentation at the SRR. The system interaction to the user is evaluated, the human engineering aspects of the system analyzed, and the interfaces and development requirements investigated. This walkthrough should be conducted by the technical manager, as supported by the systems engineering staff and should result in baselining of the operations concept through the PSL.

3. **Software Requirements Walkthrough (SRW).** Evaluates the basic proposed architecture of the software system and the initial allocation of requirements to the various components of the software configuration. This walkthrough should be conducted prior to the SDR by the technical manager supported by the system engineering staff. The initial software architecture and structure should be baselined through the PSL after this review.

4. **Functional Design Walkthrough (FDW).** At each level of the functional decomposition, a walkthrough should be conducted to ensure technical integrity and validity. The walkthrough should be the responsibility of the technical manager; however, the parallelism inherent in the review process requires delegation of this responsibility to the system engineering staff. At each level of the decomposition an FDW should be conducted, with all data at that level being baselined after review and approval.

5. **Design Analysis Review (DAR).** A walkthrough should be held for each software unit preceding the functional allocation and overall design concept. The participants should include the responsible programmer, his

or her immediate technical supervisor, and a group of peers. The participants should review the material for completeness, compliance with standards, and compliance with the requirements and interfaces defined.

6.   **Unit Design Walkthroughs (UDW).** The DW should occur upon completion of the unit design and the unit test definition, when the design is completed on paper and not coded beyond that level. The DW should concentrate on adherence to requirements, design, interfaces, and on the relationship of the module(s) to the software subsystem. A structured SW should be held for every unit to review the intended design.

7.   **Code Review (CR).** The CR should occur upon completion of coding. It should be conducted by a senior designer (normally the task leader) or the senior technical member of the staff. The CR should concentrate on acceptable coding techniques and adherence to standards. The code should be verified against the design to identify any coding errors. Upon successful completion of the CR, the reviewing authority should indicate required changes and corrections. The code walkthrough should verify that this unit implementation meets project standards and implements the unit design accurately.

8.   **Unit Test Walkthrough (UTW).** The UTW should occur upon successful completion of unit testing. The UTW should validate the final module source code, should review the unit test scope, and test materials for completeness and correct results. The responsible programmer should make required changes and corrections and conduct any necessary retesting. This is the last informal review of the software prior to the start of integration testing. As such, the manager must ensure that UTWs are conducted for each and every unit despite schedule and cost pressures. The responsible programmer delivers the tested source and matching portion of the software documentation. The program walkthrough leader should independently review the code and documentation for compliance with standards and conventions and should place them under configuration management and sign off the unit as completed.

9.   **Build Walkthrough (BW).** A build review should be conducted prior to the demonstration of a build to the Software Manager. The Software Integration and Test Plan, the Unit Development Folders, and the Build Test Plans of the Build Development Folders should be reviewed. The participants should include the technical supervisors and key programmers involved with the build. Materials to be reviewed should be provided to the participants prior to the review. Upon completion of the review, the integration test procedures and integration test results should be made available to the Technical Manager prior to the build demonstration. The build demonstration must be brought under library control prior to the demonstration.

10.   **Acquisition/Reusability Review (ARR).** An additional informal review should be conducted to evaluate software prior to acquisition by the project for use in the software system or subsystem configuration. This review

should be conducted by the Software Systems Engineering Group and, when successfully completed, should authorize procurement or application of the component. The review should be chaired by a technical member of the software system engineering staff. This group should review the proposed acquisition in the context of the system configuration. Considered should be the specific functional support to be provided by the software, the technical compatibility of the software architecture, the documentation quality, and compatibility with project standards.

Independent Software Quality Assurance

In addition to these internal reviews, an independent quality assurance representative should perform two primary activities directly for the program manager: audit the formal and informal project baseline for technical integrity, contractual compliance, and project standards; and review the project for adequacy, development integrity, and application of the requirements of the software development and second-level project plan.

Prior to each walkthrough or review, QA should audit the materials to be presented to independently assess traceability to the previous baseline and to certify completeness and technical integrity. QA should attend all walkthroughs and reviews to ensure compliance with customer and project standards and should audit all internal and deliverable and internal project documentation for adequacy, technical integrity, and compliance to applicable standards.

INFORMAL TECHNICAL PROGRESS MEETINGS

The Quality Assurance activities should provide the customer clear visibility into the project throughout the development period. For this reason all walkthroughs, project SCRB and CCB meetings, and technical and quality assurance reviews and audits should be attended by customer representatives.

In addition, a series of informal technical and project meetings throughout the project development period should be conducted. These meetings should be called by the project manager in response to a request from the performing technical organizations and should address a narrow range of technical and administrative issues. Direct customer contact on any technical or administrative issue should be through this channel or through formal or informal reviews, through customer representatives on project boards, through the software configuration management group, through the PSL, or through data supplied by program support. This should be the means used by the customer to evaluate the project integrity. Informal discussions on project issues between customer and technical project personnel should be discouraged. These discussions lead to mutual misunderstandings concerning the actual goals and objectives of the project, technical parameters and decisions, and constraints, problems and project realities.

5 Early Test Planning

Even though test planning is complete and usable, unless the manager can implement and enforce the plans from the outset, they will have no effect.

As illustrated in Figure 5.1, the planning of the system and software test programs is a multi-part process. The top-level systems test planning is normally the responsibility of the program, directly supported by the software organization. The system test plan defines the basic level 5 and 6 testing requirements. It describes the test case definition and the environment and methods to be used for integrating and qualifying the hardware and software system operational components. Also, the organizational structure, resource requirements, and system technical and management controls to be applied by the program during the system test segment are described. The system test plan also includes an identification of the requirements for each of the software and hardware test segments which feed into the system test levels, a description of the system test effort, and a description of the specific data products which are provided by each of the supporting test structures, and how these products will be used during system testing.

The software test plan, on the other hand, describes how the individual software subsystems will be integrated and qualified in an operational configuration. A separate software test plan should be developed for each software subsystem in the system configuration. These plans are consistent with the build requirements defined for the software test program. The controlling document and basic testing requirements for all the software subsystems is the Software Development Plan.

The software test plan provides the roadmap through the software subsystem test program. The plan outlines the specific test cases to be used to qualify the software, the test methods to be used at each test level, and the objectives and project criteria to be satisfied at each level. In addition, management control and reporting procedures, and a specification and requirements cross-reference matrix which defines the requirements for the test cases that will functionally qualify the subsystem at level 4 are provided.

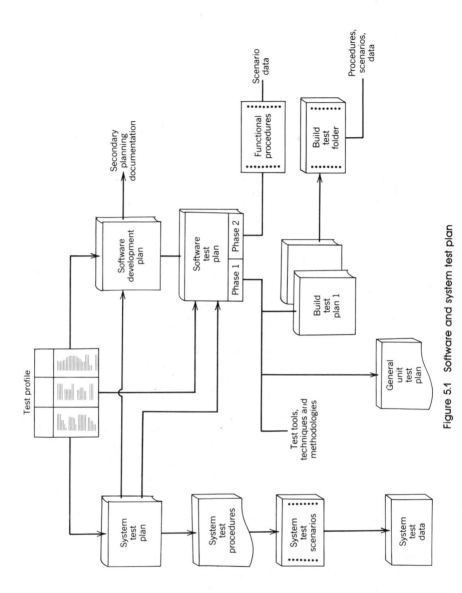

Figure 5.1 Software and system test plan

From the test plans a myriad of lower-level plans, test procedures, and supporting documentation and data may be developed which detail how the testing levels are to be implemented.

Development of the test plans should be hierarchical. At the top level is the overall system test and integration requirements. From these, specific hardware and software test and integration requirements may be defined.

SYSTEM TEST PLANNING—DEFINING THE BASIC CRITERIA FOR SUCCESS

The system test plan is normally developed by the program staff and defines how the system is to be integrated and sold off to the customer. A common early mistake made by program and software managers is not to recognize the essential relationship between system and software test planning. Often these two testing segments are totally decoupled, resulting in inconsistent test specifications, redundant tools, data, and test support, unnecessary duplication of resources, and, too often, retesting, replanning, and/or software modifications to allow integration of the software into the system configuration.

The system test plan should be the first step in laying out how the system is to be tested after completion of the software subsystem test levels. The plan is based on the system's technical requirements, the system structure, and architecture. It must be consistent with the contract, proposal inputs, program plans and the definition of the software project and program support to be provided for each test level. The administrative, management, and control requirements of the program are described, as are the inter- and intraproject data flows. Development of the test plan should be assigned to the responsible test manager with support from each of the software test managers responsible for subsystem test and integration: the hardware test manager who is responsible for test of each hardware component and the personnel test manager who is responsible for each of the major program software and hardware support areas to be used during system test.

Responsibility for development of the test plan must be delegated by the program manager to a single individual responsible for and cognizant of all aspects of the system test. This individual must be experienced in the requirements of system testing, familiar with tools, techniques, methodologies, and test interfaces to be established in support of the system test levels, and have an understanding of the contract, and the program requirements for system test. He or she must be able to direct the development of the plan, be willing to listen to opinions, yet firmly direct the staff to develop the plan, and be technically competent to select, tailor, and document the methodologies to be used during system testing. This role is extremely difficult due to the complexity of the early system test planning. The amount and diversity of data to be dealt with and the seemingly endless array of personnel associated with the program who have opinions, ideas, and optimistic technical solutions as to how to solve the system test problem make this role difficult. The system test manager must sort through these inputs, tailoring and structuring them into a plan containing the following:

1. A clear identification of the program requirements to be addressed during system testing.
2. A statement of the system testing tools, techniques, methodologies, and management and control disciplines to be implemented for level 5 and level 6 test.
3. The technical controls to be used to ensure the integrity and validity of the requirements used during test, the environment established to support the testing process, and the program monitoring and review procedures to be used to maintain visibility into the testing and evaluate its success.
4. The specific requirements for the level 6 test cases cross-referenced to the baseline documentation used to develop them.

The system test plan should be done early. The system test plan defines how to translate test requirements at all test levels into an effective program environment. The Software Development Plan, on the other hand, defines what software project requirements are essential to the success of the program test program, and each of the software test plans describe how individual software subsystems are to be integrated and qualified prior to use in a system test configuration.

Areas of the software project affected most by the system testing requirements are described below.

Configuration Management—Controlling the Baseline

During system testing, the requirements for configuration management are in two separate segments: baseline management and data management.

The baseline management segment is concerned with the management and control of customer-approved and baselined project data. Baselines are reference points or plateaus in the software system development cycle that are established by customer review and acceptance of baseline specification documents. The disciplines used will identify and control approved software system data products at discrete points in time. Baseline configuration management will systematically control changes to approved configurations. This configuration management segment will maintain the integrity and traceability of the approved data products throughout the development period.

Unlike data management functions which control and manage evolving data within the software project, the baseline configuration management functions manage and control software or system end items that have been submitted to or approved by the customer. These end items are in three categories:

1. **Baseline Specification Documentation.** Documentation approved by the customer that specifies the requirements for the software configuration or describes the technical characteristics of the "as-built" system.

2. **Support Documents.** Documents approved by the customer that describe how the software is to be developed.

3. **Technical Data.** Data approved through either customer or project reviews that describe the operation of the system and require customer approval or review to modify.

During system test, baseline management requirements ensure that the product built is indeed the product desired. In order to maintain this data integrity during system testing, three customer-approved and controlled baselines are established during the development life cycle. These are:

1. **Functional Baseline.** This baseline denotes the end of the top-level system design activities. The system requirements, interface specifications, and basic software functional requirements are included and approved at the System Requirements Review (SRR).

2. **Allocated Baseline.** This baseline denotes the end of the preliminary design activities. The baseline is composed of a complete functional specification of software and derived requirements, a specification of the data and control interfaces for the software, and a definition of the software and data architecture. The functional baseline describes the system requirements while the allocated baselines are assigned to individual software subsystems. These baselines are approved at Preliminary Design Reviews (PDR) held for each subsystem.

3. **Product Baseline.** This baseline describes the "as-built" software system and subsystem in terms of its functional, performance, and operational characteristics. It is first established with approval of the software subsystem design at the Critical Design Review (CDR). It continues, in effect, through software implementation, integration, and software demonstration. The final product baseline is established after successful accomplishment of software qualification and system acceptance testing. These results, when approved through an end-product audit, represent the completion of the development.

The formal control of data during system testing is critical to ensure that software and system capabilities and data products are evaluated against approved, traceable requirements and acceptance criteria.

Data management requirements during system test, on the other hand, provide that means by which data products locally approved by the software project are managed and controlled. Unlike baseline management policies and practices, the data management component of configuration management controls informal project, functional, allocated, and interim product baselines, and monitors and controls the development of informal project data products. The data management requirements during system test consist of:

1. Technical control and project monitoring of software content and quality.
2. Facilities for controlling the content and structure of software products.
3. Reporting procedures and structure for standardized reporting and processing of software design or implementation issues and documentation of library contents of data products.

The software products to be controlled consist of documentation, source code, executable code, and status records for all major software elements.

The primary role of data management during system testing is to ensure all software requirements, design, code, and test materials used during system testing have been reviewed and approved by the project manager. Technical content is to be known and traceable, and all changes to controlled software or project data is to be formally reviewed and approved prior to inclusion in a system configuration.

Project Organizational Strategies During System Testing

The structure of the program organization during system testing should be a basic consideration in defining the structure of the software support required during system testing. Generally, there are three effective alternatives for organizing during this period of the project.

1. An independent test team staffed and administered from within the software organization.
2. Total organizational autonomy.
3. Project level system integration and test team integrated with the software development team.

The advantages of using an autonomous test organization are objectivity and testing independence. This testing organization is especially effective when high confidence and traceability are required between system requirements, design, code, and testing parameters. The disadvantage is cost and organizational difficulties associated with implementing and supporting this form of testing structure.

The second form is to define an independent test group within the software organization. This group will integrate and demonstrate the software in a system configuration. The advantage of this technique is that a degree of objectivity may be retained since the team does not participate directly in the implementation. The independent team may also be staffed from within the program or software systems engineering and design organizations. This provides a means for retaining trained personnel familiar with the basic system structure through the system testing period. The disadvantage is the project trade between retaining software system engineering and designers at the expense of maintenance personnel. This could have a disastrous effect on the project if major problems are found.

The third organizational structure is to assign system integration responsibility to software engineering and staff it with the implementors who developed the code. The advantage of this approach is that software maintenance resources are retained at least through the system integration period. This minimizes the risks associated with finding critical or difficult software problems. Two primary disadvantages, however, limit the application of this organizational structure to the system integration effort.

First, the development staff will not have the time to properly plan and develop a system integration environment. This lack of planning will inhibit the effectiveness and success of the program during the demonstration. Secondly the team cannot maintain a system perspective. Primary emphasis will be placed on looking at individual software components rather than on how they execute together which will inhibit the success of the integration effort.

Early selection of an organizational approach is critical since the decision has a major impact on how resources are allocated, budgeted, and controlled.

External Simulation—An Alternative to Risk

A second early decision that must be made is how test data to be used during system testing is to be provided to the system and how external data resulting from system execution is to be recorded, analyzed, and reported. The reason for this early decision is twofold. First, if a decision is made to develop external hardware or a system environmental simulator, an extremely long lead time must be taken into account. Second, and more important, the development of a simulator for system integration may have application to earlier testing levels if the simulator is properly defined, the requirements understood, and the various test environments built around the use of simulation. If a decision is made to build a simulator for system integration, this same tool should then be used during the build functional and build integration test levels.

The simulator is a hardware and software tool which executes outside the test system and provides controlled, reproduceable test data through actual external system ports. The simulator also records output data and, depending on the sophistication built into the tool, dynamically reduces and evaluates the results. Two major advantages lead a software manager toward the application of a simulator during system integration. First it abrogates the risks of nonoperational system hardware and hardware schedule slips. Secondly, the use of a simulator during integration will establish a controlled, predictable testing environment which may be planned from the outset of the project.

The major disadvantages associated with the use of a simulator fall into two categories: development cost and hardware usage. Simulators are expensive both in hardware costs and development resources. Often these costs cannot be passed to the customer and it is difficult to convince management of the need to commit funds for a tool that will not be used until late in the program. Second, the early use of a simulator for software and system integration will significantly affect the amount of time that hardware and software are in integration. This reduction of integration time may have a negative effect on the ultimate reliability of the system and, if problems are found in the hardware/software interfaces, testing schedules may slip out.

A third disadvantage is that the simulation is only as good as the time and resources applied to it. If an inadequate or incorrect tool is used, the resultant qualification may be compromised. The simulation development should be done by project personnel not involved in the systems design so that faulty system analysis is not duplicated.

Regression Testing

In the system test environment, regression testing is the means by which new software releases are qualified before being distributed for use in the system environment. If planned for from the beginning of the project, the time and resource requirements associated with regression testing is minimal.

The degree to which software system releases are regression testing prior to use in the system test environment must be based on the inherent reliability required in the system after delivery, the form and structure of the test program, and the time and software resources committed to support the period of system demonstration. In the context of system testing, regression testing is the rerunning of specific design, functional, or integration test levels to ensure that a system release works adequately across a range of conditions and in a variety of prequalified system environments. Generally, the more extensively a system is regression tested, the more reliable the final product.

The difficulty in applying regression testing to the system test levels is twofold. First, the test levels are organizationally split, with the test development and analyses being the responsibility of the system demonstration and hardware/software integration testing being the responsibility of the program organization. Software Development and execution of software testing levels, as well as the software/software segment of level 5 testing is the responsibility of the software organization. If the organizational conflicts are not clearly resolved early in the project, they will preclude successful integration and regression testing during the period of system testing.

Secondly, in order to ensure that regression testing overhead may be minimized, the execution and analyses of the test cases should be automated. If properly planned, the process of regression testing may be simply a matter of starting a test tape from the beginning of a test file and allowing the test to cycle through each of the individual test cases that makes up the test configuration. Unless the tests are automated, or at least simplified where they can be run without a large overhead in terms of operator or support requirements, the project impacts associated with running the tests prohibit their use. Early planning can avoid these impacts.

Hierarchal Testing—Integrating the System in an Execution Sequence

System testing is concerned with taking qualified software subsystems and integrating them into an operational configuration. Two primary testing techniques are effective when accomplishing this test requirement: hierarchal integration, which integrates software subsystems in their execution sequence, and thread testing, which links the software through its system and software interfaces.

Hierarchal testing takes small segments of the software and integrates them into some larger component in a hierarchal fashion. This component is then integrated into a still larger component using hierarchal techniques, and so forth until the system is fully integrated. The advantage of this phased technique is that software integration emphasis is focused at the interactions and interfaces that must be qualified at each level of the software integration. Each phase is being qualified through some test step before being used in a higher or more comprehensive level of testing. The disadvantages of this approach is that it is highly sensitive to slips in software development schedules. Even small slips in the completion of a major component of a test configuration may have major impacts on the integrity of the software integration schedule. Also, it is difficult to define, develop, and input data into a test configuration that has many levels in the test hierarchy. It is difficult to force the software at the lowest levels to take predetermined execution paths with data injected from above.

Thread testing is an alternative integration technique that can demonstrate the operation of key functional capabilities early in the system integration activity. A thread is a string of software components which, when executed in sequence, support a distinct processing function and in most cases have an identified input source and output product. This form of testing is most appropriate in applications with a dynamic operational environment since it provides a controlled means for qualifying support components prior to using the software in a random functional support environment. This integration form is less sensitive to software schedule slips than hierarchal testing. When using thread testing techniques, the software configuration must be instrumented to isolate problems that result from prior improper execution of software in the thread or from the execution of related interfacing software threads.

Random Testing—Breaking the System

In order to evaluate operational integrity, a period of time should be provided between the completion of system integration testing and the start of the system demonstration. This time is for the unstructured operation of the system in the operational configuration to ensure that the software reliability meets the operational expectations of the end user. During this period, individuals familiar with the operational characteristics of the user and technical environment exercise the system in a realistic, controlled, but unplanned manner in an effort to force a failure.

The advantage of this analysis is that in order to assess how reliable a system will be in the field the system should be subject to a representative system load and typical operator interactions to evaluate performance. In systems where these interactions are unpredictable, as in real time support applications, the specific execution environments are impossible to project and, as a result, can't reasonably be simulated in controlled tests. By allowing an unstructured evaluation of system performance, operational randomness of the support environment will be exercised and reliability will be demonstrated in a quasi realistic environment.

Two primary disadvantages often preclude use of this technique. First, the costs are significant, since during this period of testing, critical project resources must be diverted or reassigned. Second, the tests are only as valid as the experience, technical ability, and "system savvy" of the analyst assigned and, because of the unstructured nature of the testing, it is difficult to evaluate accurately their effectiveness or measure their success.

Software Instrumentation—Internal System Monitoring

The purpose of system integration testing (level 5) is to evaluate the internal integrity of the software, first in relation to the design and architecture of the software and, second, in the context of the hardware and system support environment. The purpose of software instrumentation tests is to monitor system internals rather than demonstrate external characteristics.

In order to collect performance data, instrumentation should be incorporated into the software.

During system testing the application of instrumentation is required only if internal system parameters are required to evaluate system performance. During system integration, however, internal parameters are the only means by which software execution may be evaluated. Three categories of instrumentation should be considered for inclusion in the system integration environment. Internal real time dump routines will record the settings of key data values during periods of actual support. Trace routines collect data which describe the paths followed by the software in response to various system conditions. A third category allows the tester to dynamically vary the system environment during periods of execution by changing internal data values and system conditions. The requirements for the type and form of the instrumentation are a function of the technical, functional, and execution characteristics of the software application and the size and complexity of the software system. The use of instrumentation will significantly alter performance of the system and, as such, must be used judiciously. If the instrumentation requirement is defined for the systems demonstration, proper specification of requirements will allow application of the same tool set to the software test levels.

System Test Plan Contents

Once these basic program and software project parameters have been identified and analyzed, a decision must be made as to how they will be supported. This information must be translated into the system test plan.

The plan should contain the following information.

1. **Introduction and Scope.** Documents the purpose and scope of the system test requirement, scaling the program test requirement to the system application.

2. **System Test Methods.** Describes in the context of the program environment how each of the system test levels are to be implemented, the technical approach, tools, techniques and methodologies to be used, and the flow of data and program responsibility as data transitions from the development organizations through the system test levels. The system integration and qualifications techniques and support requirements are also defined.

3. **System Test Environment.** Describes the program environment during the system testing. The relationship between the various segments of the program (configuration management, test, and integration quality assurance program controls, and the program development and technical aspects) should be described as well as how each of these are to be integrated into a productive program environment. The program review and monitoring procedures, how and when the individual reviews are to be applied, and the data products to be reviewed at each individual review should be discussed.

4. **System Test Objectives and Test Phase Summary.** Defines the requirements and objectives to be satisfied by each of the test levels. The plan should identify a common objective for the test program and it should ensure satisfaction of the overall test objectives. This part of the system test plan identifies the objectives for each testing level and the way that each

of these objectives is to be integrated into a consistent, achievable test program.

5. **System Test Requirements and Criteria.** Describes the specific test case by test case requirements for system testing at both the integration and qualification levels. These test specifications should be concise, identifying the objective of each test and providing a summary of each of the test steps which make them up. This test specification should be input to the system test cross-reference index that documents which requirements are satisfied by each test step and the major software and hardware components exercised by each.

The plan should also document test case success criteria. These criteria will serve as the basis for defining acceptable performance and establish the basis for execution of each test case analysis of the output and acceptance of the results.

6. **Test Controls.** Describes the specific technical, program, hardware and software controls to be applied during system test to ensure the integrity of the software plans being used, the validity of requirements, test plans, data, and test specifications, and the requirements and design upon which the tests are based. The plan should specify requirements for configuration management, quality assurance, and budget, schedule, and resource controls which monitor program progress against expenditures.

The plan should also describe how data from each of the developing organizations should be controlled during system test and procedures for authorizing data for use in a system test configuration.

7. **Organization and Responsibilities.** Identifies the program organization to be used during system testing. The discussion should include an identification of the roles and responsibilities of each component of the organization, the communication and data flow between organizations and how the system test and support organization interface with development and support organizations within the project.

8. **Documentation Requirements.** Identifies the specific requirements for system level test documentation, how the individual elements of the documentation are to be produced and controlled, and which specific organization is responsible for each document.

The system test plan describes how the individual parts of the system are to be integrated into an operational configuration and how this configuration is to be qualified. The plan should be developed in two segments. The first documents information available early in the program. This information defines the hardware and software test requirements. The second release provides data, available later in the program, consistent with test schedules and required for development of procedures, scenarios, data, and test support requirements.

A common and often catastrophic, program planning error is to decouple the development of the system test plan and the software and hardware test planning activities because of organizational or programmatic consideration.

SOFTWARE TEST PLANNING

Unless planned for, the test requirements defined at each level will overlap and be duplicated. The software development and test requirements often conflict, and many times essential interfaces between the test levels and implementation requirements are ignored or, at best, poorly defined.

As illustrated in Figure 5.2, development of the test plan is a two-step process. The first step is to integrate the system level test requirements as defined in the system test plan with the software project requirements as defined in the Software Development Plan. These software project requirements define what software testing levels will be supported during the development, what project activities will support the testing process, and how, within the project, the project testing activities are to be managed and controlled.

The iteration of the Software Development Plan based on the requirements of the system test plan ensures that the software project will adequately interface with the program during the period of system testing. The Software Development Plan review will also ensure that the various specifications for the software test levels are consistent, properly scaled, and adequately defined in relation to the defined system test requirements.

From the Software Development Plan, the test manager must ensure that a software test plan is developed for each subsystem.

The initial release of the software test plan is the basis for all subsequent test planning, development, execution, definition, and integration and project testing interfaces. The plan must be sufficiently detailed to allow the software manager the option of initiating critical or long lead time testing tasks which, if not completed in a timely fashion, could limit or constrain project programs. The software test plan is the basic testing document establishing testing rules, criteria, organizations, and specific test case specifications for the functional test case.

Interfacing to the System Test Levels

In order to plan a smooth transition of test responsibility to test activities, and an effective flow of data and responsibility between system and software testing, several software project parameters should be defined. These should act as a precursor to planning the software project environment. These parameters defined for software testing are software subsystem specific.

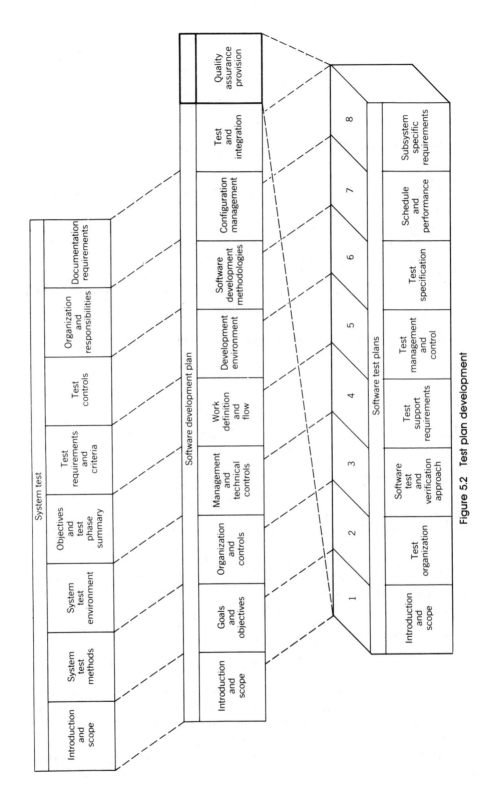

Figure 5.2 Test plan development

They are dependent on the characteristics of the subsystem and may differ depending on the technical and execution attributes of the software.

The project parameters which most affect requirements for the software test environment fall into two categories: those which result from the projected system test environment and those which are a result of the functional and technical characteristics of the software subsystem. The system test interface issues to be evaluated include:

1. How complex is the software subsystem environment to be integrated at level 5 and how functionally autonomous is each subsystem.

2. How coupled from a data and operational standpoint are the subsystems and how critical is this coupling to the integrity and operational effectiveness of the integrated system.

3. Is the projected system integration environment phased or serial. If phased, can builds which track the build requirements be defined, enforced, and consistently applied throughout the software project?

The project requirements for software testing, besides being influenced by the system level requirements, are impacted by the technical characteristics of the software subsystem. These characteristics are similar to those used in defining system test project requirements. The attributes of size, complexity, number of separate and unique components, complexity and number of interactions, interface characteristics and functional divisibility must all be defined at a software subsystem level. They must adequately specify software subsystem qualification environments. This data cannot be specified accurately early in the project; however, adequate data is available in proposal and contract specifications to facilitate initial level 3 and 4 test requirements definition. These requirements must be updated before detailed requirements for the software test environments may be defined. The segments of the software project test environment which require early analysis are defined in the paragraphs which follow.

Configuration Management During Software Test

During software testing the project configuration management requirements are most critical and must be integrated effectively into the project if control over the project data is to be maintained. Baseline management requirements during this phase of the project must be stringent, preplanned, and rigorously enforced to control formally approved project data. The most volatile project baselines are those requiring frequent updates during software testing to reflect operational and execution experience. These changes must be controlled and monitored. All changes must be documented, qualified, and incorporated into system releases in a controlled fashion.

Data management requirements are also demanding due to the frequency of updates to controlled software. The project must manage and control small data elements used by many segments of the project. If control over these data elements is lost, or if the documentation, data base, code, design, or requirements get out of phase, the project has little chance for success.

The software configuration management requirements must include both software test support requirements and system testing support requirements. At the system level, the primary emphasis is on ensuring that baselines established between the contractor and customer are maintained. Traceability between software system data products and the approved operational and user requirements must be ensured. At the software test levels the configuration management function must provide a smooth, controlled flow of data and ensure integrity and traceability between software requirements, design, code, and test. The requirements for software configuration management must interface effectively to system level configuration management functions while also supporting and controlling the development of all subsystems using a common structure.

Regression Testing—Qualification of Software Subsystem Releases

In the system integration and demonstration environment the requirement for regression testing new software is important, being influenced by the reliability, fiscal, and program requirements of the system and program environment.

During software testing (levels 3 and 4), however, the requirement for regression testing of new software is absolute, being the only way that the validity of software modifications may be confirmed and the integrity of previously made changes guaranteed. The rigor to be followed and the degree to which regression testing is to be applied to the qualification of individual software subsystem is heavily influenced by the technical attributes of the software subsystem and the reliability and execution characteristics of the software application. It is not feasible in most project situations to reintegrate and requalify all modifications to software subsystems using the full suite of previously run level 2, 3, and 4 tests. Besides being nonessential, it is often prohibitive in terms of time and resource requirements. The specific number of tests to be rerun for each release and the test level to be returned to before requalifying a release for qualification testing is a decision to be made after the technical attributes of the software are defined, and should be modified on problem-by-problem or release-by-release basis. The general requirements for regression testing should be identified at this planning stage, as should the general requirements for retesting for each individual software build.

System Simulation During Software Test

If the system has new unproven hardware, if the external interfaces are difficult to establish and support in a controlled manner, or if the software test environment is difficult to establish and reproduce for a particular subsystem, then a data simulator is required. Proper early planning will assure that any simulation requirement developed for level 5 will be usable at this level of testing as well.

Organizational Autonomy During Software Test

The organizational structure to be used for software testing is a critical early decision, impacting not only the cost projections but also the staffing profile and scheduling. The management alternatives are as described previously for level 5 and 6 testing; organizational autonomy independence within the software organization, or total project integration of the testing functions. As with level 5 and 6 organizational requirements, the arguments for or against each organizational technique center around testing objectivity and autonomy versus increased cost.

These arguments concerning the project organizational structure are more difficult to resolve at the software test levels, since the costs of totally independent testing teams, or even dedicated teams within the software project, are significant at this test level. The costs are multipled by the number of parallel software test requirements needed to support subsystem development schedules. The arguments for objectivity at this level of testing also become more persuasive because of the necessity to demonstrate functional, derived, and software subsystem performance requirements which are most likely to be misinterpreted by designers and implementors. These requirements must be evaluated by an objective analysis conducted through software testing. These requirements will not be demonstrated completely at any other test level.

Incremental Qualification During Software Test

Early definition of the structure of the software testing is an essential precursor to the definition of software schedules, budgets, and the technical structure of project. Incremental testing will qualify the software subsystem in pieces with each increment scheduled in accordance with inherent subsystem functional relationship, development, and schedule realities, and the overall requirements for level 5 and 6 testing support.

Incremental testing is an extremely efficient means for qualifying software subsystems. As software is released from level 3 integration it is immediately placed in a qualification environment and functionally validated. This "build a little—test a little" structure will result in a more reliable, functionally valid quality product.

The disadvantages in the approach fall into two categories—cost, and management complexity. The extended software test period resulting from incremental qualification of software subsystems requires the parallel accomplishment of test planning, development, execution, and analysis if it is to succeed. This parallelism is good for the project in one respect since it offloads software testing responsibility from the development staff. As with any additional project requirement, the support requires a commitment of resources and additional costs.

Additional integration of software testing with level 5 activities and the level 3 software integration requirements requires that the project manager consistently orchestrate the activities of the testing staff. The requirements for this control, due to technical or development complexity, appear too difficult during these early planning periods; alternate software testing structures should be investigated.

Software Instrumentation—Internal Performance Monitoring

The requirement for instrumentation during software testing has two aspects:

1. **Instrumentation During Test Dry Runs.** During the early periods of software test preparation, inclusion of instrumentation is essential to collect test data information.

2. **Instrumentation During Software Demonstrations.** Software instrumentation during the demonstration phase of software testing may impact performance and, as a result, negate the validity of the testing. This software may, however, be the only means to collect data describing system execution. During software testing, the instrumentation requirement should be scaled to the project and to the needs and requirements of the subsystems software test.

If instrumentation is defined for software testing at the subsystem level, the tools should be made available to all subsystems and to related system test level.

Normally tests for this level execute in a controlled environment, using predefined data and highly structured environment. Real time subsystem applications, applications with extensive operator interaction, and subsystems characterized by random software interactions to interfaced equipments or software components often cannot be fully demonstrated in a controlled environment and require that a degree of randomness be integrated into the test situation. The requirement for randomness must be defined early in the initial planning and used to set the structure for the test environment and degree of reproduceability, control, and direct traceability to requirements. Whether tests are random in nature, or are totally controlled, all software tests must be firmly based on previously approved software functional requirements and be documented in test plans, procedures, scenarios, and test data.

Software Test Planning

Careful planning early in the project is an essential prerequisite to success. This planning has the following components:

1. **Purpose and Scope.** A clear understanding of the purpose, expectations, scope, and limitations of the software testing program should be made, documented, and agreed to by all parties associated with the test effort. This early agreement is essential, for it provides the basic criteria on which organizational relationships and project responsibilities will be made.

2. **Test Organization.** The organizational roles and project responsibilities should be identified, documented, and approved by each project organizational element. The responsibilities should be consistent with the identified test purpose and scope and reflect the organizational commitments, goals, and objectives of the test program.

3. **Test and Verification Approach.** The test and verification requirements and general approach toward satisfaction of the requirements should be defined, documented, and agreed to through the software test plan. They should address each phase of the testing, individually identify how each segment will be supported via the test program, and specify requirements by phase that must be supported to complete the test effort. In the preliminary test planning phase, the emphasis is on what is to be accomplished by the test and verification approach to each phase of the testing rather than on how the requirements are to be satisfied.

4. **Test Support Requirements.** The planning should identify the test environment required to support each phase of testing, the flow of data between the test phases, and manual and automated tools, techniques, and procedural support requirements that will support the satisfaction of test goals and objectives during each test phase.

5. **Test Management and Control.** The requirements for management of the test program at all levels, as well as definition of requirements for the control and flow of data as the testing proceeds through each test phase, should be identified, documented, and reviewed with each test organization.

6. **Test Specifications.** The specifications of requirements for each test case to be developed for functionally qualifying the software at the build functional and system functional tests should be identified.

7. **Schedule and Expected Test Program Performance.** General task categories for support of each phase of testing should be identified. The schedule requirements and task phasing should be described, documented, and agreed to by the responsible test organizations. The software test plan should be available and coordinated through the various management levels and project organizational areas before any software tasks are initiated on the project.

A single test plan should be developed for each subsystem. Once approved by the customer, the test plan becomes the basis for implementing test activities in the programming process. The test plan may be modified as approved changes are made to the program requirement's specification or to reflect changes in the planning process. The latter would generally involve the customer and the programming organization.

The software test plan is the basic description of how the test and support requirements defined in the Software Development Plan are to be implemented in the project environment. Development of the plan should be the responsibility of the software test manager, as should direct test implementation responsibility.

TEST PROCEDURES—DETAILING THE TEST CASE REQUIREMENTS

Functional Test Procedures are developed from the software test plan. They document the detailed step-by-step execution requirements for each level 4 test case documented in the software test plan. The procedures should be developed exclusively from the functional, performance, and interface documentation. These procedures, when developed exclusively by an independent organization familiar with externally specified system parameters, rather than internal design or execution characteristics, provide an objective appraisal of system compliance to specified software operation requirements.

The procedures should be functional in nature, traceable to a specified set of approved specifications, and contain nine separate categories of data, as follows:

1. **Purpose, Scope, and Limitations.** Describes the purpose of the test case, the scope of the test, and expected limitations.

2. **Software Inventory.** Describes the specific software and data components which must be integrated into an executable configuration before the test case may be executed.

3. **Test Support Facilities and Tooling Requirements.** Documents either specifically or by reference the specific test environment required to execute the test case. The description should include not only a specification of the requirements for the test case environment but also describe the integration, qualification, and availability schedule required to keep test case schedules.

4. **Test Conditions.** Describes the specific conditions which are required to be in place to ensure test validity and success. These conditions include essential state of the software configuration; essential state of the hardware, software, and support configuration; simulation, emulation, and instrumentation requirements; and execution analysis, review, and acceptance requirements.

5. **Test Inputs.** A description of the input test configuration, the input data sources, and how the input is to be generated, provided to the target

system, controlled, varied in response to test conditions, and reproduced. Also included is a description of the specific test message formats and control inputs.

6. **Test Outputs.** A description of the test output ports, how test data is to be monitored, collected, and reduced, and how test outputs are to be used to construct essential test responses and conditions. Also included is the expected output message formats and ranges of acceptable values for each major parameter.

7. **Test Procedure.** A step-by-step time-phased description of the external test control and data inputs and the expected software responses and test outputs. This procedure details how the test is to be executed and the expected results which are to be monitored and serve as the criteria for success.

8. **Test Constraints.** Describes the constraints on the test case imposed by hardware, software, environmental, personnel, or test resource limitations or restrictions. The constraints section should limit the expectations of the test personnel and ensure the validity of the test analysis and acceptance.

9. **Test Analysis.** Describes how test results are to be analyzed and evaluated, the tools, techniques and procedures required to evaluate performance and success, and specific criteria upon which acceptance may be established.

The test plans and procedures are the basis for all test activities. They document the structure for all levels of test and establish the environmental requirements for the project during development, software and system test. Adequate planning forces the test managers to think through the process of test, anticipate the problems which will befall the project, and establish links between the levels of test.

6 Motivating the Work Force

Planning is useless if the test manager can't motivate test personnel.

Translation of the software development and software test plans and procedures into a smoothly functioning project environment is a difficult, complex task. Unlike early requirements analysis and software design tasks which have early visibility and a reasonably early payoff to the project, the test tasks have a longer-term project significance. Unless these early testing milestones are treated with a sense of urgency by the testing staff, the milestone will almost certainly drift. If not corrected this drift will ultimately invalidate the test schedules and impact the success of the project. Translation of plans into project action requires clear direction through the management chain and use of effective scheduling techniques, which stress timely satisfaction of near-term milestones.

MANAGEMENT DIRECTION—TASKING THE STAFF

The software test manager must initially organize the test staff to support the development, review and control of the test products. The software test organization must be structured to develop integration and functional test plan procedures, scenarios, data, tools, and support facilities for each subsystem. Responsibility should be centralized in a single test manager. This manager should have focal-point responsibility for all software testing activities, interfacing directly to the system test organizations, the project support organizations, and each of the development groups. The critical nature of these activities, coupled with the difficult management and control requirements implicit in the test problem, requires use of effective management techniques from the outset. Critical components of software test management are described below.

TASKING AND CLEAR DIRECTION

Before initiating any test planning or development, the test manager should ensure that clear direction is received from the software project manager. This direction should include a specific statement of the test tasks, schedules, and budgets, an identification of milestones, and criteria for success. This tasking represents the contract between the software testing organization and the software project. As such, the test manager and software manager should negotiate the terms of the testing task before budgets, schedules, and technical responsibilities are put in place and work initiated. This early negotiation is critical, establishing a firm basis for performing the testing tasks.

Once the software project and software test managers finally agree on the scope and responsibilities of the testing activities and agree to budgets and schedules, the software test manager must communicate the requirements of the tasks to the staff and motivate them to accomplish them within the cost and schedule constraints. This is the point at which many projects fail. The manager calls the responsible individual into his office, tells him to do a particular task, and tells him to return when he has a planned approach and progress to report. The difficulty with this scenario is that the individual receiving the tasking does not understand what the software test manager expects, the acceptable level of performance and criteria for success, or how the job, in the view of the manager, should be conducted. They should ask for:

1. A schedule for completion of the activity which is responsible, attainable, and agreed to.
2. A strawman illustrating what is expected and the form of the products to be delivered.
3. An identification of the interim milestones, reviews, and audits to be used by the manager to evaluate performance.
4. A definition of the limitations, constraints, and problems associated with development of the task.
5. A discussion of the program and management interfaces which must be supported and considered during the execution of the task.

The individual who is responsible for the task must ensure that all work associated with test conduct is assigned and delegated through the same communication method.

A CLEAR-STRUCTURED, WELL-DOCUMENTED ORGANIZATION

The myriad tasks implicit in the planning, organization, execution, and evaluation of a software test program requires participation and support of diverse and organizationally distributed disciplines and expertise. In order to ensure that these relationships and the hierachy of responsibility within the test organization are clearly understood by assigned test personnel, the test manager should have a current organizational block diagram available for all personnel to see. The diagram should identify the internal organizational elements comprising the test group and how each of these elements relate to the software project and program organizations. The individual responsible for each area should be identified, as should all personnel assigned. This staffing profile should be kept current. For each block on the chart, a list of responsibilities should be identified, as should the flow of data between organizational elements. The organizational structure must be retained on a current basis and communicated throughout the test organizations through regular updates and a responsibilities chart. The test manager must act as the clear leader within the specified test organization. Communication must be direct; flowing down and throughout the test and support organizations. Tasking must be clear, coordinated by the manager and consistent with documented test plans, procedures, technical specifications, project plans and documented requirements.

Without the effective coordination between management, the organization, and test tasks, the development execution, analyses, and support activities will overlap and be characterized by redundancy and ineffectiveness.

MANAGEMENT IMAGE—ACTING LIKE A LEADER

The software test manager is responsible for myriad activities within the project. These require the application of a wide range of technical expertise, experience, and support capabilities with the staff. The manager must control and have the respect of technologists versed in the technical aspects of the software project, requirements experts familiar with the needs and requirements of the end user and customer, and systems engineering personnel who understand the hardware, software, and interface characteristics of the system. In addition he must deal with support personnel who develop and support the tools and products of the test program, management and staff personnel within the program, and the software project and customer organization.

It is to the software test manager that all these individuals turn for information, guidance, and direction concerning all aspects of the test program. The test manager must be clearly in charge. He or she must understand all tasks which comprise the test program and the relationships between them in sufficient detail to meaningfully assign responsibility to task leaders or line managers, coordinate their activities, and monitor their progress and success. The manager need not understand the technical detail of each task, nor need he or she understand the detailed assignments of all personnel directly working on or supporting the testing.

The software test manager must be willing and able to make decisions based on limited or nonexistent information and have sufficient resolve to implement these decisions in spite of torrents of criticism and direct and indirect verbal abuse. The test manager must understand that in a software testing environment, because of the complexity and multifaceted nature of the problem, there is never an ideal solution or absolutely correct decision to every issue that must be dealt with. Decisions must often be made based on conflicting or nonexistent data and the test manager is the individual who stops the buck.

The worst thing a test manager can do is to defer or avoid making key decisions for any reason. When a critical decision is outstanding in a project, personnel, resources, or other project activities are being impacted. These impacts will continue and get worse until the decision is made and the results felt within the project. Making a poor or improper decision is not necessarily a negative impact on the project. True, a poor decision may result in misdirected resources and, perhaps, some embarrassment; however, these may be corrected through redirection of the testing activities, where a lack of decisive action cannot be remedied. Deferred decisions ensure that resources are being misapplied, often wasted, and there is no guarantee that when action is finally taken, the results will be optimum.

Personnel being impacted by the lack of positive direction will rapidly lose respect for an indecisive manager. They see themselves as pawns, forced to work extra hours and commit their time and energies to take up the slack caused by a poor manager. Respect is not easily regained by the manager, which results in long-term motivation and productivity impacts. The ability to make, implement, and enforce timely decisions is an essential element of successful test management.

FOCUS AND DIRECTION MUST FLOW FROM THE TOP DOWN

The process of software test and integration is an area of the project where it seems everyone has an opinion, a better way, or a reason why a particular approach won't work. There are an infinite number of "technically superior" solutions, proven methodologies, and superior techniques which the staff swears are the only way the software can be tested. Often these approaches are overlapping, conflicting, and are inconsistent with the technical and development environment of the software project. They often do not consider cost and schedule constraints or the expertise or training of the technical personnel assigned to the project. "Qualified experts" abound. In order to implement the planned test approach, the test manager must initially convince the staff, management, and customer personnel and continually reinforce the concept that the documented test program is the way the testing will be conducted. The manager must be, many times, "a snake oil salesman," convincing, cajoling, and often dictating the merits and details of the test program within the organization. This ability to sell is an acquired and essential element of test management skill.

The software test manager must direct, focus, and channel the activities of the test staff. The manager must have a clearly identified set of testing goals and objectives and have identified documented strategies and tactics for carrying them out.

Finally the software test manager must look and act like a leader. He or she must present a positive image to staff, customer, and management personnel. This does not mean being technically superior to all personnel on the project, or working harder or longer hours than the staff, or any other visible attempts at staff recognition. It does mean being responsible and accountable for both successes and failures, both passing achievements and credit through the staff and taking positive action to correct problems before they affect productivity or success.

The software test manager must ensure that the emphasis of the test program is always channeled towards the "bottom-line tasks," which result in quality, reliability, and customer acceptability. The manager must avoid crisis or reactive management, which may get the test program to the milestone but preclude delivery of an integrated, qualified system.

The test manager must ensure that the various segments of the test project communicate effectively, and that test meetings are successfully conducted, even between individuals, groups, and organizations who don't like or respect each other. The manager must blend technology with planning and good common sense to develop an effective, coordinated approach test structure. In order to achieve this blending, the manager must listen to the many opinions within the project, filtering that which is nonsense, tailoring that which is usable, and incorporating that which is functional.

Everyone related to the test project must feel that their contributions to the project are significant, appreciated, relevant, and meaningful in the context of the overall success of the project. Even if the individuals' contributions are not used, particularly effective, or even smart, the individual who made the contribution should be made to feel that he or she has provided a significant part of the project success.

PERSONNEL PSYCHOLOGY—THE MOST DIFFICULT TASK

Many well-planned test programs prove unsuccessful not because of basic structural or environmental issues but because of the inability of the test manager to deal with the day-to-day issues of managing a technical staff. The manager folds when faced with a requirement to confront a staff member or take unpleasant actions which may affect a career or result in bad feelings between the manager and his staff.

Successful test managers recognize that although a significant majority of the project staff must respect them if they are to succeed, the staff may or may not like them personally because of the difficult decisions which must be made that are contradictory to the wants, needs, or desires of the staff. Popularity is not a prerequisite to test management success.

Many times the software manager will publish what he or she considers to be a well-planned, structured, organized document describing how the test program is to be run and will be astounded at the criticism and negative comment it elicits. The technologist may find the plans technically naïve, the less technically orientated may find the plans overly ambitious, and there always seems to be a segment of the staff who, for no identifiable reason, find the plan just plain stupid. Unless the test manager anticipates this reaction, he or she may find it demoralizing, and retreat to the safety of his or her office, spending profiles, and manpower projections. By retreating, the manager has removed himself or herself from risk. However, this person has now become a software test monitor rather than test manager. Once this happens, the test program loses its center and will evolve in accordance with the desires of the most vocal members of the staff, rather than following a preplanned structure or path. The test manager must have a thick skin, accepting and evaluating criticism graciously while doing what is necessary to maintain a productive test structure.

The manager must also recognize that, at least within the test organization there will be three categories of personnel which he or she will have to motivate: fast trackers, average performers, and poor performers.

Fast trackers are those individuals who every manager wishes he or she had unlimited access to. They always have innovative, often brilliant solutions to the difficult problems of testing. They are the ones who cause the breakthroughs and break the log jams on the project that otherwise would preclude project success. They are goal-oriented and need little direction or monitoring to succeed. Motivating these individuals is reasonably straightforward, as they desire continual challenge. The fast trackers respond well to recognition and like the feeling of achievement for a job well done. The effects of failures should be minimized, since these individuals will quickly recognize the error and do what is necessary to correct the mistake. The test manager must listen to the fast trackers, for these are the people who have their fingers on the pulse of the project. They must be heard. Fast trackers must be given responsibility commensurate with their contribution to the project. This does not mean that they should be promoted to positions they are unqualified for, but it does mean that they should be groomed for progress and put quickly into roles consistent with their abilities. Fast trackers should be distributed judiciously throughout the organization. They should be balanced in groups with average performers and nonperformers since they have a tendency to bring everyone up to their level. And, finally, they should be rewarded for their achievements through a variety of means, including, but not necessarily limited to, financial reward. For this type of individual financial compensation is only a secondary motivator behind personal achievement, success, and personal recognition.

The average performer, on the other hand, requires firm direction on a regular basis to succeed. These individuals make up the bulk of the project, are more task-oriented, and have a tendency—when faced with unclear or difficult tasks—to throw up their hands and wait to be told how to proceed and what is expected. This category of personnel is extremely susceptible to peer pressure. When dealing with organizations heavily loaded with average performers, the manager should recognize that performance is analogous to a flywheel—it is difficult to start; however, once the manager starts motivating the staff, provides the plans and direction, organizes schedules, and initiates the testing tasks, the effects of peer pressure, short milestones, and clear direction will keep the project moving towards the specified goals. If the manager can't start the flywheel, the project will bog down.

The average performers require a clear set of tasks to follow, and identified milestones which are close, ideally requiring no more than a week to achieve. The test manager should reward the average performer through peer recognition. By making achievements visible throughout the organization, the test manager is making the individual feel that his or her contributions are not only appreciated by management but are also critical to the way he or she is perceived by coworkers.

Financial rewards are more important to the average performer than to the fast tracker. Increases in compensation are the visible "strokes" that tend to reward good performance. To the average performer, financial compensation is the measure of recognition and success.

Compensation is not a good short-term motivator to the average performer, however. Test managers often make the mistake of attempting to gain the support of the average performer through financial means. Experience has shown that with the average performer compensation is far less effective than peer pressure as a short-term motivator.

Failure or poor individual performance must also be dealt with in a positive, constructive, and timely manner. Because of the complex interactions within the test organization, and the intricate technical and scheduling relationships between the testing organizations and the other segments of the software project and program organizations, poor individual performance cannot be tolerated. In a short time, poor individual performance will impact testing productivity. The fast tracker will recognize his or her own poor performance and do whatever is necessary to get back on track. The average performer, on the other hand, will occasionally drift and, unless corrected by management action, will continue to perform poorly until the problems become acute. The aware test manager will recognize the early symptoms of this drift; lateness to work, poor attention to details, excuses absolving poor performance, and repeated poor schedule performance and frequent budget overruns. The test manager will take immediate, decisive action with the supervisor responsible for an average performer whose work has dropped to an unacceptable level. The effective test manager will ensure that the supervisor understands the actual cause of the performance problem and takes steps to correct the problem. If correction is not achievable in a short time, or if the individual is unable or unwilling to perform adequately, swift action is imperative. These personnel actions are often the most difficult for a technical manager, yet they are essential if the test program is to be productive and efficient. Procrastination or unfounded optimism that the individual's performance will improve only make the test problems worse and increase the personal defeat the individual will experience when the situation explodes.

The third personnel category, the nonachiever, is unfortunately found on most projects. These are the individuals who for one reason or another can't perform in accordance with project requirements and are unable to keep up with the technical demands of the test activities. Many times the fault lies not with the individual but with the way he or she was assigned, the overly optimistic expectations of management, or the simple fact that the individual got off on the wrong foot and never could get back on track. In any event, these individuals represent an unacceptable burden to the test segments of the project and, if not dealt with early, will act as demotivators, first to the test organization and finally to the project as a whole. As difficult as it seems, the test manager has an obligation to the other personnel on the project to take swift and effective action to avoid the poor performer's impact on the project. This action initially should include working closely with the responsible supervisor to attempt to solve the problem without reassigning the individual. If this doesn't work, the only other action possible—and one which should be taken quickly—is to reassign the individual to a job more consistent with his or her desires and talents or remove him or her from the project.

OVERTIME—CHALLENGE VERSUS BRUTALITY

The use of overtime by a test manager is an obvious and often effective solution to be used to get a troubled schedule back on track or to resolve a difficult technical problem. It is often the first alternative thought of, the most readily accepted by the technical staff, and seems to have the least affect on project morale or well-being. Unfortunately, managers often don't realize that when individuals are forced to work through threat or coercion, project morale will drop quickly and productivity will be poor.

The test manager must be aware that he or she, more than any other manager within the project, will need substantial commitments of personnel time late in the project to maintain project test schedules. If the manager oversteps the individual's tolerance for overtime early in the project to support early milestone production or other project needs, he or she will not be able to gain the support needed to see the test program through to a successful completion.

Overtime should be treated like any other critical project resource—it should be budgeted and used judiciously. Early in the project scheduled overtime should be kept to an absolute minimum and used only when there is no other alternative. Later, when overtime is required to meet test schedules, the manager should point out to all that the use will be carefully controlled, scheduled fairly, and—although mandatory—will not be for extended periods without relief. All required overtime, should be compensated.

Casual overtime should be avoided or eliminated. Although it may seem harmless for an individual "to drop in for a few hours to catch up on a few things," this time is time away from family, friends, and recreation. If the use of casual overtime becomes excessive by an individual, these segments of his or her life will begin to exert pressure that will ultimately affect willingness to work essential extra hours. On the other hand, there is a segment of the staff who willingly work significant extra hours because of interest and motivation, or career or personal objectives. These individuals are easily recognized and they should be allowed and encouraged to establish their own priorities, work schedules, and goals. If they work extra hours, however, the work should be towards predefined project goals and should be compensated on an hour-by-hour basis.

Everyone on the project should be expected to drive hard during the normal workweek. This workweek should be set from the outset as a maximum of 5 days, 10 hours a day, with anything above this being looked on as overtime and compensated accordingly. Unless absolutely essential, weekend work should be discouraged.

KNOWING WHEN TO YIELD

The test manager is the focal point for a myriad of critical, diverse activities which directly or indirectly support the test program with the software project. As such, he or she must deal with a variety of management and technical personnel, each having differing motivations, goals, requirements, and expectations. Often these conflict with the testing constraints and must be negotiated, ameliorated, or supported by the test manager, even though he or she doesn't agree with or understand the motivations.

Invariably, these goals for testing differ substantially depending on who the test manager is dealing with, and they almost always conflict with the consistent implicit testing budgets, resources schedule, and technical capability.

The customer wants something "good" but can't identify exactly what it is. The customer wants to have confidence that the software project generally, and the software testing specifically, will minimize risk and result in a quality product responsive to his or her needs, objectives, and unspecified desires. The test manager, when dealing with the customer, must present an image of competence and exude confidence, goodwill, and a desire to support the customer in all essential test areas. The goodwill must, however, be tempered with realism. The customer's desires must be only one input to the test manager and, when they differ substantially from test plans, procedures, constraints (e.g., cost and schedule) or environmental issues, they should be adapted, scaled, or ignored, depending on the characteristics of the inconsistency.

The program manager has a heavy responsibility for coordinating, focusing, directing, and channeling the many diverse activities of the program towards a common set of goals and objectives consistent with the contractual and technical requirements of the program. The program manager and his or her staff are often overwhelmed by the number of activities that must be monitored and controlled, the difficulties associated with maintaining visibility into the system development process, and the impossible task of providing each functional and development group with adequate resources, schedule, and technical support to perform their required tasks. In this environment, the test manager is only one element in a seemingly endless array of technical, administrative, management, and control activities—all essential if a system is acceptable and successful to be fielded and supported.

Below the level of the work package the program manager has little ability to control the activities of the functional organization. The program manager and his or her staff reluctantly must have faith that the functional organizations are competent and have the best interests of the program at heart. This confidence is not always rewarded.

Schedules often slip, technical work is often poorly done, and budgets are not rigorously adhered to. The program manager thus becomes increasingly frustrated. This frustration is felt by the test manager directly through increasing levels of monitoring and attempted steps to control, and indirectly through increasing distrust of reported achievements, performance, and potential for success. The test manager must realize that, although the decisions of the program may appear naïve, shortsighted, technically inept, unfair, and damaging to the test program, they are made based on the program manager's assessment of what is best for the entire program, not just the software project or testing elements.

The test manager must attempt to "get the best deal" for the test organizations. During the early stages of the project the test manager must recognize that the testing problems, although critical and seemingly overwhelming to the manager, will often receive secondary program emphasis while the program staff comes to grips with the "bigger bears in the woods." During the latter stages of the project, the entire focus and emphasis of the program will be towards the test and integration activities. During this period the test manager will have more visibility than he or she wants and will spend an inordinate amount of time reassuring, reinforcing, and reacting to suggestion after suggestion as to how the test program may be better run. The primary motivation of the program manager when dealing with the systems and software test organizations is to ensure that the job will satisfy the contract with the minimum commitment of resources, budgets, and schedules. There is normally only passing interest in the technological aspects of testing, advancing the state of the art, enhancing the expertise of the technical staff, or using the latest tools, techniques, or methodologies in the pursuit of testing excellence. In short, the program manager is most interested in the "bottom line" and how the various segments of the test program minimize the programs risk in all three areas: technical, cost, and schedule.

The software project manager has direct responsibility for all software development and support activities which are required to sell a software system to the program and customer.

The software manager is accountable for the work packages assigned to the software development and test organizations and must plan the fiscal, administrative, management, and contractual requirements of the project. The software project manager must motivate the project technologists who feel that esoteric, state of the art solutions are the only road to success, the project naysayers who preach doom and gloom from the beginning, line management personnel who are constantly vying for increased budgets, schedules, and responsibility, and a variety of support and technical personnel who have many different goals, personal expectations, and motivations.

The software manager must also deal even-handedly with the positive members of the staff who seem highly motivated, dedicated to the project, and committed to its success, as well as those who seem less motivated and dedicated to the project. The software project manager is continually inundated with information, most of it negative, concerning how the project is proceeding and its prognosis for success. Extended exposure to the software management role makes it extremely difficult to maintain enthusiasm and an open mind when dealing with the day-to-day problems of the software project. The test manager is initially looked on by the software manager as someone who has an easy job because of the seemingly long lead times associated with the early products of testing. Later, the software project manager looks on the test program with disbelief, not understanding how it can take so long to develop such a seemingly small amount of data. Finally, the software manager looks on the software test program with concern as the test schedules stretch out due to unforeseen problems or test complexity. Optimism and hoped-for schedule recovery are dashed on the rocks of reality.

The software project manager wants to find a segment of the project which will perform as advertised while completing tasks within cost and schedule constraints. In short, the software manager would like a little peace.

The technical staff is perhaps the most frustrated segment of the project the software test manager must deal with. Initially, the individuals assigned to the testing staff all were either promised a role, or had certain expectations concerning their roles in the project when assigned to the test program. These expectations might have been technical challenge, advancement, career enhancement, security, or a variety of other tangible or nontangible factors that were keys in their acceptance of the test position. Initially, there was a general feeling of optimism within the project. "We'll do it right this time" was the widely held belief within the project.

Shortly, the technical staff becomes disillusioned when they realize, usually before management, that there is not enough time to accomplish critical testing tasks. Unless the test manager deals with these early problems, chaos will set in. The commonly heard statement will be, "If we can just get to the next milestone we'll be all right." Finally, the problems, unless dealt with effectively, result in a staff feeling that the project can't go any further. The initial enthusiasm becomes disillusionment, the early optimism becomes pessimism, and the initial energy becomes fatigue. The test manager, when dealing with the technical members of the staff, must exude optimism. He or she should be upbeat, realistic, and always positive. The test manager need not appear to be a technical guru, but should understand the general requirements of the test program and be sensitive to the needs and problems facing the staff.

HIRING TEST PERSONNEL

Selection of qualified test personnel is an essential skill of the successful software test manager. Staffing the test organization is more difficult than hiring development personnel because of the limited number of available, qualified, proven test individuals. These individuals need a high experience level, have to be able to maintain a general system understanding, and be able to synthesize a test structure from many small pieces of technical data.

The first thing to look for when interviewing test personnel is a good self-image. Personnel who are working on the problems of test and integration are going to deal with problems which, on the surface, seem insurmountable within the constraints of the project. Unless an individual has confidence in his own ability to succeed, he will often throw up his hands and retreat into the safety of obscurity. The self-image is clearly evident during the interview through the individual's responses to questions.

Look for people whose primary goal is a sense of achievement and who are willing to make the absolute commitment in time and personal sacrifice. Achievement-oriented individuals are what the manager should seek out since these are the ones who will become the fast trackers.

Avoid hiring people just because they are willing to work for low wages. There is always a reason. Individuals whose careers have not kept pace may have had the following experiences:

1. Problems beyond their control, such as layoffs, may have affected their career. These individuals may become the best and most dedicated members of the staff.
2. The individual may be nonaggressive, ineffective, or unreliable. These particular types should never be assigned to testing positions since they will not provide support at the critical points in the project when test schedules become short.

The manager should strive to hire individuals who are more intelligent and capable than the manager himself. The test manager's success is measured by how effectively personnel assigned to the test segments of the project perform the many technical and nontechnical tasks associated with testing. The personnel assigned to testing are the means by which the manager achieves success and gains recognition.

Unfortunately, when interviewing personnel many managers fail to recognize the essential relationship between the competency of the staff and their own success. When interviewing individuals who are clearly superior to themselves in intelligence, experience, or capability, many feel threatened and pass such individuals up for less capable personnel. Test managers who make this mistake limit their own ability to succeed by limiting the capability of their own staff.

The software test manager should ensure that he or she has at least two individuals who can take over the test manager position. The software test manager is in the fortunate position of being in a field where there is a limited number of proven individuals and an expanding demand. Within most companies, software test personnel are at a premium.

Managers who do not ensure that there is a designated, qualified replacement for their position have limited their own career potential by ensuring that they will not be able to be released from their current position if a better position becomes available. Many test managers fall into the trap of running the test program as a "one-person show," not sharing or delegating responsibility within the organization. All test plan problems are theirs alone. They deal directly with the test issues, personally planning, allocating, and applying resources to the project without coordinating with their staff. They have made themselves indispensable. Despite exceptional performance, these managers will be passed over for promotion, not considered for better positions, and will not be released from their current positions because of potential project impacts.

The wise test manager will ensure that there is always a clearly qualified, identified management backup. The backup should be cognizant of all management decisions, open issues, and test activities. He or she should ensure that the backup manager can take over at any time in the event of enhanced opportunity, nonavoidable personnel requirements, or reassignment.

LEADERSHIP—THE CRITICAL MANAGEMENT SKILL

The test manager must be an effective leader capable of bringing together, focusing, and directing the many activities, organizational elements, and experience and talents of personnel assigned to testing.

The test manager should be a clear, rapid thinker capable of assimilating large amounts of information and translating the data into accurate and correct decisions. He or she should be able to express ideas, easily and persuasively, in a concise, focused manner. The test manager must be analytical, extracting meaning from many small, unrelated pieces of information and technical inputs. This person must be objective and capable of making decisions, evaluating information, and observing progress in an impersonal manner. He or she should not let predefined opinions or personal prejudice influence thinking. The test manager should retain an impersonal perspective, forming ideas from facts rather than attitudes. He or she should trust insight, realizing that many times this is correct despite indications to the contrary. The test manager must be patient because, when dealing with testing personnel or technical issues, impatience or precipitous actions will have a negative project effect. The test manager must act as the interface and buffer between individuals and groups who don't like or respect each other. He or she must be tactful when dealing with people, orchestrating the activities of individuals with the test project, and must have poise amid the apparent chaos of the test planning, development, or execution. The test manager should show self-restraint, ensuring that the test program is not run in response to unplanned criteria. This person must have a sense of humor and be able to communicate easily with personnel. He or she must understand what motivates and drives the different levels of the program and software staff, and must stay in tune with the needs, desires, and problems of the test staff.

Effective leadership is the discriminator between an effective test manager and one who experiences management difficulty.

7 Test Specification

Planning and implementation of the test structure is the responsibility of the test manager, and must be smooth, structured, and rigorously enforced.

Once the planning, scheduling, and personnel assignments have been made, the real work of test development begins. As illustrated in Figure 7.1, these early activities fall into four categories. These are conducted in parallel by separate organizational elements.

1. **Test Support Development.** Support planning and application of the automated tools and test facilities support, test control, test review, and audit practices and procedures, development of the specific test methodologies, and definition of the flow of test data, responsibility, and project interfaces.

2. **Development Test Planning.** Development of generic requirements for the development test category and implementation of the support environment, project controls, and reviews and audit requirements.

3. **Build Test Planning and Development.** Definition, documentation, and implementation of build plans, test scenarios, and data procedures for each software subsystem, and identification of the tools, testing techniques, and methodologies to be used to integrate and qualify each build.

4. **Functional Procedure, Scenario, and Data Development.** Detailing of step-by-step functional test requirements from the test specifications in the software test plan, the requirements which are the basis for the software development, and the functional specifications which detail the derived requirements and software data interfaces.

These four areas of test development translate documented test policies, practices, strategies, and requirements into a set of detailed test specifications which define how each individual design and functional requirement is to be validated and how each individual software component is to be verified.

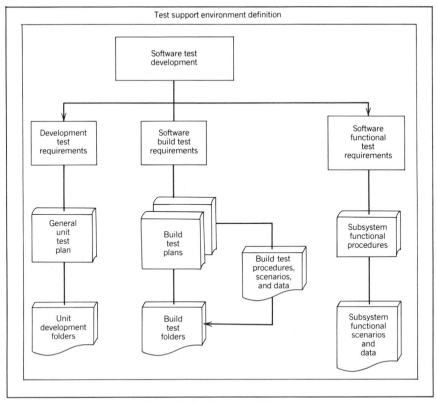

Figure 7.1 Early test activities

From the manager's perspective, these tasks often represent the most difficult to accomplish and control since they:

1. Require a long time to complete. There is rarely sufficient structural information—data flows, data base design, detailed algorithms, to do an effective planning job as early as it should be done prior to the testing period.

2. Require that personnel synthesize large amounts of detailed technical information into a reasonably limited set of testing specifications.

3. The interim product of these levels of test development are difficult to evaluate, are abstract in nature, and are hard to review and audit in a piecemeal fashion.

4. The close relationship between each of the three levels of test development and the specification and development of the test support environment is critical to the effectiveness of the test program but is difficult to ensure.

Direct control of personnel during this phase of test development is extremely difficult, even if production schedules and earned value techniques are applied to plan and monitor progress.

Personnel easily bog down in the morass of technical detail, finding it difficult to synthesize test requirements from evolving and incomplete system functional and design requirements. Even with short milestones and regular reviews, test personnel will lose sight of the test schedules and long-term goals and requirements of the test program, and may drift away from the planned testing structure. Personnel will forget that the segment of testing they are assigned, whether it be development, build, functional, or support, is only a single component of an overall test structure and, unless frequently reminded by the test manager, will treat their area as an end in itself rather than an integral part of a larger piece. Finally, integration of the software test activities with system test planning and development will quickly be lost during the period of software test development if not constantly supported and maintained as a high-priority activity by the test manager. This drift is subtle, occurring first as small production schedule milestone slips, and slight drops in earned value productivity measures, later as significant schedule and productivity problems, and finally as a general inability on the part of the test manager to maintain any schedule commitments or reasonable productivity. If allowed to continue, problems associated with poor test development productivity will become an almost insurmountable problem defying easy solution. Early problem recognition provides the test manager with the flexibility to deal with the situation before it becomes critical, and if decisive action is taken, impacts to cost, schedule, and productivity can be avoided altogether.

These indications, plus earned value and production schedule discrepancies, require an early assessment on the part of the test manager to isolate the basic problems causing the condition and require quick, decisive action to correct.

Once the basic test structure has been defined and documented the test implementation process begins. This process starts with the development test levels. These tests are the most informal and are controlled by the development organizations. They are initiated by the development of unit test planning and the implementation of these plans as an integral part of the code development.

INTERFACING TO SOFTWARE TEST LEVELS

The relationship between development tests and tests used to integrate and qualify software subsystems imposes certain requirements on the techniques, procedures, and control disciplines used by each of the development test levels. These development test requirements fall into two categories.

1. **Test Disciplines.** Those components of the development test environment which result in the planning, execution, and evaluation of module and unit testing. These tests provide confidence that the software unit is of sufficient quality and integrity to permit integration into a subsystem configuration.

2. **Testing Management, Control, and Monitoring Procedures.** Those segments of the development test environment which plan, manage, and control the process of module and unit test and monitor progress for quality, adequacy, and adherence to project standards.

The development testing disciplines exercise small, stand-alone segments of the software. The techniques and the criteria for successful completion are determined by the attributes of the individual software element, rather than the need to demonstrate interface or system performance. During development testing, several project disciplines should be tailored to the development test environment.

Configuration Management During Development Testing

During the development test period, project control of individual data products associated with module and unit testing should be limited to programmer controlled and administered configuration management practices and procedures. The characteristics of the data products during this period, the instability, the use by only one individual within the project organization, and a lack of interim milestones to evaluate software integrity and monitor development performance limit the degree to which formal baseline and data management techniques may be applied. Although the baseline and configuration management practices are used at this stage of the project to control requirements and software design, their early application to control of developing code will slow coding progress and unnecessarily inhibit the prerogatives of the programmer.

Formal project controls over unit design is established through successful completion of a Unit Design Walkthrough (UDW). Project control of the Unit Development Folders (UDF), and module and unit code and test data after successful completion of the Unit Test Walkthrough (UTW) are essential to maintain the integrity of the data and to insulate the project from changing unit design, code, and unit test specifications. During the period between these two walkthroughs, the programmer should be in charge, with responsibility for the integrity of the software being developed and the adherence to project requirements. After these walkthroughs, formal project controls should be applied if the software data products meet the following criteria.

1. They will be used by more than one individual or organizational element of the project.

2. Changes to the data items affect related baselines or the technical integrity of the software requirements, design, code, or testing.

Any configuration management and control procedures implemented for development test should be an extension of those used for software testing. New procedures, modified project controls, or unique project policies, practices, or configuration management techniques should not be necessary to support the control requirements during development testing.

Reviews of Data Products During Development Testing

Development testing deals with two categories of information: data being generated by individuals or single organizational elements within the project, and data used by more than one organization or by more than one person. While the data products are under development, use is usually restricted to the organization developing the product. As a result, absolute technical integrity is not established until the product is complete. Impacts associated with poor data control, inadequate specification, or misinterpretation of technical requirements are localized to the project group doing the work. Frequent peer-level reviews within the project organization will provide the checks and balances essential to ensure the ultimate integrity of the data being developed. These reviews are consistent with the volatile nature of the software products during this period. Premature attempts to review, freeze and control code and test parameters at a project level before the product stabilizes will negate the effectiveness of the baseline and data management components of software configuration management. This premature control will force the project to control many small pieces of data which are undergoing frequent change and have not been reviewed or approved at the project level. Frequent, formally structured walkthroughs and reviews of developing or evolving data prior to and during the development test period will provide assurances that the quality and integrity of the data are consistent with project standards. If problems are found, there is sufficient time to correct them without affecting software or system test schedules.

These reviews are costly, however, in terms of personnel and schedule requirements. As such, the degree to which they are applied to the project, their frequency, and the specific requirements for their conduct should be balanced against the technical characteristics, and operational and performance requirements of the application.

Test Tools During Development Test

During the period of development testing, the test environment and automated support options available for application to the test problem are limited by the uniqueness of individual module or unit testing requirements.

Essentially, qualification of each module and unit requires execution of the paths through the software which must be tested. Completion of this path testing is essential if the unit is to be considered ready for integration into a subsystem configuration. Reliability and internal integrity must be demonstrated if the unit is to be considered ready for integration and the functional, interface, and operational characteristics must be demonstrated at the unit level. Based on these parameters, requirements for the automated aids, testing, tools, and software control environments may be defined. These requirements, because of cost, complexity, potential nonusability at higher test levels, and the disposable nature of the tools after development testing, make it necessary that before any requirements for unit testing tools, techniques, or methodologies are specified, the overall requirements for the test environment should be specified. Considerations should include commonality of tools across the spectrum of development testing, consistency with the software test levels, and minimization of development complexity, and cost for tools specified for the development test levels.

Specification of requirements for development testing is a multilevel process. As previously described, the basic level 1 and 2 test requirements are identified in two parts.

1. The Software Development plan defines what is to be accomplished during development testing and the development testing management and control procedures.
2. The Software Subsystem test plan defines how the level 1 and level 2 test requirements are to be satisfied and supported on a subsystem by subsystem basis.

These documents are the basis for the definition of detailed module and unit test requirements. The basic module and unit test requirements are documented in a subsystem-specific general unit test plan by each of the development organizations.

The general unit test plan is the basis for the individual unit test specifications included in the Unit Development Folders. As such, the general unit test plan should provide guidelines to be used for all unit test planning, a structure for the unit test planning segment of the Unit Development Folders, and rules for unit conduct and general criteria for success.

The general unit test plan should define, at a minimum, the following categories of information.

1. **Functional Relationships.** Identifies the requirements, top-level design specifications, and detailed design relationships. This section describes how the functional relationships are to be established and allocated, how they are to be specified and controlled, and how they are to be documented in the unit development folders.

2. **Functional Index.** Identifies how the functional requirements are documented in the Unit Development Folders and how the unit test cases are to be related to the requirements.

3. **Organization Rules and Responsibilities.** Define how, in general, the process of unit testing should be organized and structured and how the support functions are organizationally interfaced to the unit test process.

4. **Unit Test Procedures.** Define how the individual unit test cases, both integration and functional are to be documented in the unit development folders, how the unit test scenarios and data are to be defined, developed, and reviewed, and who within the development organization is responsible for development and conduct of the test cases.

5. **Unit Test Reporting.** Defines how and by whom the results of unit testing are to be documented, evaluated, and reviewed.

6. **Unit Configuration Definition.** Defines how the individual unit configurations are integrated, documented, and released from unit test conduct. And how corrections are made, documented, and incorporated into the test configuration.

7. **Project Interfaces.** Define how the unit test activities integrate with the related levels of software testing, how the relationships between unit test and the configuration management segments of the project are defined and maintained, and how support resources are requested and provided.

8. **Unit Test Tools, Techniques, and Methodologies.** Describe what generic tools, techniques, and methodologies are available throughout the software project for use during unit testing and what the rules and constraints are for tailoring these to specific unit test application.

The general unit test plan is placed under configuration management and control after a walkthrough. This walkthrough is chaired by the software project manager and is attended by the technical manager, all task leaders responsible for development, and the software test manager. At the walkthrough the "what ifs" of unit testing are reviewed against the general unit test plan parameters, the units testing technical and project constraints and limitations are identified and discussed, and the project expectation and requirements for unit test are identified and reviewed. At successful completion of the walkthrough, the project walkthrough authority approves the plan and releases it to the PSL, and from then on it can only be modified through SPR action.

Development of the Unit Development Folder—The Unit Test Plan

The second part of unit test planning takes place when the software developer translates the parameters in the general unit test plan to a specific test structure. This is documented in a unit test plan in order to be incor-

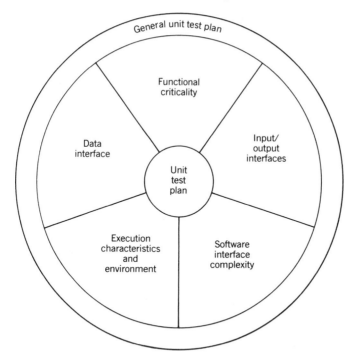

Figure 7.2   Unit characteristics

porated later into the unit development plan. As illustrated in Figure 7.2, there are five primary unit characteristics which determine the specific structure for unit testing.

The test planner should evaluate the degree of functional criticality the unit has in the context of the software subsystem. Unit testing is the only point in the overall test cycle where the internal aspects of an individual unit may be exhaustively exercised and evaluated. As such, the amount, degree, and rigor associated with unit testing should be scaled to how critical a problem in the unit will be to the functional integrity of the software subsystem. Noncritical units have less of a requirement for rigorous unit testing than does a central subsystem unit.

The number and complexity of the external unit input/output interfaces determines how much rigor is to be included during functional unit testing. If the unit executes on the extremities of the subsystem—that is, it deals with the external system or subsystem data interfaces—each individual interface must be qualified before the software is released for the software test levels. This testing may require that each interface be simulated during level 1 and the internal and functional processing characteristics of the unit be evaluated through the application of thread analysis.

Software interface complexity also impacts the structure and requirements for unit testing. As with the external interface problem, units which must interface with a large number of related units in a complex environment require more extensive testing of internal functional support team than does a unit which must support a simple set of interfaces or executes in a noncomplex environment.

The execution environment that the unit must support has a major influence on how the unit is integrated and qualified. A unit which must execute in a highly dynamic environment with a random set of inputs and outputs requires a different unit testing structure than that used for a status unit environment.

The nature of the dynamic unit execution environment presents problems which must be dealt with through rigorous unit testing practices. The unit test environment for dynamic software units executing in a dynamic environment must be integrated and qualified in accordance with the interface and physical characteristics of the unit. In addition, the unit performance should be evaluated.

The unit should be exercised in a nominal as well as anomalous stand-alone test environment. Performance should be measured and compared against budgets assigned to the unit. This performance qualification for this category of software is essential to establishing the execution and integrity of the unit before it is integrated into subsystem configuration.

The data support and interface characteristics of the unit influence the extent to which the internal aspects of the unit are exercised and the degree to which changes to data values are monitored. The data monitoring requirement determines the instrumentation required to monitor the data as well as the complexity of the test environment and drivers to be used.

The unit test plan segment of the UDF should then be structured in accordance with the guidelines included in the general unit test plan. The requirements for unit testing should be reviewed and evaluated during the unit test walkthrough. At the unit design walkthrough the unit structure is evaluated against the functional and design requirements of the unit. The unit test plan is evaluated against the design and execution characteristics of the unit.

The Unit Test Walkthrough (UTW) is the last informal review of the software conducted by the developing organization. This walkthrough is conducted after completion of the unit testing and it evaluates the conduct of the tests in relation to the test requirements in the UTW. At the UTW the following is evaluated.

1. That all interfaces have been incorporated and tested.
2. Software has been coded properly, complies with project standards, and is consistent with the requirements of the design.
3. The code meets the functional, performance, interface, and design requirements, and the unit tests verify compliance.

4. The unit test plan requirements have been completed, the test execution has been in accordance with the requirements of the plan, and the results have been properly analyzed and documented, and corrective action has been taken.

5. All problems identified through the testing have been corrected or the corrections are scheduled and assigned.

After completion of the UTW, the unit responsibility will transition from the developing organization to the PSL for release to level 3 testing.

SOFTWARE TESTING—INTEGRATING AND QUALIFYING SOFTWARE SUBSYSTEMS

As illustrated in Figure 7.3 the software test requirements are developed from requirements defined in the software development and test plans, from the design specifications and from the functional specifications identifying the performance, functional, processing, and software interface requirements. These test requirements detail, on a subsystem-by-subsystem basis, exactly how each software build is to be integrated and qualified.

As previously described, the software testing requirements are defined in two parts: the level 3 requirements which are designed to qualify the internal execution characteristics and level 4 test requirements which functionally qualify the software from an internal perspective.

The software test plan is the first step in laying out the structure of the software builds. This plan describes and defines the requirements for the planning and conduct of these tests. The plan provides the basic schedule for the planning, specification, execution, and completion of all build tests. The functional requirements for the build are defined in the plan, as are the tools, techniques, and methodologies to be used. The controls and project support requirements are described and the specific software inventory, configuration, and architecture is defined.

From this plan the software functional requirements are allocated to specific builds. These builds are incremental in nature, each layering a new set of software capabilities with those integrated and qualified in the previous build. As illustrated in Figure 7.4, builds should be allocated according to five basic criteria.

1. All builds should be functionally compatible. The software build should represent a reasonably complete block of the software system capability. Execution of the build tests should require minimum simulation of interfacing software and test software when establishing the test environment.

2. Each build should integrate and qualify software components developed under compatible implementation schedules. All units, test tools,

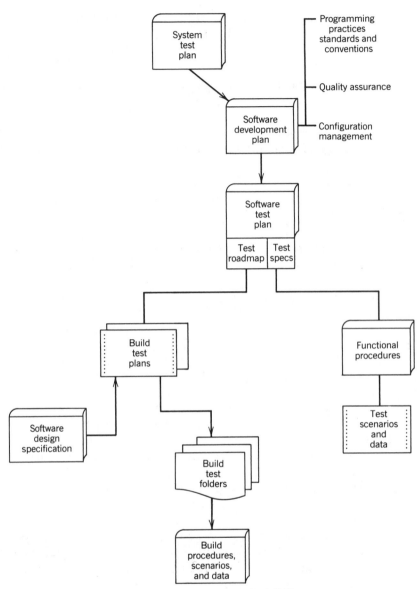

Figure 7.3   Test requirements definition

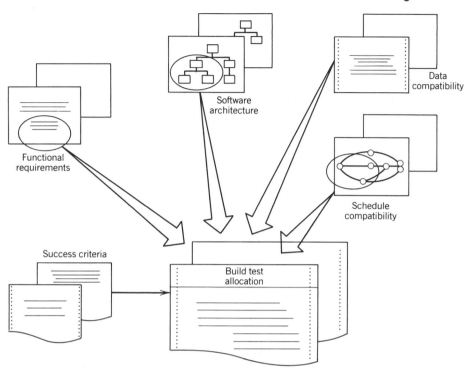

Figure 7.4 Build allocation

and support facilities should be available when required according to the overall build schedule. This will minimize the requirement for generation of drivers, emulation, or simulation to complete.

3.   Each build should be data compatible. The software configuration exercised by a build should include an integrated, defined set of data, structured in accordance with the architecture of the software.

4.   Each build should be verifiable, allowing the integration success to be measured and functional integrity to be evaluated.

5.   Each build should be traceable, to the software design for level 3 testing and to the functional requirements allocated to the subsystem.

The definition of the builds is the focus of all planning and scheduling from this point of the development. All unit development schedules must be phased to the build requirements; all reviews and audits are keyed to the builds; all documentation production and customer reviews are tailored to the build plans; and all tools, automated facilities, project controls, test procedure, scenarios, and test data must be in consonance with the requirements of the software builds. As the build requirements change, the phasing and adequacy of project resources and plans must be reevaluated and readjusted if necessary.

Often managers fail to give the proper emphasis to the selection of the builds. Faced with near-term scheduling and planning milestones, rather than following a proper procedure for selecting the builds, the manager succumbs to the temptation to quickly define a structure, thus "taking the heat off." There is hope that there will be plenty of time later to fix the build structure and readjust the plans. This is never the case. These poor decisions won't become visible or critical for a long time and have a way of becoming "cast in concrete." Personnel in the project will forget how the build architecture was defined and will assume that there was a firm technical basis which, for one reason or another, can't be violated. There is often significant pressure to hold to these schedules in spite of increasing project difficulty. In the end the build structure is finally redefined, but only after much project pain and difficulty. The build structure should always be based on a complete and effective analysis of technical, schedule, support, and resource realities.

Once the builds have been determined, the work package schedules should be readjusted and development of the build test plan for the first build should be initiated. As illustrated in Figure 7.5, the software project has become a series of parallel "mini projects" supported by different segments of the organization. The activities of the various areas are coordinated through the work package schedules, focused through the production

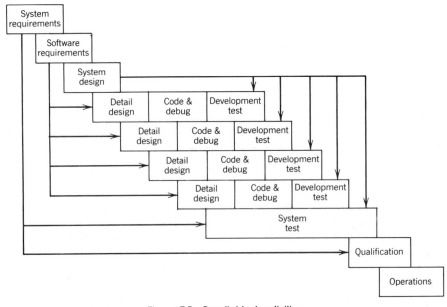

Figure 7.5 Parallel test activities

schedules, monitored through the reviews, audits, costs, schedule control procedures, and the earned value system, and controlled by formal and informal configuration management, project control, and test management procedures and practices.

Development of each build configuration is initiated through development of a Build Test Plan. The Build Test Plan is the responsibility of the build test leader. The build test leader is normally assigned from within the software systems engineering organization. He or she plans and schedules the build, acts as a focal point to other segments of the project for all issues concerning the build, schedules, allocates, and controls the application of resources to build requirements, and supports all project reviews and audits.

Depending on the level of testing being supported, the role of the build test leader varies. During level 3 testing, the build test leader will direct, at least functionally, the activities of several technical levels of the software organization.

1. The software systems engineering organization, which plans, develops, implements, and performs the tests, while initially evaluating the results and documenting observed problems.
2. The PSL and SCRB, which are responsible for the integrity of all data products used during test and provide documented software releases and maintenance versions for test.
3. The software development organizations, which correct problems uncovered during testing and update affected technical documentation.
4. Project support organizations, which provide test tools, data, ensure the integrity of supporting systems, and provide organizational and administrative support.
5. Quality Assurance organizations, which review the integrity of design and test materials, monitor the adequacy and effectiveness of the test activities, and ensure the consistency and technical validity of baselined data used during software test.

The build test leader orchestrates the activities of each of these organizational and support areas, ensuring that they "play together" in support of the software build test requirements. He or she often must act as an umpire, bridging the different goals and objectives of the areas of the project and dealing with the polarization which will invariably take place during level 3 testing. The build leader must provide the test manager with clear and accurate status information concerning all build issues. He or she must take action when necessary to ensure that software build schedules are maintained, elevating those issues outside his or her purview to the SCRB for resolution or action. During this period of the project, the build test leaders are the "first line" of supervision, focusing the roles of the project toward the integration of a software subsystem.

During the period of functional, or level 4 testing, the build test leader takes on the role of coordinator. During this testing phase the build test leader, rather than directing the activities of the test staff, will coordinate the various segments of the project and focus them toward the functional test activities. The build test leader will continue to act as a focal point, fighting the battles essential to test success, and speak with a single voice about test problems and successes, while ensuring that the rigor and functional test structure is retained even in periods of stress and project pressures. The leader should deal with the problems of project polarization, orchestrating the activities of groups within the organization who do not like, respect, or understand each other's goals, objectives, and motivations. He or she is responsible and accountable for the functional test integrity, interfacing with the program, customer, configuration management, and support organizations on any functional test issues. This is the individual who plans, executes, and "sells off" the functional test and has a major influence on the customer's acceptance of the software subsystems. If properly planned, the build test leader can take advantage of the overlaps between the test levels, minimizing the work required to support each level of software testing and ensuring a smooth flow of data between the levels of software testing.

As illustrated in Figure 7.6, the allocation of software and functional procedures to builds is accomplished as a result of several factors. As previously described, the issues of schedule architecture, functional and data compatibility are essential ingredients of an effective build structure. From these parameters, and in accordance with the project requirements of the software test plan, a structured allocation of software builds is developed. The build allocation schedule is the bridge between the overall software testing requirement and that required for each specific segment of software test. It is not meant to be a plan but rather a visual means of showing how and when particular segments of the software subsystem are to be integrated and qualified. The allocation schedule is a precursor to finalization of the work package schedule, requiring an interaction of the subsystem schedule. In order to maintain software schedule validity, three pieces of information are included in the build schedule: the software units to be included in each build as defined in the schedule; the functions to be qualified at each build as documented in the functional specification; and the major data elements required to support each build as specified in the software design specification.

The allocation schedule is developed by the software test manager and reviewed at an initial build walkthrough. This walkthrough is attended by senior technical personnel from the software system's engineering, software development and software test organizations. The purpose of the walkthrough is to evaluate the integrity of the proposed test architecture, in-

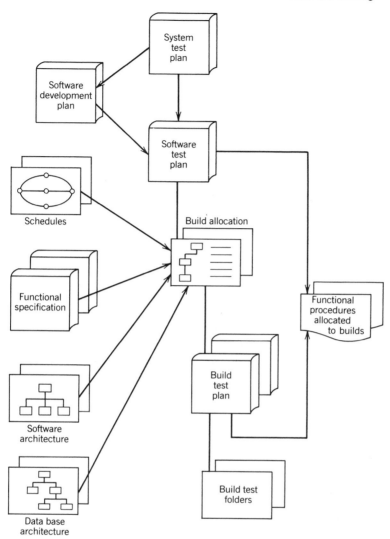

Figure 7.6   Test requirements allocation

vestigate technical feasibility in relation to resource constraints, and identify and plan for contingencies which may impact progress or productivity. This is where the "what ifs" are asked concerning the test structure and proposed allocation of testing.

After successful completion of the walkthrough, the build plan for the initial build is developed. This document should be completed before any test development, implementation, or execution for that build is initiated. The build test plan should be terse. It should detail how the particular build is to be integrated and qualified, what resources and software components are required, what functions will be demonstrated, and what are the measurable criteria for success. The plan consists of six sections as follows.

1. **Purpose, Scope, and Limitations.** Define and circumscribe the build requirements defining the purpose of the build, the scope of the build structure, limitations of the build resulting from the selected software or functional capabilities, and what measure of success may be expected.

2. **Functional Definition.** Identifies specifically or by reference the requirements for functional demonstrations as well as describing the software performance parameters which must be monitored, measured, and evaluated to ensure functional integrity.

3. **Software Architecture.** Documents specifically or by reference the software units to be included in each build, the expected degree of completeness, and the architecture of the build.

4. **Test Tools, Techniques, and Methodologies.** Describe specifically or reference how the build is to be integrated and qualified. Identify the specific test tools to be used, where they will come from, and how and when they will be qualified for use. Also, this section of the plan should document the procedures and techniques to control the build test process and ensure the integrity of data and adequacy of the testing.

5. **Resource and Personnel Requirements.** Document the requirements for resources and personnel for each level of testing to be conducted for the build. The requirements should be keyed to specific scheduled events and identify not only availability requirements but also expected sources from which the resources are to be acquired.

6. **Contingency Plans.** Documents specific problems which are anticipated during the integration and qualification of the build. This section should describe not only the problem but also the project actions which either have been or will be taken to avoid or minimize the impacts on the project in the event the problem occurs.

Completion of the build test plan is a precursor to any testing beyond level 2. This plan determines, to a large extent, how the software testing is to be phased and the specific steps to be accomplished. The level 4 requirements are further detailed in procedures as previously defined. Level 3 requirements are less structured, being defined in the Build Test Folder (BTF). There is one BTF for each level 3 test case. The BTF is the means by which the integration team describes tests to be run in order to integrate the software, documents the results of the tests, and describes schedules, problems, test configurations and notes which provide critical, informal test information.

Development and maintenance of the BTF is the responsibility of the individual assigned test case responsibility. He or she uses information from all staff and organizations participating in the build planning, execution, analysis, or test control functions. As with the Unit Development Folders, the BTF is stored in the PSL, and controlled through the project software configuration management and control practices.

With the exception of the UDF, the other test planning documents are a before-the-fact specification of the planned test approach. The BTF, on the other hand, is an in-process documentation of the conduct of software level 3 and 4 test cases.

Development of the BTF is evolutionary. Initially, it defines the software integration and functional test schedule, initial test configuration, and data required for test conduct. The initial build walkthrough evaluates these data items. Later the BTF contains a record of the build test case experience. The BTF documents the tests executed, the problems experienced, the approved modifications and regression test history, the record of tests run, and the software performance history. These later additions to the BTF are reviewed at the final build walkthrough conducted by the build test leader. The walkthrough evaluates the testing adequacy, conduct, documentation, and results.

The BTF consists of ten separate categories of data resident on PSL files. These are:

1. **Build Configuration.** The latest software and data build configuration released by the PSL and documented by a Version Description Document (VDD).

2. **Functional Index.** A functional traceability index or matrix which maps the functions to be tested to the software components. This serves as the Verification Cross Reference and is essential in making the test case meaningful.

3. **The Production Test Schedule.** Details the plan and schedule for conducting the test cases and completing critical build test milestones and reviews.

4. **Test Input Sources.** To be used in the level 3 and level 4 test configuration. This section describes essential modifications to the input sources described in the software and build test plans on a test-case-by-test-case basis.

5. **Test Output Support Requirements.** Identifies on a test-case-by-test-case basis the output interfaces to be established and essential data reduction requirements.

6. **Organization Roles and Responsibilities.** Identifies the organizational responsibilities in the execution, analysis, review, or approval of the case.

7. **Test Step Design.** Details the test execution sequences, the software units exercised, the major data modifications resulting from the test, the interim outputs either from the test instrumentation or the software itself, and the conditions which define a test run as successful or unsuccessful.

8. **Test Operation.** Details how the test conditions are to be set and initialized, how the test and target software is to be loaded and initialized,

how the test is to be operated and controlled, how test conditions are varied by the operator, what to do in the event of a deviant test condition, and how to terminate the test normally.

9. **Test Execution Log.** Records the history of the test case executions, describing the data and performance of the test, the software, test, and data configuration used, the software problem reports open or closed by the test run, and the test operator and analyst.

10. **Notes and Observations.** This section is the repository for any informal notes and observations concerning the test case, test materials or support, software configuration, test conduct or analysis, or any other information useful in executing, evaluating, or analyzing the test case.

Test Case Design—How Should Level 3 Test Cases Be Defined, Designed, and Structured

The definition and design of the level 3 test cases can only be achieved after completion of the allocation software and functions into a build configuration. This allocation determines which software subsystem functions and components are to be tested in which build. From this, each individual test case may be designed and developed.

The basic objective of software testing is to exhaustively exercise the software and to uncover and correct as many errors as possible as early in the development period as feasible. The objective is not to pass a set of predefined test cases. The effectiveness of the test environment in satisfying this objective has a significant effect on the development costs, overall productivity, and the reliability and operational effectiveness of the software subsystem.

During integration testing one focus is on the checking of the internal logic of the software on a unit by unit basis. Goals for this testing are:

1. Exercising every unit with all units interfacing to it.
2. Exercising all logical paths through the software subsystem.
3. Exercising every major subsystem decision element.
4. Exercising every major data base structure.
5. Exercising the software from each external stimulus.
6. Executing the software subsystem in sufficiently realistic and controlled environments to measure the performance and timing of individual units.
7. Evaluating the accuracy of all software algorithms and data elements in nominal and irregular system conditions.
8. Executing and evaluating all recovery aspects of the software and responses to abnormal system conditions.

Due to project cost and schedule constraints, complete satisfaction of these goals is not achievable in any reasonable level 3 environment. However, the use of automated aids, the application of various integration techniques, and the use of incremental testing will optimize the testing effectiveness.

The testing should be structured so that as it progresses through level 3 there is a natural and logical flow to the tests. During software subsystem integration, the test emphasis is with internal verification of subsystem interfaces, computational accuracies, timing, data relationships, and control paths. During level 3, the latter stages of the tests are directed at evaluating how effectively the subsystem components perform in relation to the subsystem design requirements.

If properly defined, the level 3 test cases can easily be modified and restructured for level 4 testing. If not defined with this in mind, two completely separate test sets may be necessary, along with the tools and support materials.

Integration testing occurs in several progressive stages and results in first an executable subsystem configuration. As illustrated in Figure 7.7, the first group of test cases should initially demonstrate that the software units execute together and when linked, the subsystem cycles.

The second group should evaluate the control paths through the software. This phase of integration testing ensures that the subsystem controls supported through terminals and other external sources are adequately

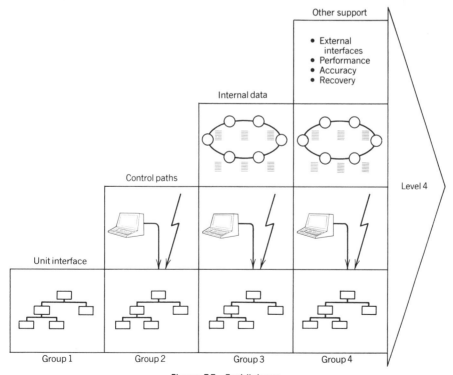

Figure 7.7   Test linkage

supported by the software and that internal control paths, and internal software performance monitoring functions have been implemented in accordance with the design.

The third group of level 3 tests consists of tests designed to evaluate the internal data integrity of the software subsystem. These tests are designed from the standpoint of the data to be monitored rather than the software being executed. These tests require instrumentation to monitor data values and isolate system conditions which are critical when data values change.

The final level 3 test grouping, group 4, evaluates the performance aspects of the software from an internal execution perspective. These tests should be driven to the maximum extent possible from data external to the target system. These test cases evaluate the adequacy of support to external software interfaces, software performance and accuracy, and software error recognition and recovery attributes.

This phasing of test case structure and execution should be consistently applied to each build.

During integration testing the test configuration instrumentation almost always affects execution and often invalidates performance measurements unless the test cases are structured to take the instrumentation into account. Until the final build, the test configuration is incomplete. It requires simulation, emulation, software stubs or drivers to allow the test to execute. The test case design must anticipate this incomplete configuration, and must exercise those units execution characteristics and data elements which are the object of the test case.

Integration testing rigor is a function of many previously identified factors. It is reasonable to assume that a large, complex system requires more extensive, rigorous integration than a smaller, less complex applications.

Independent of other factors, the size of a software application has the major effect on the complexity of the development both from a technical and managerial standpoint.

Using source statement size, Yourdon has classified software products into discrete categories. His categorization ranges from simple programs that are less than 1,000 source statements to what he describes as "utterly absurd programs" that contain between 1 million and 10 million statements. For each category, he specifies the approximate number of programmers involved, schedule length, number of software elements, and the number of subsystems. These parameters may be interpreted to identify the escalating extent and complexity of the testing that would be necessary for each category. Software systems in Yourdon's "absurd" category have been built, but, with a few exceptions, have not been delivered within originally planned schedules and budgets.

Yourdon's observations are particularly valid when defining and designing a suite of integration test cases. It is easier to test software exhaustively in small units. It is here that structurally oriented testing goals, such as number of logical paths traversed, percentage of statements executed, number of possible inputs to be tested, and so on, are applied. A very large percentage of errors can be discovered and corrected at this level and the cost of doing so will be minimal. It is less feasible, both technically and economically, to attain these objectives after software units are interconnected. The testing on this early level emphasizes the verification of logic, computations, data handling, timing, and sizing.

In extremely large systems the isolation of small, individually testable elements is difficult. By structuring the test cases for each build as previously described, and breaking the system into many small builds, the problems of the large system may be minimized.

A second factor which must be considered when selecting a primary integration technique is the type of application. As described in Chapter 3, an early decision must be made about the general technique to be used in integrating the software.

Real-time software is characterized by communication exchanges that are initiated or driven by the random receipt and time-dependent processing of data messages. Processing is controlled by interrupts and processing signals which occur in an unpredictable manner. The system interaction is often network-orientated, requiring interaction between independent processing elements.

Data exchanges and system processing requirements essentially are randomly initiated by the receipt of data, occurrence of an event, or existence of a specific system condition. The nature of real-time functions and the associated complex, time-dependent interactions present testing problems not encountered by more predictable application categories. These problems are in two major areas.

1. System performance and loading characteristics must be an integral part of the testing environment, demonstrated at all levels of software and test.
2. The testing environment must support the random, stringent, and interactive environment characteristic of the system.

Adequate performance and loading testing must be a fundamental part of each level of test. The performance of individual modules and units should be assessed at level 1 and 2. Affects of loading on the performance and integrity of the module and unit should be assessed through emulations of the software configuration and the impacts on unit performance resulting from changing environments. During software testing levels 3 and 4 the performance of the software subsystem after receipt of a data message should be monitored and evaluated and the timing of individual functions isolated. The testing should investigate the effects of system loads and the impact of stress conditions on the integrity of the subsystem support. This layering of performance testing between development and software testing is the means by which accurate measures of software performance may be made. System test levels 5 and 6 evaluate the aggregate performance and support characteristics of the operational system. The use of external system monitors must be planned into the test environment and the system operational environments must be modified to evaluate the affects of changing stress conditions on system integrity. The performance tests should have the following characteristics.

1. **System Interactions.** The interactions between system, software subsystem, and data components are complex and unpredictable. The tests should execute each test component individually and then in increasingly more complete configurations.

2. **Repeatability.** Because of differences in timing, the same sequence of test case inputs, phased slightly differently, or executing in a different configuration or loading conditions may result in different outputs or execution characteristics. Nonrepeatable test cases are invalid, since the results cannot be anticipated or predicted.

3. **Equipment Interaction.** The interactions between individual system components in a network configuration and the data and control exchanges should be thoroughly and exhaustively exercised. These tests should be simulated at first and then repeated with the actual hardware.

4. **Program Interaction.** The asynchronous interactions between software components within a software subsystem must be tested, first in a stand-alone, simulated configuration, and then in an integrated subsystem.

5. **Reproduceability.** All test cases, particularly in a real time environment, should be reproduceable. In the event of a failure, the exact environment and test conditions should be achievable and any failures re-created.

Thread testing is a technique of integration that can monitor the integrity of interfaced software elements as they respond to an external stimulus. A thread is a string of programs which, when executed, accomplishes a specific set of functions and results in a single or related set of outputs.

Testing begins with the exercise of single threads and then progresses to the testing of multiple threads. The phases of thread testing are:

1. **Phase 1.** This consists of testing individual elements, testing threads one at a time, and monitoring software execution paths through each thread by varying the inputs and system conditions. The thread configuration must be instrumented and should use a simulator to provide the inputs and collect and monitor the outputs.

2. **Phase 2.** This again tests threads one at a time and traces execution paths through the threads. During the previous testing, interfaced threads in the software configuration were simulated. During this phase of testing these simulated threads and support are replaced with the actual software threads and the relationships between the interfaced threads is executed. The addition of this support is compatible with build schedules.

3. **Phase 3**. This phase expands the input conditions used during the previous phase and develops a more realistic subsystem execution environment.

4. **Phase 4**. This is the first time the entire software subsystem configuration is tested. Simulated inputs are used to test more than one thread at a time in order to uncover inter-thread execution problems, interface inconsistencies, and performance and support problems. A major objective in this phase is to stress the subsystem and determine its throughput capacity. By loading subsystem queues, limiting or filling available buffer space, and restricting the available time and support resources, the effects on system support and integrity may be assessed. During this test phase, both nominal and anomalous data and system conditions are used and the emergency, error-processing and recovery aspects of the subsystem are evaluated.

5. **Phase 5**. In this phase the on-line terminals are incrementally connected. The testing begins with a single terminal; one thread test evolves into a multi-terminal test.

6. **Phase 6**. The transition from artificial to real entries is made in this phase. Again, the number of terminals participating in the testing is gradually increased.

7. **Phase 7**. This phase consists of a trial operation period. The period concludes when the incidence of problems is reduced to an acceptable level, and the system performs smoothly.

These thread tests are applied during group 4 integration when the internal integrity of the software has been established. This testing is a natural forerunner to the level 4 testing categories. By modifying the instrumentation, varying the test inputs and acceptance criteria, and mapping the test cases to the individual functional capabilites the thread test cases can serve as the basic level 4 test set. When considering the requirements for scenario and data development (to be discussed in the next section), this saving is significant.

Group 1, 2, and 3 integration tests as well as tests of static or non-real time applications, may require a different integration technique than that used during group 4. During these early integration tests, the emphasis is on the orderly development of an executable software subsystem capability. Rather than evaluating software subsystem execution characteristics, these tests build a system from single units and data elements. For simple, non-real time, or small applications, these tests may be all that are required at level 3. As discussed in Chapter 3, there are several methods which are used with varying degrees of success: hierarchical testing, bottom-up testing, and thread testing. Hierarchical integration testing takes qualified units which have completed level 2 testing and integrates them in a top-down fashion until an executable configuration is reached.

As illustrated in Figure 7.8, the top-down approach nominally begins at the top, or control level of the software hierarchy. The units which comprise

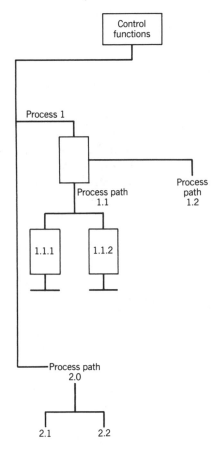

Figure 7.8   Top-down testing

this path are integrated first and this serves as the driver for the next level in the software integration plan. The second level takes units qualified through level 2 and integrates them with the control level above. Data is injected directly from the actual units above, and units at the level below are simulated with "stubs" which simulate performance of the lower level software units. As software becomes available at the third level, it replaces the stub for the software using data injected from above until all levels of the hierarchy have been filled.

Two problems often inhibit the effectiveness of this form of integration when used for complex or other than simple projects. The technique is extremely sensitive to slips in development or test schedules. As unit schedules slip, they impact the hierarchical relationships essential for success. If this slippage is broad, the entire testing structure can break down.

A second problem with pure top-down testing techniques is in the provision of data down through the software hierarchy. As the software configuration levels increase it becomes increasingly difficult to define and input data which, when injected at the top, will reasonably drive the lower level units. Many of the test conditions deal with processing situations or are environmentally defined and require modifications to the data, performance, or creation of processing loads.

Bottom-up testing is a third technique which may be used to integrate qualified units into an executable configuration. Under this test approach a driver which simulates the execution environment of the unit is written and used to prequalify the software before it is included in a subsystem configuration. When the unit executes properly with the driver it is released for level 4 testing. This testing technique is less sensitive to schedule and data problems than top-down testing but it has several problems which inhibit general use. First, the drivers are the key to the success of the bottom-up testing. They are often difficult and expensive to develop, are throwaway, and must exactly emulate the execution environment of the limit. If the driver is not exact, problems will be found at level 4 which should have been caught at level 3. These problems are often extremely difficult to isolate and correct and will have a significant negative impact on testing success.

In reality, a combined top-down, bottom-up approach to group 1, 2, and 3 testing is most frequently applied. As illustrated in Figure 7.9, when using this technique a software hierarchy is defined as if the software were to be integrated in a totally top-down fashion. Before software is integrated into

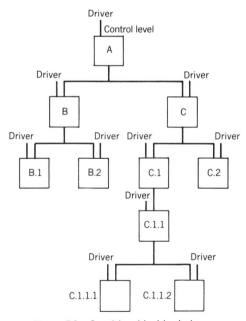

Figure 7.9   Combined test techniques

the hierarchy, it is first prequalified using a driver which simulates data and control inputs. All lower-level outputs are stubbed. When the unit executes properly with the driver, and if the interfacing units have been incorporated into the architecture, the unit is incorporated into the hierarchy. The stubs from the higher level are removed and the software is driven for the driver at the next level up in the hierarchy. Using this approach three advantages accrue.

1. The testing is insulated from the vagaries of software schedules.
2. The number of levels that must be driven by data is reduced by the use of drivers.
3. A test bench for testing software changes is developed through the hierarchy of test drivers.

Level 4 Test Case Design—Demonstration Rather Than Qualification

The definition and design of level 4 test cases is accomplished parallel with the development of the level 3 test cases. The initial specification of the level 4 test cases is provided in the second release of the software test plan. This is the point at which many test planners bog down. They attempt to define an optimal test set in relation to the functional or performance requirements of the software subsystem, only to discover that in fact there is not an optimal configuration, but a set of tests which correspond to the build requirements.

The build requirements define which functional requirements are to be demonstrated by each build and the schedule to be followed in executing each test case. The most effective way to schedule these test cases is to allocate functional requirements into the following generic testing categories.

1. **Subsystem Load.** Those functions which load the various software, and data base components of the subsystem.

2. **Subsystem Initialization.** Those functions which initialize all software, hardware, firmware, and data subsystems.

3. **Non-Real Time Data Input and Control.** Those functions which support the analysis and initial processing of non-real time input data. These tests also demonstrate the subsystem control functions initiated through operator action.

3. **Real Time Input Processing.** Those functions which support the input of real time data in an operational software configuration. These tests will demonstrate the handling of any communications protocols supported by the subsystem, the functions which input and route real time information, and the scheduling and execution initiation functions which cause selected subsystem functions to be executed.

4. **Subsystem Processing Functions.** Those individual processing functions which are supported by the software subsystem. Each traceable and

testable processing function should be demonstrated in such a manner that the performance may be monitored and the results clearly evaluated.

5. **Non-Real Time Outputs and Subsystem Reports.** The functions output those reports and external indicators of subsystem health, status, and performance.

6. **Real Time Outputs.** These test functions format, output, and maintain the real time interfaces. The output protocol processing functions, the communications and real time interfaces, data collection and formatting, and message processing functions are tested.

7. **Error Recognition and System Recovery.** These functions monitor the integrity of the software, recognize and process anomalous conditions, and initiate and support recovery or shutdown procedures.

8. **System Termination.** These functions respond to a termination request and perform those functions which result in an orderly subsystem shutdown.

The first step in designing the level 4 functional test is to define the general functional groupings to be used, and then allocate the functions, data, and other requirements of the system into these categories. This allocation is exclusive of schedule or build requirements and serves as the basis for test case definition.

The second step is to break each functional category into a set of test steps which will perform a small, reasonably complete set of related functional requirements. Each test step should be characterized by a set of inputs which are readily established or readable by the system and a set of outputs or subsystem conditions which may be monitored. This initial test step allocation should not require extensive analysis nor should it take a long time to complete.

The first steps, irrespective of the functional groupings, are then combined, into a set of test cases which have the following characteristics.

1. They are technically sound; the test case emulates the operational environment of the subsystem.

2. They track the level 3 environment, making maximum use of the test cases and data used during the later stages of level 3 integration.

3. They may be suballocated into the defined build architecture and development schedules.

4. Each subsystem function, interface, and data element is exercised and demonstrated at least once in one of the test cases. Test cases should have defined breakpoints which allow the monitoring of data values and permit restart without loss of test integrity.

5. All test cases should be driven from external sources not requiring manipulation of internal data values to initiate test execution.

6. All test cases should provide parameters which may be monitored to assess the performance of each test individual requirement.

7.   There should be clear success criteria for each test case identified and the requirements for test completion should be clearly spelled out.

Each test case should have a primary object. For example, if the test object is non-real time input, the predominant number of test steps will exercise these functions with other functions being exercised as required to provide test execution integrity.

As previously described, each test case is then summarized in the software test plan and detailed in a test procedure. These procedures may then be split into test configurations consistent with the software subsystem build requirements. This split should be made by test step.

SYSTEM TEST DEVELOPMENT

As previously described, system testing is normally a program responsibility. During levels 5 and 6 of testing the program system engineering staff designs and develops a set of test cases which will integrate multiple software subsystems into a system executable with the system hardware, and finally qualify the software against the operational requirements in the system specification. System testing development techniques are directly analogous to those used during software testing with several exceptions.

1.   Instead of using a Build Test Folder for definition of the level 5 requirements, all system integration design and experience is documented in a System Test Folder (STF). The STF has somewhat different format and structure than the BTF, yet serves the same function.

2.   The level 5 test cases are exclusively concerned with data interfaces between subsystems and hardware/software components external to the subsystem configuration. Each subsystem is assumed to be a "black box" which is functionally sound.

3.   The level 5 tests are externally driven with inputs being provided from an operationally qualified or externally simulated data source and outputs being interfaced to the input point of the related hardware or software component.

4.   The level 6 test cases are complete configurations of hardware and software and certify system operational integrity. As such, all external data, unless technically impossible, should be provided from the actual data sources and operational environment of the system.

The planning for system testing was described in Chapter 4. The basic planning document, the System Test Plan, documents the requirements for the level 5 and 6 test cases. This plan defines how the tests are to be developed and executed, and defines criteria for measuring success. From these requirements both level 5 and 6 test cases may be defined.

As with the software test development, a focal point from within the program's system engineering organization should be responsible for all system integration test activities. This system integration leader is the core of the integration effort, having technical as well as schedule responsibility for the development, conduct, control, and reporting of all level 5 test cases. He or she is the one who interfaces to other areas of the project concerned with system integration test status or progress. He or she sits on all program boards and committees which affect or impact system integration testing. He or she is responsible for ensuring that all essential resources, personnel, and support are available, when required to avoid impacts. Finally, the integration leader is the "umpire," coordinating the activities of the various segments of the program to support the test activities and resolve any problems and difficulties between organizations with regard to system integration issues. Unlike the build test leader, who is assigned responsiblity for integrating individual builds, the system integration leader is responsible for all level 5 activities.

System Test Case Design

The system integration test case design is initiated after completion, review, and approval of the system test plan. In this plan, the relationships between the various test levels were defined, the techniques, procedures, and control practices which link the activities and data products of each level together were identified, and the test tools, techniques, and methodologies to be applied to each level were related. From these parameters, an STF is established to document the requirements for and the experience of the system integration activities.

System integration testing differs from software integration testing in that it is not concerned with the internal performance of individual elements of the test but only with the interfaces between them. The interfaces between individual software subsystems tested through level 4 are qualified first. As each build becomes available from the software organization, the interfaces between the various releases are integrated until the software system is complete and fully integrated. All new, unqualified hardware components should be simulated during the initial software integration stages, with the actual hardware being phased in as it is qualified through hardware testing. This prequalification of hardware before use in a test configuration is essential to ensure that only one untested object exists in any configuration. For this case the objects are hardware/software interfaces.

The goals of system integration testing are:

1. To exercise every subsystem interface in nominal and anomalous conditions using valid and invalid data combinations.
2. To exercise the software system from all external sources using valid and invalid data combinations.

3. To test the integrated software system in various load conditions and in realistic environments to ensure adequate performance.

4. To evaluate all error-processing and recovery aspects of the integrated system.

5. To execute all interfaces between new hardware and software subsystems at least once with all documented message formats.

6. To execute all operator control options and ensure that the system correctly responds.

7. To ensure that all performance monitoring and reporting functions are correct and that the data is valid.

The system integration may proceed in a hierarchical fashion as described previously, a bottom-up fashion, or using threads techniques. The selection and use of these particular test techniques is not to evaluate functional performance of the individual subsystems but rather to provide a vehicle for the software organization to isolate problems in the event of a test failure. The techniques used for software and system integration should be common.

The system integration tests should be structured to permit the orderly and incremental addition of more complicated interfaces after qualification of the simpler ones. As illustrated in Figure 7.10, this structure may be in four separate groups.

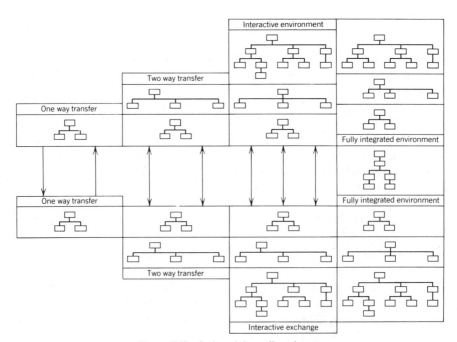

Figure 7.10   System integration stages

The initial set of tests qualifies interfaces which are essentially one way; that is, a data item which is set by one subsystem, does not require a response, and is not critical to the integrity or performance of the other. The second grouping consists of two-way transfers. These are data items which, when sent between subsystems, require a response or affect the performance of the interfaced components.

The third grouping are those interfaces which are interactive. These require a "data dialogue" between the interfacing subsystems.

The final set of tests support fully interactive data environments, real time, and communications interfaces (if part of the system environment), and use real hardware as much as possible.

The level 5 test requirements are documented in the System Test Folder. As with the UDF and BTF, this folder is an in-process record of the requirements and execution experience for conducting level 5 tests. STF development is phased, first defining the level 5 test schedules, test configurations and resource requirements, support, tools, and facilities essential for test conduct. These initial parameters should be reviewed by the system test leader prior to conducting the specified level 5 test cases. This review should be a technical and readiness assessment of the test case status. It should be informal, conducted as a walkthrough. Completion of this review should ensure that the test cases adequately reflect the technical and documented requirements of the program allocated to each test and that the tests are ready for execution. Later the STF will contain specifications for all level 5 test cases to be executed, a record of the test execution experience, and a log of discrepencies. The STF also records configuration information, an update history, and the modifications made to the system. The format and structure of the STF is the same as described for the BTF. The STF deals with system level test requirements, configurations, and interfaces rather than subsystem build or functional requirements. This more universal application impacts the detail, content, and planning requirements included in STF.

System integration testing should track the software build schedules. The software releases should be integrated as they are qualified by the software organization.

Level 6 Test Case Design

The development of level 6 test cases is accomplished from the requirements in the system test plan. The procedure to be followed is the same as described for level 4.

First, an initial set of test categories is identified. Those general categories previously described for level 4 are adequate for this purpose, except they must be modified to reflect the system level demonstration. The approved operational requirements are allocated individually to the test grouping and test cases, and are then developed. These are then documented in system test procedures which are structured as described for level 4.

Test Planning—Completion of the Planning Effort

The previous chapters have described the requirements for planning the overall test program. These requirements form a significant portion of the overall test requirement, and necessitate the commitment of significant resources and schedule to complete. Many test managers attempt to "short circuit" the process through inadequate planning. Too often managers attempt to skip test levels, or turn technical personnel loose to test the system without prior planning. They delude themselves into thinking that they are adequately testing the system, only to find that when the functional capabilities of the system are to be demonstrated the software subsystems don't work. The interfaces are improperly implemented, the software subsystems don't "play" together, and the essential relationship between code, design, and system requirements is lost. The time which was saved by not planning is more than used up by ineffective test practices, system rework, and redefinition of nonresponsive software. Segments of the software are extensively tested while others are hardly tested at all. Personnel testing software tend to test those components they are most familiar with, while deemphasizing those components which are difficult or unfamiliar.

Unless the planning is accomplished early and progress continually assessed, or the test manager is blessed with exceptional good fortune, poorly planned testing will result in development, productivity, and project performance problems.

8 Test Development, Tooling, and Execution

The demonstration of functional and user requirements is the bottom line to software development, and requires careful planning, effective development, rigorous execution, and continuous salesmanship if it is to succeed.

As illustrated in Figure 8.1, once the planning of the test program is completed, the builds defined, and the test cases designed, testing transitions from planning to implementation, execution, and analysis.

Once the test cases are designed, whether they be software integration, software function, system integration, or system demonstration, the implementation and execution steps are generically the same. Development tests, on the other hand, are less structured, requiring a unique set of implementation steps and activities. This chapter will describe the steps to be followed in the latter stages of each level of testing. The techniques discussed will ensure that the test cases when implemented are consistent with the test case design and that the tests are executed in an orderly and controlled fashion.

UNIT TEST IMPLEMENTATION

Implementation of level 1 and 2 test cases is based on the test requirements in the UDF. Test implementation and execution responsibility is with the development organization.

During this period of the project, when software units are being coded and informally tested, it often seems to the test manager that he or she has no control over, and cannot affect, the adequacy of the unit test activities. To a large measure this is true. Despite the critical effect that unit testing has on the reliability of the software, the developing nature of the software and the inherent unreliability of the code require that any testing and test

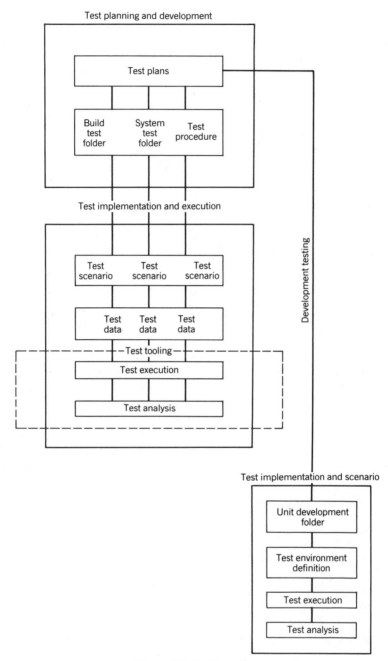

Figure 8.1 Test transition

configuration be flexible and capable of rapid modification to react to problems in design or implementation.

Unit test environments and test conditions are established through the use of drivers. Drivers are coded by the development organization responsible for the unit's implementation. They implement the test requirements demonstrated in the Unit Design Walkthrough (UDW). Drivers have the following attributes.

1. The driver accurately reflects the execution environment that is required by the test.
2. The driver simulates all major software interfaces, reflecting the actual calling sequences of the software design.
3. The driver allows the software unit to interface within simulated data structures which accurately reflect the design of subsystem data base.
4. The driver should force execution of all paths through the software unit and test all interfaces between modules which make up the unit configuration.
5. All decision points in the unit should be exercised by the driver.

The drivers are coded from the approved unit test specifications. The drivers are essentially only to be used during this phase of testing. Although they may later be usable as vehicles for regression testing, the test software is essentially thrown away after completion of level 2. Later drivers serve a different purpose and require redefinition and recoding.

In certain application categories, the unit can be tested in the hierarchical configuration that reflects the execution sequence of the software subsystem. In these cases, as previously described, the actual software architecture serves as the driver. "Top-down testing," if appropriate, provides a means by which unit testing and the initial group 1 level 3 requirements can be combined. Whether drivers or top-down testing techniques are used the unit test plans and execution should be reviewed at the Unit Design, Code, and Test Walkthrough.

Unit test execution is essentially the responsibility of the programmer who codes the software. These tests are conducted using software, data, and test support facilities from the working files in the PSL. All activities should be planned on working schedules, and progress measured using earned-value technique. The short milestones which are characteristic of these schedules will keep the unit testing focused and provide schedule completion milestones from which progress can be measured and performance judged.

In-process, technical responsibility for the conduct of development tests lies with the chief programmer or task leader responsible for the implementation.

Tests are executed by the programmer who implemented the module and who is responsible for integrating modules into the unit. He or she executes the test driver, monitors the test execution, evaluates the results, and makes any necessary corrections to the software. He or she need not document implementation problems, but only ensure that the UDF is maintained and that functional and data descriptions, design, code, and test descriptions are consistent and current. Unit tests are normally complete when one of three conditions is met:

1. The schedule for conduct of the unit test is exhausted.
2. The budget for unit test execution is spent.
3. All technical requirements for unit testing as documented in the UDF and approved at the UDW are successfully demonstrated and the unit executes without error.

Unfortunately, the realities of a software project environment are that, in a large majority of cases, completion is determined by criteria 1 and 2 rather than by the technical correctness of the unit. In this instance, a determination is made by the chief programmer as to the actual state of the unit and its adequacy for use in level 3 group 1 tests. He or she evaluates functional support, internal integrity, module and data completion, and the stability of the unit configuration. He or she reviews the test requirements in the UDF against the experience of the testing and evaluate each open problem, whether it be formally documented on an SPR or is being informally worked on by the test personnel. Based on this analysis one of two decisions may result. First, additional time and resources may be required to complete the unit tests. In this case, a "cost to complete" projection must be made by the chief programmer, reviewed with and concurred with by the technical personnel, and authorized by the software manager. Despite the frequent, apparently small impacts associated with these situations, the software manager, chief programmer, and technical staff must never lose sight of the fact that these represent a real slip in the overall project schedules and require an increase in the budget requirements for the project. It should be clearly understood that any software project schedule and budget tends to overrun a little at a time rather than in one large dramatic slip. If a small slip is identified and dealt with either through production schedules, performance earned value shortfalls, or through an inability to meet a walkthrough, milestones with adequate technical product resources must be reallocated, schedules must be readjusted, and project commitments must be reevaluated. This "real time" management will ensure that software managers are not faced with cataclysmic slips later in the program when schedule, budget, resources, and options have been depleted.

The second alternative a chief programmer has when unit test schedules and budgets are exhausted but the unit is still not technically complete is to document the discrepancies and proceed with the unit test walkthrough. In this case each individual technical deficiency is reviewed, the technical and performance limitations on the unit are assessed, and the inability for integration is determined. If it is determined by the chief programmer that, despite the problems, the unit is acceptable for integration testing then each open problem is documented on an SPR and placed in the UDF for review at the Unit Test Walkthrough (UTW). At the UTW the configuration and technical adequacy of the unit is reviewed and each open problem is evaluated for impact. The performance of the unit in relation to the UDF requirements is assessed and the integrity of the implementation is determined. From the UTW one of two results may happen. The unit may be rejected for level 3 integration, in which case the cost and schedule impacts are assessed as previously described and the unit is returned for rework or completion. A second possible action is to approve the unit for level 3 testing. Each open problem, in this case, is formally documented through a SPR and processed through the SCRB and project configuration control practices.

These problems are treated as "latent defects," and are corrected in the same manner as problems found during level 3 and higher test levels.

If the tests resulted in technically complete and error-free completion of the level 2 test set, the UDF is also subject to a UTW. This walkthrough is conducted as if there were latent defects, and results in either acceptance or rejection of the project level for configuration control.

PROJECT TESTING—SOFTWARE AND SYSTEM

Implementation of test cases for the level 3 through 6 test levels is a two-step process, whether the test case design is documented in a BTF, STF as described for integration tests, or in procedures as described for functional or system tests. The first step is to detail the test script in the form of a test scenario. As illustrated in Figure 8.2, these scenarios are built from the test specifications contained in the test folders or procedures. The test specifications describe, on a step-by-step basis, the inputs required to initiate each test step and the test outputs which, when monitored, indicate the performance of the software subsystem. The scenario is an expansion of test requirements, detailing specific subsystem control, data, and interim data output values and messages which cause the software and system to execute in the predefined manner. As illustrated in Figure 8.3, the scenario is time phased to the beginning of each test step and breaks the test into individual events each represented by a single data or control stimulus and resulting in a recognizable output or subsystem action. The scenario contains eight pieces of information.

1. **Test Step Identification.** Identifies the test step described by the scenario, referencing it to the test case, the procedure, or folder identification, and the time reference to the start of the test case creation.

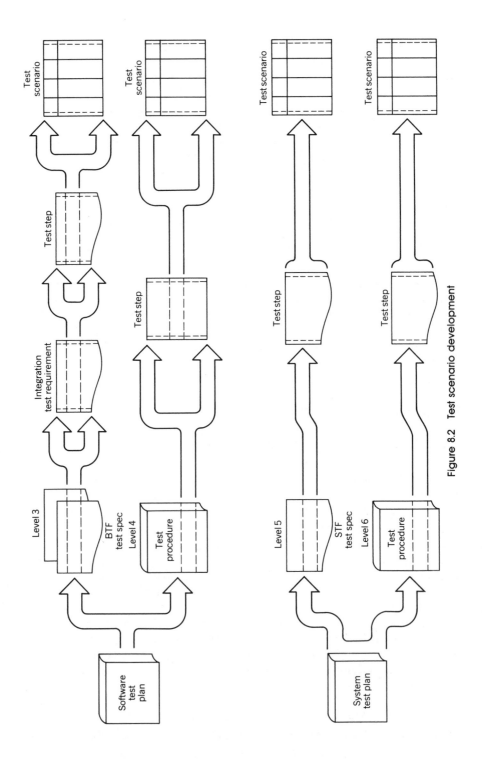

Figure 8.2 Test scenario development

Test scenario

Test step ID			Test event ID		Input data mess- age	Input control mess- age	Input data source	Data base setting	Interim data out- puts	Formal test out- puts	Output format	Notes
Folder or proc	Test step	Test time	Test event ID	Time refer- ence								

Figure 8.3   Scenario format

2. **Input Data Message.** Documents the specific data contents for the data usage which initiates the test event. Multiple data messages may be required for each test event and, if so, each must be identified and have a time reference.

3. **Input Control Message.** Documents the specific control message or system action which will initiate the test event. The control stimulus may be sufficient to cause the test event to execute or the test stimulus may require multiple control and data events. Each message must be identified and have a time reference.

4. **Data Source.** Inputs the specific source which will input the data. The input source specification includes device type, access specification, device address, protocol information (if required), and any other information essential to input the data. For every message, whether it be control or data, there should be a data source description or reference to a previously defined description.

5. **Data Base Settings.** Describes any data values which must be set to enable execution of the test event. If the value is set externally during the test event, the means of setting it should be described and a time reference provided by which the setting must be made.

6. **Interim Data Outputs.** Identifies any outputs which result from embedded instrumentation. This data should be sequenced to the input messages and need not be time referenced. Each nominal, predictable output message should be identified specifically and deviant or error indications which are possible but not expected should be described. In all cases the output source should be identified in sufficient detail to allow definition of the output configuration by the test event.

7. **Final Outputs.** Identifies those expected nominal and anomalous test outputs which result from execution of the test event. As with the interim data outputs, these should be sequenced to the input messages and need not be time sequenced. The output sources should be specified in sufficient detail to allow test event configuration.

8. **Output Format.** Documents the specific output message contents which occur during execution of the test event. For each output message identified a format should be provided. The format should include protocol requirements, structure, content, and nominal data values. If previously described, or described in the BTF or STF or procedure, the format may be referenced.

Test scenario development is the most difficult of the test implementation tasks. It matches the requirements of the test case to the software test execution characteristics. Scenarios detail the test environment and if properly defined, will build predictability, reproduceability, and control—the three elements of a successful test program—into the test configuration. Without a properly defined scenario predicting or reproducing a specific set of test conditions is not easily achieved.

When completed, the test scenario serves as the script for the test execution, the basis for developing the test data for the test case, and the specific criteria for test evaluation.

Development of the test scenario requires an understanding of how the software subsystem and system is supposed to operate from a functional and design perspective. Procedures and test folders, on the other hand, require higher level understanding as documented in users, requirements, interface, performance, and operational specifications. Unlike scenarios, these higher level test specifications are oriented toward how the system is supposed to operate rather than the internal specifications of what the software is to do during test.

For the sake of objectivity, functional test procedures and scenarios should be developed from documented system requirements and operational specifications. The team developing the procedures and scenario should be independent from the development and integration team and should be the same team which will execute the tests.

The integration team, on the other hand, should be assigned from the system engineering staffs. This team should develop the folders and scenarios as well as conduct the integration test cases and evaluate the test results. Using this technique the manager gets an independent view of the operational integrity of the software. This is not based on assumed design or implementation characteristics or undocumented tradeoffs. The tests are based solely on the specified requirements of the system as interpreted by the test team.

Test Data Development

Development of test data from completed scenarios is straightforward if scenarios are properly specified and complete. For each test event defined in the scenario, a specific data or control message is developed. The messages are time phased according to the requirements of the scenario and formatted accordingly. The individual data values in each message are set as specified in the scenario, and any data required to transfer the test message into the system are constructed from the scenario requirements. This data is then used to construct a set of data messages which, when read into the system and executed in concert with the other requirements of the scenario, create the required test environment. This test data is the basis for the testing, and along with the products of testing development and implementation should be placed under configuration control when reviewed by the test manager and approved through a walkthrough.

This walkthrough is the basis for test control. Walkthroughs should be frequent, conducted at a peer level, and should evaluate the integrity of developing scenarios as data. The walkthroughs are conducted informally after the completion of test data and after execution of the test cases. When the data is defined it is structured in an input format consistent with the requirements of the test tooling and the configuration requirements of the test system. Once the data is defined and the test input structured and properly formatted, the test is ready to run when the software becomes available.

Test Tooling

Planning, developing, and applying the proper suite of tools when required to enhance testing effectiveness is essential if the test program is to be valid. The use of automated aids to support development, software, and system testing is essential if the goals, objectives, and test requirements of each level are to be satisfied. As discussed in Chapter 3, early planning of the use of tools ensures that the tools defined for one level of testing are consistent with those defined for other levels. Early test tool planning will also ensure that the tools defined for use at each test level are those needed by that level and that they are tailored to and structured in accordance with the actual requirements of the test level they are to support.

Test tooling is an area of the project where a software project manager and test manager can expend significant resource and schedule with very little return. Unless defined in response to a specific set of project methodology, support, or testing requirements which clearly require automation for support, the manager will find that the tools are ineffective and inconsistent with the test support requirements, and that the test methodologies and project requirements will need to be modified and tailored to effectively use the tools. In this case, the tools often will be discarded and replaced with simpler, less esoteric support. The manager will find that the resources expended to build the "junked" support was wasted and that he or she is forced to "scramble," often unsuccessfully, to avoid productivity, cost, and schedule impacts.

Although there are many individual tools which are effective testing aids, they cluster into four major categories: simulation, emulation, instrumentation, and a miscellaneous category which groups a variety of diverse capabilities.

SIMULATION—TESTING WHEN THE ENVIRONMENT IS NONEXISTENT

By using simulation, the performance of the software may be observed at an earlier date, and the software development and test is insulated from the vagaries of hardware test development schedules and availability. Many times, the actual operating environment may not as yet exist; delivery of the software may be one of the requisites for commencing operations; or the users of an existing system may not wish to have current operations disturbed until the new software is ready for a level 5 test.

Two classes of simulation are often used in the required test environment, both executing outside the target system.

1. Environment simulation.
2. Interpretive computer simulation.

Environmental simulation feigns the environment in which the software will eventually perform. The environment includes other programs operating in parallel or in series, noncomputer hardware, and external inputs in the program.

Many times the control program and/or operating system may not be available at the time the applications software first becomes available for test. Initial testing then utilizes a simulator for the absent software; this simulator can incorporate many useful debugging features that would probably not be available with the operational versions of the programs.

It is often necessary to control test inputs via simulation tools. With particular reference to real time systems, it is often necessary to use simulation to generate a sufficient volume of test input data to stress the system. For some systems, this has involved simulating the output of various external equipment. On interactive systems, simulators prepare scripts of input requests that normally would have been generated by operators at display consoles. Remote terminal simulators have been used to present input messages to the main computer before the terminals are in place. These simulation scripts provide a chronology of inputs that is identical from test run to test run; hence, repeatability of inputs is attained.

Interpretive computer simulation is employed to simulate the behavior of the operational computer when the machine is not available for testing the software. These tools simulate the instructions of the operational computer by using a microcoded program running in another computer. Prior to implementation, analytical simulations, which model the performance of a computer system parametrically, may be utilized to verify loading, throughout, and capacity. Such simulations have also been used to determine allocation of storage and to determine which programs should be kept in memory and which should be kept in other storage devices.

Of all the tools which support testing, often the most critical are simulators. After the initial analysis of the level 3, 4, and 5 test environments, if it is determined that significant risk is associated with the availability, reproduceability, or control of any essential components of the test configuration, the manager should initiate development of a simulation of the support. This early start is essential because of the long lead times often associated with development of the capability and the fact that these tools often represent the last "safety net" the manager has in running the tests. If the simulators are not available when required, testing delays will invariably occur.

EMULATION—A REALISTIC SYSTEM ENVIRONMENT

The use of environmental emulation constructs an execution environment for a test which is representative of the actual operational environment expected for the software subsystem or operational system configuration. Unlike simulation software which executes outside the target system configuration, emulations execute within the target system. The software changes the loading characteristics of the system dynamically and modifies the internal data base settings as required to construct a test configuration. It also establishes expected nominal and anomalous system environments to monitor software or system responses. Emulation software executes as a "shell" around the test configuration, dynamically varying the test environment in response to operator or test inputs.

The use of software instrumentation allows the real time collection and monitoring of internal test information during the execution of a test case.

Instrumentation should be conditionally compiled with the test system or available as a standard configuration. The tools include:

1.   A static dump which formats and outputs, to a selected device, memory content of a system component. This tool violates the integrity of the test configuration by changing execution characteristics.

2.   A dynamic dump which takes specific data values during the execution of a test, formats the data, and outputs it to a selected device. The dynamic dump should not violate the test configuration, allowing the test to restart after the dump is taken.

3.   Checkpoint/restart tools allow the test execution to be suspended for a particular reason, and restarted with the identical environmental conditions. The checkpoint capability should be conditionally compiled with the test software; however, the restart component may stand alone.

4.   Trace routines collect information which provides traces of the execution sequence of the software. These tools collect information, format the data, identify which components of software are using a particular block of data at a particular time, and trace the occurence of particular test events. These trace routines are conditionally compiled with the software under test.

5.   Test environment structuring tools allow the test environment to be dynamically modified or restructured as the test is being executed. The settings of key data values may be varied, the sequence of test execution modified, and the configuration of the test modified, or restructured in response to changing system, test, or operator requirements.

MISCELLANEOUS TOOLS

These tools provide the "other support" which, if properly defined and applied, will significantly enhance the software and system effectiveness. The tools include:

1.   **System Design Analysis.** Automated design tools which provide a rigorous methodology for stating design requirements and evaluate and define the testability and traceability of the requirements and design. Automated simulation tools model the system hardware/software to study its characteristics and provide an analysis of the integrity of the architecture of the system and software subsystems.

2.   **Source Program Static Analysis.** Tools for code analysis perform syntax analysis on the source code and look for error-prone constructions. They provide program structure checks which generate graphs and look

for structural flaws. These tools provide proper module interface checks to detect inconsistencies in the declaration of data structures and improper linkage among modules. They also provide event-sequence checking which compares event sequences in the program with conventions of event sequences (e.g., I/O sequences).

3. **Source Program Dynamic Analysis.** Tools for monitoring program run-time behavior which collect program execution statistics. They provide automated test case generation which aid testers in constructing test cases that will comprehensively exercise the code. These tools provide for checking assertions which detect violations of assertions embedded into the code testers and provide tools for inserting software defenses which provide security modifications.

4. **Maintenance.** Tools for documentation generation which record information extracted during coding analysis and program structure analysis for documentation. These tools provide facilities for validating modifications which aim at predicting the effect of proposed changes.

5. **Performance.** Tools for program restructuring which assist in reorganizing programs for optimization. These tools extract and validate parallel operations which identify parallel tasks to aid parallel processing scheduling.

6. **Order of Merit.** Software quality validation tools which strive to assign a figure-of-merit to a program on the basis of comparison to desirable characteristics' attributes.

USE OF TOOLS DURING TESTING

The proper tooling of a test configuration can greatly enhance the effectiveness of all levels of testing. There are several considerations which must be addressed.

1. Will the tools impact the software performance or test configuration to such a degree as to invalidate the test?

2. Is there sufficient additional hardware, over and above support resources needed for the test, to allow implementation and effective applications of the tools?

3. Are the tools operation easy to understand and are test personnel sufficiently familiar with tools operation to allow effective test operation, analysis, and evaluation of data?

4. Have the tools been qualified and are they sufficiently reliable to use without affecting the integrity of the test?

5. Can the tools be easily configured out of the test without having to make any changes, other than a conditional compilation and/or a data base modification, to the software under test?

The use of specific tools in a test configuration is the responsibility of the build or system test leader based on the recommendation of the technical staff. This review should be ongoing, reviewing the tools as they are designed, implemented, and before each is integrated into a test configuration. Tools should be an integral part of the test configuration and should be planned into the test case design from the outset. All tools used should be controlled through the PSL and should be available to other areas of the software project if their application makes sense.

Test Execution

The execution of test cases should be an orderly activity characterized by a smooth and controlled data flow transition of responsibility between organizational components and effective technical analysis of results and correction of errors.

During the execution of the various test levels, the primary categories of errors will include:

1. **Logic Errors.** Logic errors are normally the most common type of program function. Most testing efforts are justifiably directed toward these problems. Logic errors are solid and repeatable. If a test input exposes the presence of a bug, then the same input, when presented to a program a second time, should expose the same bug in the same way.

2. **Documentation Errors.** There are some programming applications where a documentation error can be just as serious as a logic error. In most cases, errors in the user documentation, the requirements, and design can still allow successful application of the system. There are other situations, though, where errors in the technical documentation could be considered critical.

3. **Overload Errors.** It is also important to test a program to find out what happens if various tables, buffers, queues, or other storage areas are filled up to or even beyond their capacity. This is an especially critical area of testing in many on-line and real time systems (e.g., what happens if all the terminal users type an input message simultaneously?), but it can be just as important in many batch-oriented programs.

4. **Timing Errors.** This is a category that is usually relevant only to real time systems; in this case logic errors that cannot be easily repeated. The errors are usually a function of timing conditions or coincidental combinations of events within the program. In a "normal-time" program, there are a finite number of cases to be tested (even though the number is so large that we are usually quite unable to perform exhaustive testing). In a real time system, though, the number of possibilities appears (at least at first glance) to be infinite.

5. **Throughput and Capacity Errors.** This error category is prevalent in real time systems, though batch-oriented programs also experience problems

in this area. These errors are concerned with the performance of the program. Even though the software generates the correct output, it takes an unacceptable amount of computer time to do so, or it may use an exorbitant amount of memory, disk space, and so forth. This is critical for many on-line systems because the performance of a program is often immediately visible to the user in terms of response time. In a batch program, we might still want to specify (and then test) that the program be able to process one transaction per second, that it take no more than 100,000 bytes of storage, and so forth.

6. **Fallback and Error Recovery.** For a number of system applications, the concept of recovery and fallback is quite critical. If there is a hardware failure (or possibly a software failure), an unrecoverable program can cause several hours of lost machine time, or in the case of a real time, on-line system, great confusion and chaos among the users. Testing in this area should ensure that the programs can be continued from some checkpoint, that files are not damaged, that the entire recovery process can be performed in a reasonable amount of time, and that users, computer operators, and others are not confused by the recovery process.

7. **Hardware Errors and System Software Error.** In most cases, the programmer feels that it is not his or her responsibility to ensure that the hardware and the vendor's operating system work correctly—and, in most cases, he or she does not have such responsibility. However, if the testing involves an entire system and if that system is to be delivered to a noncomputer-oriented user, then someone should have the responsibility of ensuring that the hardware and the vendor's operating system do work. The user will generally not appreciate it when the programmer complains, "But it's not my fault that the on-line order operating system just crashed and lost the entire day's input—it was a hardware bug!"

8. **Standard Errors.** Programs should be tested to ensure that they adhere to various programming standards: that they are modular, well-commented, free of nonstandard programming statements, and so forth. This is of increasing concern among organizations that are beginning to realize the magnitude of the maintenance effort. This class of errors should be treated with the same rigor as those of the other categories.

9. **Test Case Errors.** Finally, problems in the test materials will cause the erroneous execution of a test case.

The purpose of all levels of integration test execution—levels 1, 2, 3, and 5—is to uncover and correct as many problems as possible. As such, the execution environment established for these test levels should be flexible enough to anticipate frequent, often critical problems which affect large segments of the software configuration. Problems will become increasingly difficult to analyze and correct as the testing progresses. The number of parallel project activities relating to the test will increase as the test levels increase.

Schedule control during integration testing is difficult because of the imprecise identification of the amount of work required to get to the next milestone. It is not possible to anticipate how many problems will be uncovered, their complexity and severity, and the resources and schedule which will be required to correct them. As a result, the scheduling technique must provide early warning of impending slippage and the effects of these slips must be clearly defined and understood by the test manager. These levels of testing are the areas where production schedules and earned-value techniques are of greatest benefit. They ensure that management and project visibility is focused toward the occurrence of specific integration milestones and that any schedule drift is identified and corrected early enough to avoid larger, more significant impact on the test schedules.

Problem Control

During the execution of integration tests, the software project organizational relationships also become critical components of success. The independent test team is comprised of the systems engineering personnel who designed the integration test levels and the individual test cases. They execute the tests according to the requirements in the procedure or test folder and associated scenario. They then analyze the results and, if successful, schedule a peer walkthrough through the build or system leader for levels 3 or 4 to authorize test completion. If any problems were noted, they are either documented in the UDF if the tests are at level 2 or on SPR forms for unit design requirements problems or any software products at level 3 or higher test levels. These SPRs are provided to the PSL and placed on the SCRB agenda. During this period of the project the SCRB meets much more frequently than earlier in the project; often daily to avoid delays associated with the processing of problems. Complete documentation of all problems discovered or suspected during these test levels is critical to the success of the test program, since this is the only means to keep track of open discrepancies and monitor corrections. The SCRB will evaluate each individual problem, assess impact, schedule the correction, authorize resources to be committed, and assign correction responsibility to an organization. The work assignment will, besides committing resources, also specify the data products which must be updated and the regression tests which must be run before the problem correction is complete and may be released to the SCRB for approval.

As a general rule, all software data products, whether code, documentation, test products, or data elements, should be updated before a correction is approved and the changes moved to the controlled library. Reality often dictates, however, that in order to satisfy critical schedule requirements, software changes may have to be approved prior to completion of the documentation or other supporting data. In these the SCRB will conditionally approve the correction, releasing it to the PSL for a system build. The SPR remains open, however, until all data is brought into compliance.

The development organization corrects and requalifies the software before release to the SCRB. This requalification is accomplished through informal execution of the specific test cases defined as regression test requirements by the SCRB. These tests are run using the updated software in the working library. This limits the number of unknowns in the test and runs, and limits the number of variables which must be considered in the event of a failure.

When a correction is completed, the entire package: software source code, documentation updates, and test results are assembled in the configuration management area of the PSL and released to the librarian for SCRB review and, hopefully, approval. The SCRB has two options. First, it can reject the update, in which case the indicated changes by the individual must be made before the SPR can be reconsidered. Secondly, the correction may be approved, in which case the PSL will review all data to ensure its completeness, update the controlled segments of the library, and either build (with other updates) a new system from the controlled source files or generate a source tape for use by the target system in building a new version of the software. In either case, the PSL generates a Version Description Document (VDD) for use as the new base version.

The new release must be regression-tested by the test team before being released for general testing. This is extremely critical in order to avoid the "damping effect" described previously. Regression testing will also ensure that, as far as the test sample can show, the system release is as reliable as the previous version. It is not feasible to fully regression-test every version using every test case at every test level. The time involved is prohibitive and the project benefits would not justify the expenditure. As described in Chapter 3, the degree of regression testing required is determined early and should be based on such factors as application requirements, system delivery and contractual commitments, customer and project expectations, and the criticability of the software components in the context of the software subsystem or system environment. If test tools have been properly specified, the regression test problem becomes significantly simplified. The test case configuration is determined by the build or system test leader, a test tape or file is constructed which interacts with the simulation or simulation software, a build is made with the test tools embedded, and the test file is started. Each test case is then run automatically according to the scenario and the only time the test is stopped is when a malfunction is recognized. If, during the running of the regression test, any test fails, the version problem is documented on an SPR and processed in a normal manner.

As illustrated in Figure 8.4, the test stabilization problem is most significant after a new release and until the software configuration stabilizes. Later on, after stabilization of the new version, the actual problems inherent in the software or system version can be uncovered.

For each new build a new set of tests are run, as specified in the build plan or system test folder. These new tests exercise the system from an

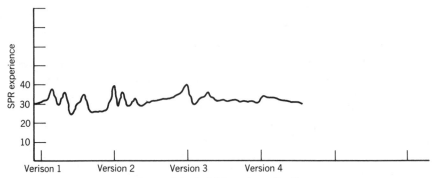

Figure 8.4   Test "damping effect"

entirely new and often untested perspective. As would be expected, there is an immediate and dramatic increase in SPRs opened as a result of test execution. As illustrated in Figure 8.5, this increase can catch a software test staff unaware and be demoralizing to the test manager, his line supervisors, and the test staff. Qualification of a build requires significant time and personnel commitment. Individuals work hard, long hours, solve seemingly insolvable problems through diligence and perseverance, and have a right to feel that things are getting better. The test manager buoys staff and line supervisors with promises of a better world to come, and during the latter stages of integration of a subsystem or system release these promises are realized. The configuration which has been built through the sacrifices of so many suddenly begins to work as it was supposed to. A general feeling of accomplishment and optimism pervades the project. Suddenly a new release is received from the PSL with instructions to first run a set of regression tests which have long since been successfully run and then run a new set of tests which have neer been executed. Mayhem

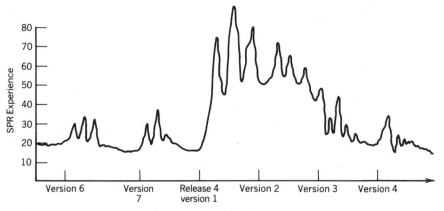

Figure 8.5   Problem increase

sets in. The system crashes even when running simple tests and the number of open SPRs increase dramatically, often by a factor of 10 or more. The feeling of optimism is lost and reality sets in. Much more hard work is required before the tests will be completed. The test manager must treat the process of testing as a continuum. He or she cannot use the number of SPRs as a measure of testing success or failure. He or she should use progress through the test levels and completion of test cases as a measure of success. The manager should point out that the number of SPRs is a measure of testing efficiency and that the purpose of these tests is to find errors rather than demonstrate system success. The more problems found during a test the more successful the test execution. Throughout all levels of integration testing, measuring reliability by SPR summaries by technical, management, or customer personnel is invalid and will prove counter-productive during integration testing. It will become increasingly difficult to keep the team motivated, eventually reaching a point where testing productivity will drop to unacceptable levels.

When To Stop Testing—Completion Versus Tradeoff

The completion of a set of integration tests is the milestone which establishes a build and authorizes the release of a new system from the PSL. Ideally this should be when all tests and all SPRs are successfully completed. Unfortunately, this is rarely the case even after the software is fully integrated, qualified, and incorporated into a system configuration.

When schedule and budget problems demand that the software version be complete even though SPRs are still open, the manager must decide whether to move on with testing or to correct the outstanding problems. This decision can only be made by categorizing the problems into three groups: critical, noncritical, and nonessential. All critical problems, such as nonreproduceable crashes, misrouting of data, and system performance discrepancies, should be evaluated on an individual basis. Those deemed critical in the context of the software environment must be corrected immediately. The second category, serious problems, may be treated as latent.

Correction of critical problems should be scheduled using a production schedule and carefully managed using earned value techniques. In order to stabilize the software test configuration only those tests required to complete the critical problem corrections should be run during this period until the build is complete. When the build is completed the new release may be authorized by the PSL.

FUNCTIONAL AND OPERATIONAL DEMONSTRATION

After a software build is fully integrated at level 3 or a system build is completed through level 5, functional level 4 tests for that build may be initiated or the level 6 operational tests may be started using the level 5 configuration. Execution of these tests is an activity parallel to the integration tests. As previously described, the PSL builds and documents the releases and versions of software being used by each level of test.

The tests are run from the level 4 or 6 procedures and are totally independent from the integration levels which preceded it. When a problem is found, there is no attempt to evaluate the failure, only document the symptoms on an SPR. These SPR's are processed as with any other test level and assigned by the SCRB for correction. When a correction has been made and qualified at the integration levels which precede it it is available for SCRB approval, then included in a release through the PSL. When a new release is received it should be qualified by running the full suite of all test cases for that build or system release to ensure functional or operational integrity.

Except where essential, the test system should reflect the operational configuration. Emulation and instrumentation should be avoided. To the maximum extent possible level 4 tests should use simulation to ensure reproduceability, control, and automated execution. Completion of these test levels for each build should follow the same procedures as described for the integration levels.

SELLING THE CUSTOMER—THE BOTTOM LINE

Despite the care and rigor which goes into laying out and structuring the test program, there is all too frequently a problem convincing a customer that what has been built is consistent with what has been contracted for. Many times the results prove not to be what is wanted after the customer sees the system run. The needs that seemed so clear at the beginning of development become fuzzy at the end. The initial flush of enthusiasm early in the program turns to disillusionment, impatience, and distrust at the end. In short, the early partnership between customer and developer too often turns into an uneasy truce when it comes time to sell the system.

Establishing an effective working relationship between the customer and contractor is essential if the system is to be consistent with the needs and expectations of the user. Unfortunately, early concurrence between the customer and contractor is not easily achieved. The goals and objectives of the two camps differ significantly. The customer wants something that will solve a set of needs which, although they cannot be clearly expressed, are essential if the system is to serve its intended purpose. The developer, on the other hand, is concerned with building a system at minimum risk and within cost and schedule constraints. Bridging the gap between these two diverse goals is often a painful and difficult negotiation. Many times one or the other group will give in just to minimize the controversy.

From the customer's perspective, this "backing off" is simply the trading off of an immediate project difficulty for a potential longer-term catastrophe. Poorly specified, nonuser-responsive system requirements will greatly compound the development problem and make it extremely difficult to sell the product through a level 6 test set. Well-defined, mutually agreed to requirements significantly ease the development and test problems and will ensure that what the customer thinks he contracted for is demonstrated at the end.

Customer participation, cognizance and concurrence during the early requirements definition and stages of design is crucial to the success of the test program phase. The products described in the Software Requirements and Design Specification as such provide a nonambiguous basis for the level 6 test activities. Data products developed during this phase describe how individual subsystems will be designed and the functional requirements which will be supported by each. The performance of these subsystems, although critical to the overall integrity of the system, do not constitute an end in themselves.

Later, as the design is completed and is translated into code, the requirements for customer participation become less critical. During code and development testing, customer participation in the day-to-day activities of the project should be discouraged, and encouraged to increase again as the product becomes operational. One thing that must be constantly borne in mind by the software test manager is that he or she is responsible for selling the software subsystem to the program and customer. The system test manager, on the other hand, is responsible for selling the operational system to the customer.

These two positions are key to the ultimate success of the program. Many test managers purposely or inadvertently establish an adversarial relationship with the customer, feeling that if given too much latitude the customer will hold up progress, inhibit productivity, and, most importantly, ask questions which can not be answered honestly. Test managers may try to keep the customer at a distance. This approach, though seemingly effective in the short run, fails to recognize that there is a "payday" at the end of the development when the customer is asked to accept the product. If the customer has participated throughout the development he or she is more apt to accept the software or system, albeit conditionally, than if the state of the system is a surprise and does not perform as expected. Effective test management, besides requiring planning skills, also requires large measure of salesmanship if it is to succeed.

When dealing with the customer, the test manager must first coordinate all contacts with the software project manager. The software project manager is responsible for all project activities and for reporting all progress.

Understanding the Customer

As illustrated in Figure 8.6, the project concerns which plague a customer and must be addressed by the software project and test manager are hierarchical.

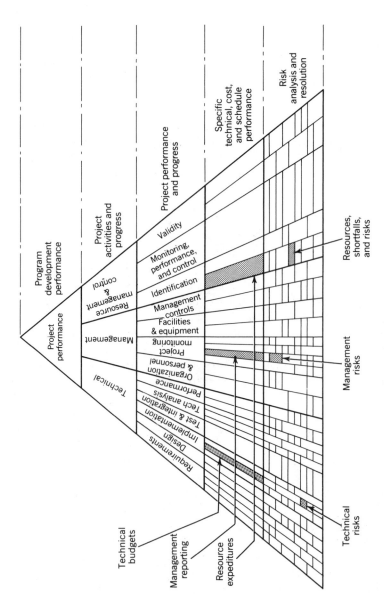

Figure 8.6 Customer concerns

TOP LEVEL—CUSTOMER CONFIDENCE

At the top level is a general concern that the contractor is adequately developing the proper product. The customer has a basic fear during the early stages of the development and, if not dealt with adequately by the contractor, in increasing degrees as the software is produced, that the product will be late, nonmaintainable, of poor quality, and not usable in his environment. This is a general feeling which must be countered by confidence betwen customer and contractor that the entire project staff is competent, committed, capable, and adequately supported.

This early confidence is built as much through perceptions as project performance. If a customer perceives the project as going well, actual performance, in terms of customer confidence, is secondary. Many managers erroneously assume that the way to establish a positive project image is to pass on only good news, while holding back or repressing negative data or real project problems. This common misconception is often devastating to the customer's perception of the project. He or she looks on the manager as naïve, not cognizant of the actual state of the project and incapable of anticipating problems before they occur. Many of the project situations which were not reported eventually reach a point where they must be dealt with and require customer action to resolve. By not having included the customer early on, the software project manager has "dumped a surprise" on the customer and has removed any options that early warning would have provided. Early and consistent forthrightness between customer and contractor is essential to customer confidence.

SECOND LEVEL—PROJECT DELIVERY AND FORMAL REVIEWS

Establishing a customer feeling of project well-being and confidence also requires a clear understanding on the customer's part of how the technical, support, and resource aspects of the project are to be managed and controlled. This second level of customer concern is reflected in the project plans and documented technical requirements of the software project as provided by the contractor. Many software development test managers and project managers feel that it is better to submit a second-rate product to the customer on time than to be late with a quality product. They fail to understand the motivations of the customer's staff who will review or use the data and do not "prenegotiate" the contents or determine the customer's expectations prior to delivery. They "throw the data over the fence" and then wait for a response.

Invariably, the submissions are unacceptable, the data must be redefined and redocumented, and, more importantly, the customer's view of the contractor is now tainted. The first level of visibility that a customer has into a contractor's capabilities is through the data the customer supplies. These submissions are the basis for all opinions, observations, and assumptions. If they are of acceptable quality to the contractor, and the contents, form, structure, and style have been prenegotiated, the problems of acceptability are diminished. Data of unacceptable quality or data which has not been reviewed within the project should never by submitted to the customer even if it means slipping project schedules.

THIRD LEVEL—CUSTOMER VIEW OF SECOND-LEVEL PLANS

The third level of customer concern is in the ability of the software managers and test managers to develop a project structure and to synthesize a software design from the project planning documentation and from the technical requirements allocated to the software. These second-level specifications are both formal and informal. Formally they are submitted to the customer for approval and reviewed at a formal project review. Informally they are developed by the project for internal use and reviewed at an informal project review. In either case, the customer should be afforded the opportunity to attend all project reviews, whether formal or informal, and to have early visibility into the process of development. By allowing this continued participation, the astute software project manager and test manager are drawing the customer into the problems of development and significantly reducing the risks of a surprise or negative reaction to a project data product.

FOURTH LEVEL—DAY-TO-DAY ASSESSMENTS

The fourth level of customer concern is in the day-to-day performance of the development and test aspects of the project in relation to technical, management, cost, and schedule commitments and constraints. This is the point where the project and test managers must consciously and cautiously open the project and testing to the customer and make in-process information available for scrutiny. The previously described levels of customer concerns could be dealt with through a customer review of complete, structured pieces of data or documentation.

At this level the customer is being provided fragmentary, incomplete data packages and, unless the limits and expectations of these reviews are clearly defined and understood, erroneous conclusions may result, false opinions may be made, and, most significantly, the confidence of the customer in the competence of the contractor may be eroded.

FIFTH LEVEL—PROJECT INTEGRITY

The lowest level of customer concern is the ability or inability of the project to smoothly and effectively deal with project problems and crises without affecting the development or technical integrity of the project. As described previously, a mark of a well-run software project, particularly in the areas of test and integration, is the ability of the project to anticipate and avoid problems associated with development crises. If not dealt with, these can have a severe affect on the productivity of the project and the integrity of the development.

When viewed by the customer the occurrence of a crisis within a project can have the following effects.

1. If dealt with effectively by the software contractor, it reinforces that the project is "on top" of the problems and enhances confidence that the software and system will be adequate to suit the customer's requirements.

2. If not properly dealt with, these problems or crises will create a staccato project flow. The productivity stops and starts are very destructive to the integrity of the development and the confidence of the customer in the effectiveness of the project.

Crisis avoidance decisions should include the customer if the effects are felt by the customer.

As illustrated in Figure 8.7, the participation and visibility of the customer in the day-to-day activities should vary depending on the phase of the project and the stage of development. The segments of the software project which are areas of concern to the customer and provide visibility into the day-to-day activities of the project are:

1. **Technical Visibility**. During the early stages of the project, customer understanding and concurrence with the technical aspects of the project is

Project phase	Requirements definition		Functional design		Detailed software design and code		Test and integration		
Project activities	System requirements definition	Software requirements definition	Requirements allocation	Functional decompo-sition	Detailed design	Code	Development test	Software test	System test
Visibility into technical aspects of the project	Full	Full	Limited	Limited	Limited	None	None	Limited	Unlimited
Participation in project activities	Full	Full	Limited	Limited	Limited to none	None	None	Limited	Full
Walkthrough attendance	All	All	All	All	All	All	All	All	All
Visibility into project decisions	Full	Limited	Limited	Limited	None	None	None	Limited	Full
SCRB attendance and participation	Full	Full	Full	Full	Full	Full	Full	Full	Full
Project planning visibility	Full	Full	Full	Full	Full	Full	Full	Full	Full
Technical planning visibility	Full	Full	Full	Limited	Limited	None	None	Limited	Full
Crisis awareness	Full	Full	Full	Full	Full	Full	Full	Full	Full

Figure 8.7   Customer participation

essential since these decisions and technical parameters determine to a large measure what the system will do and how it will appear to the end user. As the development proceeds, the technical emphasis shifts from requirements to design and, by necessity, should become less visible to the customer. During code and development testing, all customer technical visibility should be limited to established reviews and project boards. As the product becomes operational through the levels of integration and test, technical emphasis again shifts from internal performance to design to external performance to operational requirements, and the customer visibility into technical matters should shift accordingly.

2. **Customer Participation.** Customer review of the initial stages of the software design is essential. It is during this period that the developer's interpretation of the system requirements is made. Initial system and software architecture and requirements allocation are defined and, most importantly to the user, the initial test requirements are defined. During this early project phase, the contractor tells the customer how the system will be structured and designed and how it will be integrated, qualified, and demonstrated. Unless the customer concurs with the approach, there is no guarantee that the tests run at levels 3, 4, 5, and 6 are compatible.

3. **Walkthrough Participation.** The use of walkthroughs as a vehicle for providing a customer with visibility into the process of development is extremely effective. Walkthroughs are structured, providing a clear view into the technical integrity of the software project. They deal with reasonably complete, albeit small, pieces of data and they are at a technical level that allows the customer to draw his or her own opinions about technical quality. All walkthroughs should be available to the customer. This offer should be extended, provided the privilege is not abused and project delays are not experienced because of customer interference or unnecessary analysis or investigation resulting from customer insistence. Any problems noted by the customer should be documented on SPR forms and submitted to the SCRB for resolution. Reporting observations through other channels or directly back to the customer should not be allowed and should result in customer exclusion from the walkthroughs.

4. **Visibility.** During the requirements specification and early design stages, the customer should have complete visibility into the early development activities. He or she should be permitted to view all technical materials and comment directly to the software technical manager concerning quality and responsiveness. During these stages of the project, the external attributes of the system—performance, interface, operational requirements, and control attributes—are being defined. The earlier that meaningful customer input is provided concerning these parameters, the more effective and responsive will be the development. These parameters have critical effects on the level 6 test effectiveness and on the acceptability of the end product by the user.

During the latter stages of software design, customer visibility becomes less critical. During these periods of development, the data products are internal to the development organization and do not bear directly on the end use or customer acceptance of the product. Access to this data by the customer should become the responsibility of the customer rather than being "pushed" by the contractor. If the information is not requested it is not provided. During code and development test, the code and unapproved supporting documentation, and detailed technical information should not be provided until approved through a walkthrough and placed under project control. During software and systems testing, the customer visibility into data products must increase in proportion to the proximity of the test execution.

5. **SCRB Attendance and Participation.** As with walkthroughs, customer participation in the SCRB through submission of SPRs and actual representation on the board should be encouraged throughout the development life cycle. This provides a vehicle through which the voice of the customer may be heard. Participation in this board draws the customer into the problems of development. He or she can, through the SPRs, make comments, observations, and can recommend changes. Through participation on the board the customer has an input equal to that of the contractor's technical segments of the project in the resolution of problems described on SPR's.

Customer SCRB participation should be encouraged by the contractor. It is a means of keeping the customer current with the state of the project without allowing direct involvement of the customer with lower-level technical individuals. This participation should be extended into the Program Support Library. Through the PSL librarian, and in accordance with previously described factors for participation and visibility, the customer should be provided access to controlled PSL files.

6. **Project Planning Visibility.** Full project planning visibility should be provided to the customer throughout the life cycle. These plans describe the means by which the software manager will produce, test, deliver, and control the software product. By allowing the customer visibility into how these plans are developed and the decision process used to produce the plans, the software manager ensures that there will be no surprises in the project environment and structure. This visibility should include problems being addressed, and expected limitations, constraints, and shortfalls which are anticipated.

Customer observations and inputs concerning these plans, while not always acted on, should be considered. Where change is made in a plan to respond to a customer observation or suggestion, credit should be given to the customer for the recommendation.

7. **Technical Planning Visibility.** Customer visibility into planning the technical aspects of software development, tool planning, methodology selection, project standards and reviews and audits should be controlled except for the initial and terminal phases of the project.

This control is essential in order to avoid impacts associated with customer opinions, recommended approaches, and grave concerns. The software and test manager should be aware that there will be emotional reactions on the part of the customer concerning any technical plan which is inconsistent with his or her experience, desires, understanding of development requirements, or desirable project attributes. In order to minimize the project impacts associated with assumed customer technical perogatives, the customer should be provided decreasing visibility into technical plans as the project proceeds until the completion of development testing. From that point forward, the technical plans are, hopefully, "cast in concrete" and the customer's technical visibility can be increased.

8. **Crisis Awareness.** Any problem or project crisis which is not controllable locally must be made visible to the customer in a positive and timely fashion. These problems will impact technical, management, and resource integrity of the project and, as such, require at least customer awareness and often customer action.

What Does All This Mean

The confidence and attitudes of a customer are felt by the contractor in a very real way: in his or her ability to sell the system to the customer or to gain approvals required for progress.

The software project and test managers who do not provide the proper level of concern to the customer interface or who assume that these interfaces are not critical to project success are very short-sighted. Ultimately these relationships must be corrected if the project is to be completed. Depending on the intensity of early customer/contractor antagonism, this correction may or may not be straightforward.

WHAT TO DO WHEN A SOFTWARE PROJECT BLOWS UP DURING TEST

Software testing, no matter how rigorously planned, carefully implemented, or effectively managed and controlled, is subject to a productivity catastrophe. This may be due to unresolved project drift, early project problems not dealt with adequately, or personnel, resource, or development decisions made by management which have a devastating effect on test productivity.

Irrespective of the cause, the project effects are dramatic: the project stops, the testing becomes ineffective, and the project productivity drops to unacceptable levels.

This book and other software project literature describes management of the software test process, assuming that the effort is starting from scratch. What happens when software testing has already begun and is running into cost and/or schedule problems during test? What are the special problems encountered and the unique solutions that are used to turn a troubled software development effort around? How does management initially recognize that a problem exists?

Recognizing the Problem

Software projects that experience difficulty during testing are characterized by one or more of the following symptoms.

1. General lack of motivation on the part of personnel assigned to the project.
2. Inability, on the part of software personnel, to meet schedule or cost milestones and to identify specific causes for the slips or overruns.
3. Lack of understanding of how tools will be integrated into the project structure prior to development.
4. Inability to clearly state project goals, objectives, and development methodologies.
5. Overall lack of clear project organization and communication sources.

Resolving the Problem—Right and Wrong Ways

When scheduling and cost issues become acute, software project and test management will normally pursue aggressive actions in an attempt to resolve the situation. These actions often include:

1. Reorganizing the project and shifting personnel assignments in an attempt to gain managment expertise and perspective.
2. Keeping the same management while rescheduling and rebudgeting the software project to provide sufficient time and resources to complete the effort.
3. Bringing in outside "experts" to evaluate the software development problem and to restructure the existent project by focusing it toward a goal.
4. Descoping development to reduce technical requirements, problems, and schedule requirements.
5. Canceling the project or at least reassigning development responsibility to a different organization.
6. Reassigning software management responsibility, initially keeping the same schedules, budgets, and staff while giving the new manager freedom to reestablish development parameters as required.

Experience has shown that these actions alone will not be enough. Successful project recovery during test can only be effected through redefining basic software management structures, identifying a clear and integrated set of development methodologies, and instilling a sense of purpose and basic motivation to personnel assigned to the project.

Assigning a competent test management staff that is experienced in the area of project recovery, is the most effective technique to implement project structures essential for successful software redirection. Effective project recovery techniques that may be applied by a newly assigned software test manager are described below.

1. Identifying accurate project status, performance history, problems, technical objectives and requirements, and contractual obligations.
2. Defining documentation and implementation of a project organization, structure, and development environment tailored to actual characteristics of the development task.
3. Rescheduling and rebudgeting software development tasks which provide a realistic basis for project implementation.
4. Identifying a project area that, aggressively pursued in an organized manner, would result in a series of visible, dramatic, short-term achievements.

As the new test manager assesses the situation and begins to redirect the efforts of the project's personnel, he must establish and enforce an integrated set of disciplines to support specific project software development requirements. The manager must also motivate project personnel to follow defined software methodologies and to develop the software within project constraints.

To accomplish these goals, the test manager must have a clear understanding of the tasks. Knowing how to accurately identify and acquire project support and personnel requirements, having the fortitude and capability to make firm decisions, and having the personal ability to convince both management and project personnel of the technical merit of selected development approaches are essential management prerequisites in a salvage situation. The test manager must be clearly in charge from the outset.

Assessing the Situation

The newly assigned test manager must assess the extent of the trouble he or she has inherited, and must accurately identify the software status before embarking on a recovery plan. During this data collection period, the test manager must rely primarily on his or her own perception and observations rather than on discussions with previously assigned project personnel. Any conversations with previous personnel will be prejudiced by their natural desires to have their efforts appear in the best light.

Source data for this status evaluation is to be gathered in four categories.

1. Schedule, budget, and performance analyses during the previous development and test period.
2. Documentation, quality of content, development practices, and customer visibility/acceptability of deliverables.

3. Software management control procedures documented and implemented in the development process.

4. Contractual documentation describing the development obligations.

After reviewing this documentation, an objective assessment of the status of the software project and the integrity of the test activities can be made.

The software test manager must make a series of extremely important decisions based on this assessment. The degree to which the existing project structure can be retained must be determined and include organization entities, schedule and budget viability, management techniques and procedures, and technical project parameters. Personnel must be assessed on an individual basis to identify those who are properly assigned and those who must be reassigned or removed from the project. The development methodologies, controls, and test philosophies must be evaluated for effectiveness.

Finally, an overall assessment of test adequacy must be made. This assessment is heavily influenced by project review parameters.

Once the test manager has formulated a project assessment, he or she must then convince management and customer personnel that the assessment is valid and that it must be supported regardless of internal opposition.

Decision management technique requires positive actions. The test manager must be visible, must provide clear direction, and must direct project flow in order to achieve dramatic successes.

Obtaining the Support of Customer and Management

Through the software manager, the test manager must convince higher management of the gravity of the software testing problem. There is a tendency for management to initially perceive software development problems, especially test problems, as transitory or susceptible to dramatic strokes designed to force the development back on track. Unfortunately, software problems are often deeply rooted in the basic management, technical, and control structure of the software project and can only be resolved through a significant expenditure of both schedule and project resources to redirect the efforts. This redirection requires an absolute commitment on the part of management to provide the resources required to complete the development, even at the expense of project profit or short-term project success.

Convincing upper management of the software problem can best be achieved through a series of presentations that clearly identify the causes and magnitude of all aspects of the development support. The software test manager must be willing to either raise the problems to higher management or to resign his or her position if support is not forthcoming.

Without customer concurrence, however, the salvage effort has no chance of success. The software project and test managers have an obligation to be totally open with the customer, clearly identifying project status, risks, plans, and perceived prognosis. The customer frequently has not been given accurate status and often reacts favorably to a candid assessment of status and problems.

Defining the Testing Structure/Methodology

Once an accurate assessment of project status has been made and management and customer personnel have been apprised of and support the salvage effort, the test manager must define a test structure and methodology. The structure and methodology must be consistent with the realities of software development in a project salvage environment and cover all test levels 1–6.

Defining and Disseminating the Methodology

The testing methodology to be followed for the salvage effort should be documented in a software development plan and related planning documents.

The replanning of the test activities may entail a complete replanning of the system test activities and the software project, complete software project replanning, selective replanning of segments of the software project, or a more effective implementation of existing plans.

These documents should be distributed to project management, staff, and customer personnel.

As previously described, these plans document all test aspects of the project. The plans are the basic root document for all policies and practices and must be maintained and distributed on a regular basis to all tested project personnel. Through plan updates, the test manager communicates basic criteria and project changes to staff, management, and customer personnel.

Redirecting the Effort

The steps involved in redirecting the test effort include reorganizing the test project to increase productivity, planning the efforts, and taking firm control of the project in order to implement these plans. A key item in the effort to assume control is ensuring a project success as soon as possible after takeover. This success will significantly enhance credibility and make direction easier to follow.

Enhancing Productivity

Planning and redirecting must have maximizing productivity as a key goal. Augmenting productivity in a project environment requires implementation of a structure which drives all facets of the effort through the single most productive activity. An approach toward organizationally supporting this environment is illustrated in Figure 4. The structure centralizes management responsibility by assigning configuration control and support functions, software integration and test planning, documentation, and development support to groups external to the management team. It is the responsibility of these external groups to follow the management director.

Planning for Success

Successful completion of the test plan is the most critical aspect of the salvage effort. This document defines and describes the scope, responsibility, and test flow and is the first opportunity for the test manager to take charge of the project and document his or her testing philosophy. This document need not be a literary masterpiece, but should be a complete and clear expression of how the project is to be developed. This document defines what has to be accomplished if the salvage effort is to be successful. It defines how technical and management parameters are to be implemented, and describes what tools and support are required to implement the effort. This planning effort must be personally directed by the test manager. Too often the manager delegates this responsibility and finds that the resultant plan is not what is required to complete the effort.

Rescheduling of Work

The amount of software rescheduling and rebudgeting required is a function of the degree of the problem as perceived by the test manager, the detailed planning information gathered by the manager, and the requirements defined and documented in the software development plan.

A scheduling form that is effective in a software salvage effort is a Program Evaluation Review Technique (PERT) schedule which shows work flow, constraints, and project dependencies. It is essential that the PERT schedule have extremely short milestones keyed to an integrated status accounting function. The technique for defining the schedule is for the software manager to identify all major milestones and essential constraints.

The test manager should plan the latter phases of software test first, and expend a significant amount of effort in evaluating and planning the test problem and a lesser amount of direct management effort in planning the design and coding interactions.

The manager should meet with technical people associated with each of the milestones, identify all activities required to complete them, and document these activities in the form of an unordered list. The list should then be ordered, critical constraints identified, and personnel brought in to define and lay out the PERT network without identifying any time spans. After the work is complete, each of the managers will define the spans by event. After all spans have been completed, the scheduling function will convert these spans into dates and use this information to derive milestone dates. Manpower and budget requirements for the project must then be reassessed to provide schedule credibility and allocate funding and manpower support requirements.

When the estimates, schedules, and budgets are complete, the software manager should layer this information into the PERT and present this data to management and customer personnel.

If these efforts are adequately done, convincing personnel assigned or associated with the project of their accuracy and viability is possible. If it is not adequate, the associated schedule slippage and overrun information will not be acceptable in or out of the project organization.

Taking Control—Implementation of the Structure

The most difficult aspects of salvaging a software project during test are implementing plans and methodology, focusing development efforts toward specific goals, motivating personnel to accomplish assigned tasks, and establishing a development team from individuals assigned to the project. These tasks, although required for any development effort, are extremely difficult in a salvage situation due to an almost universal feeling on the part of project personnel that the newly assigned manager is an intruder. The project controls being imposed are felt to be unnecessary and will not be supported because they represent an infringement on the technical prerogatives of the development team.

The test manager must make the technical staff understand that the job to be accomplished, although difficult, is achievable if resources are properly focused and applied. This is a four-step process.

1.   Identify a set of key decisions that are outstanding and initiate specific actions to resolve them. This decision process should be very visible to all staff members, and actions should be formally tracked. The successful and decisive resolution of outstanding project issues is an absolute prerequisite for a successful salvage effort. Indecisive or ineffective management, especially early in the effort, will preclude future staff support.

2.   Break the project into an integrated set of mini-projects tied together through the PERT. These small efforts provide for short achievable milestones and, if properly planned, provide for a smooth phasing of manpower and work flow.

3.   Provide at regular intervals a detailed projection of tasking for the next work period based on performance during the current period. Accurate status monitoring based on work projection is absolutely essential to keeping the job moving and enables identification of project problems early enough to facilitate correction. The manager must be prepared to take seemingly ruthless personnel and organizational actions to meet both short-term and long-term milestones.

4. Consistently establish, maintain, and enforce a rigorous development environment and standards throughout the project. This enforcement must "tree down" from the software manager through all organizational levels, with exceptions being approved only by the software manager. This consistency is difficult to achieve due to apparent short-term schedule and budget impacts, which can be convincingly argued as being attributable to imposition of standards or development disciplines. The software manager must be prepared to be adamant in insisting that project disciplines be followed. The manager must be willing to accept responsibility for short-term project slips in order to preserve project integrity and long-term schedule viability.

The second key aspect in taking control is to keep the project moving. If the effort stalls or waits for resources, personnel, or decisions, it will be difficult to reestablish momentum. Decisions must be made in a timely manner and planning must anticipate rather than react to project conditions.

Early Success Is a Prerequisite for Credibility

The new test manager assigned to a project is too often looked upon by project personnel as another in a long chain of solutions to a seemingly unsolvable problem. The frequent reaction is to question why this solution should be any more effective than previously unsuccessful attempts. The new manager, once planning and scheduling tasks are completed, must very quickly establish credibility with customer, staff, and management personnel. The most effective technique for establishing credibility is to identify a visible, difficult, and previously unachievable milestone and to marshal sufficient resources, management expertise, planning, and controls to successfully realize the milestones in a short time period. The selected milestone should have a single data product output and should be the key to the start of a broad spectrum of project events. Above all, the manager must be convinced that the milestone is achievable within the specified period.

The manager should first define exactly what resources are required to accomplish the task and, ignoring resource expenditures, should gather all required resources and assign them to the project through the duration of the pilot effort. Secondly, he should define and maintain a very detailed PERT schedule, adding or replacing personnel or resources as required to maintain that schedule. It is extremely important in this effort that minor milestones be met and that the schedule not be allowed to slip, even slightly.

Being the major force in accomplishing the task, the manager must provide intense direct management guidance. Besides providing management support, the manager is forging a team environment and a sense of project purpose and is defining his or her role as project leader.

The fact that the effort is achieved on time greatly enhances schedule, budget, and credibility. The software manager, when proposing the pilot project, must be prepared to insist on his or her approach and schedule and must be willing to drive people to complete assigned tasks. The manager also must be willing to compromise on structure and content in order to meet schedule dates.

This technique is the most effective approach in short-term project re-motivation. The results of this effort are transitory, however, and continued project success and direction are required to maintain the momentum. The software manager must realize that in order to successfully complete the salvage effort, he or she will have to relentlessly manage the effort or inertia will return.

The software manager is still dealing with the same project, customer, and staff. If the manager removes himself or herself or reduces the level of commitment, the project will drift. If successful in redirecting the effort, the completion of the job and the commitment of the people will be the software manager's responsibility. The intensity of support required must be understood by the manager and must be willingly given, or the project will not succeed.

9 A Testing Example

The test planning and development steps described above are critical components of a successful software project. Unfortunately, the planning requirement is often ignored due to conflicting priorities or, in many cases, a lack of experience in the management of software. The following example is a fictional account of a real testing environment. The example has been based on several actual project situations in which the planning was poorly done.

PROJECT BACKGROUND—EARLY SEEDS OF DISASTER

In the mid 1970s a contract was awarded to develop a real time, state-of-the-art software application. The project began with the usual flourish; customer and contractor congratulated each other on the quality of the specifications. They agreed that the development would be done "by the numbers" and be an example for the industry to follow. For the software manager the first several weeks of the project were a whirlwind of meetings, briefings, interviews, and a never-ending array of short-term project requirements. There was no time for planning but, in the mind of the manager, as soon as these short-term commitments were completed, there would be more than enough time to plan the project. This did not prove to be the case.

Early Schedule Drift—Project Control Problems

The first major project milestone was the System Requirements Review (SRR). This review was the responsibility of the program office. However, because of the customer's requirements and the nature of the system, a major segment of the presentation became the responsibility of the software organization. Everyone on the project worked hard getting ready and, although the preparation for the review was chaotic, the presentation was reasonably well received. The success of the SRR established a feeling on both the contractor's and the customer's sides that the project was succeeding well. This was far from the case.

Shortly after the SRR the project began to experience difficulty. People working on the project did not have sufficient direction or guidance to develop and document the next level of the requirements. The software manager had not planned for this phase of the project and momentum soon slowed, eventually stopping when requirements had to be translated into a software architecture. Schedules and budgets were ignored. The application of resources was ineffective and the generation of the functional specification became an insurmountable roadblock.

The software manager was told late in the pre-PDR segment of the project—after budgets, schedules, and resources had been depleted—that major design problems had been found and would require significant time and resources to correct. He had been "had."

What Happened—Disaster

The project problems began to snowball shortly after the functional specification delivery schedules were missed. The software manager found that, since there was no organization or structure to the software project and no plan for performing the essential development tasks, even the smallest project task could not be completed. The project slowed, and slowed, eventually stopping prior to PDR.

Early Test Planning Problems

During the early project stages there had been no attempt to plan or structure the test activities. Half-hearted attempts had been made to develop a system test plan. However, without a test philosophy or set of testing goals and objectives, this planning had been, at best, ineffective. Meeting after meeting had been spent arguing about test technique without any definition or understanding of the task at hand. Schedules slipped, progress was negligible, and the easy, loose structure of the system test group changed to a desperate, frustrated group of individuals working hard toward a goal no one understood.

Corrective Procedures—Difficult But Effective

When the project blew up, the program manager was faced with a difficult decision. He felt that he had only six possible options, none of which were attractive.

1. Reorganizing the project, shifting personnel assignments in an attempt to gain management expertise and perspective.

2. Keeping the same management while rescheduling and rebudgeting the software project to provide sufficient time and resources to complete the effort.

3. Bringing in outside "experts" to evaluate the software development problem, to restructure the existent project, and to get the project focused toward a goal.

4. Descoping development to reduce technical requirements, problems, and schedule requirements.

5. Canceling the project or, at least reassigning development responsibility to a different organization.

6. Reassigning software management responsibility while keeping the same schedules, budgets, and staff while giving the new manager freedom to reestablish development parameters as required.

The manager decided to bring in an outside expert to evaluate the problem. The consultant reviewed the project and identified 35 project areas which should be looked at. The areas ranged from methodology application through cost and schedule controls. When faced with the magnitude of the recommendations the manager was concerned. He grouped the problems and found that the five most significant were:

1. A general lack of motivation on the part of personnel assigned to the project.

2. An inability on the part of software personnel to meet schedule or cost milestones and to identify specific causes for the slips or overruns.

3. Lack of understanding, prior to development, of how tools, techniques, and methodologies were to be integrated into the project structure.

4. An inability to clearly state project goals, objectives, and development methodologies.

5. An overall lack of clear project organization and communication sources.

Based on this analysis a new software manager was assigned and told to "fix it."

PLANNING—HOW IT TURNED THE PROJECT AROUND

The preliminary software structure, project organization, and control and development environment were defined by the newly assigned manager and documented in a draft Software Development Plan, a Configuration Management Plan, a Standards and Conventions Plan, and a Test and Quality Assurance Plan.

Initial organization of the project was extremely difficult due to the critical requirement to get the job started. An initial analysis of the task indicated that staff was required in five primary areas.

1.   **Development.** The development team was organized under the technical leader and staffed with personnel previously assigned to the project.

2.   **Tool Development.** An initial evaluation of project tools indicated that they were inadequate to support development and test of the software. A group was identified to develop tools for supporting project methodologies.

3.   **Test Planning.** An independent test planning and development function was identified to verify software quality and adherence to baselines.

4.   **Documentation.** To maximize productivity, it was decided to offload as much documentation responsibility as possible from the development team. Personnel were identified to document the software.

5.   **Configuration Management.** To control the myriad of software products and baselines a strong configuration management structure was required. The functional and staff requirements were identified.

A quick review of company personnel resources indicated that initial staffing could not be achieved from within the company nor were there any guarantees as to the long-term assignment of personnel assigned to the program.

An organizational structure was then identified and an aggressive staffing plan was pursued to fill the required positions. Using a combination of known outside consultants, outside body shops, and personnel within the company, the project was fully staffed in a short time. Each individual was brought into a documented position and assigned a documented task.

Early Test Reorganization

Reorganization of the early test planning and development was a critical early task. When the new software manager was assigned responsibility, one of the first tasks accomplished was a thorough evaluation of the state of the test planning activities. He found them in total shambles.

He assigned an experienced test manager responsibility for all test planning, and provided whatever resources were required to ensure success. The new test manager reviewed the early test work and discarded it in total. He redirected the staff, placing primary project test emphasis on development of the system test plan. The plan was to be based on program delivery requirements. However, when attempts were made to find out what specifically these requirements were, they were unclear, poorly specified, and impossible to define.

The expectations of the user differed from the development plans of the program. The demonstration requirements as understood by the program were not consistent with the contract. And the program budgets and schedule constraints were incompatible with the customer's perception of the system performance demonstrations.

The test manager and assigned staff did an initial contractual analysis and extracted those technical and contractual requirements which had to be demonstrated. A set of system test cases was defined and the individual requirements were allocated through a requirements matrix.

The test cases were in two separate segments. One segment corresponded to the level 6 requirements. These tests were designed to demonstrate a contractual compliance of the system. The second test segment was designed to integrate the system at level 5. These tests were designed as a "ramp test" which, when executed in sequence, exercised increasingly larger system segments.

The test structure was then used as the basis of the system test plan. This plan was developed, in draft form, very rapidly and provided to the customer at the first project review after the redirection was put in place. The customer was encouraged. It appeared that at least the system test planning had taken on some semblance of structure, and guarded optimism slowly replaced outright customer pessimism.

Early Testing Organization

The software manager recognized that the separate categories of testing would require different management if they were to succeed. He assigned a system test manager who had total responsibility for all level 5 and 6 test planning, development, execution, and analysis.

He assigned a software test manager for level 3 and 4 and assigned level 1 and 2 responsibility to the task leaders for development. By defining the requirements for testing in reverse order (i.e., systems testing, first followed by system integration, etc.) the manager found that he could see how to narrow the focus of the test program if he could project what specific test steps would be used to integrate and qualify the software and system.

Using the system test plan as the base, and the software development plan, the software test manager wrote a software test plan which, he felt, described how the software testing was to be accomplished. He was totally unprepared for the torrents of criticism which resulted from the initial review of the plan. The program and software project managers felt that the test plans were overly complex, would be too expensive, had too much duplication, and need not be defined this early in the development. The technical staff, on the other hand, felt that the plans were inconsistent with the latest industry techniques, were technically naïve, and were overly structured. They wanted to have the option of conducting tests as they saw fit and to apply whatever test tools, techniques, and methodologies that seemed appropriate to the problem at hand.

One particularly vocal senior member of the staff went so far as to compare the proposed test structure against what he assumed the customer expected. He then proceeded to verbally make the results of the analysis available to any one who would listen, including program management personnel and technical personnel from within the project. His concerns were in three major areas.

1. He did not feel the approach was "top down" and therefore it was inconsistent with what had been previously described to the customer.
2. Many "leading edge" test technologies were ignored by the test approach and, as such, an opportunity to try them in a real project situation was being lost.
3. The rigorous testing structure and tight control of data removed the options of the testing staff, placing a "strait jacket" on their efforts and removing any flexibility to "try different things."

As a result of these activities the project was split into two camps: the technologists who agreed with the senior staff member, and the other members of the staff who were willing to follow the test plan. This testing polarization continued throughout the project, eventually causing serious problems later in the development.

The Software/System Test Split

The organizational split between software and system testing proved to be effective in the context of the program environments from the very beginning. The fact that it was based on a structure of test planning documents, that the roles, responsibilities, and technical activities had been predefined and that the relationship between the test organizations had been worked out ahead of time minimized the conflicts and overlaps between the groups. System test responsibility included planning, development, and control of all level 5 hardware/software integration and level 6 test data, tools, and support facilities. The software test organization, on the other hand, was responsible for integrating the four software subsystems into an operational configuration. Software configuration management and tool development was the responsibility of the software organization, as was system and software documentation development, production, delivery, and control.

The early project efficiency was significantly affected, however, by a program office decision. In order to minimize the effects of cost overruns in the system engineering and hardware development areas of the program, it was decided to combine the level 4, 5, and 6 test responsibilities under one test manager who would report to systems engineering. Level 3 test, and the lower software test levels, would remain with the software test manager. The idea was that this organization would reduce the amount of work by limiting the test case documentation and development requirements. In fact, this did happen, although the program slipped because of problems uncovered at level 5 that should have been found during level 4 testing.

Requirement specification	Software design specification	Software design specification	Software design specification	Subsystem function specification	System specification	System requirements specification
Test review	Unit test walkthrough	Unit test walkthrough	Build test walkthrough	Test Readiness Review / Functional configuration audit	Program test review	System acceptance review
	Level 1	Level 2	Level 3	Level 4	Level 5	Level 6
Test level	Module test	Unit test	Software subsystem integration	Software subsystem functional	System integration	System functional
Test object	Module implementation	Unit design/ functional allocation	Software subsystem integration	Software subsystem functional	Sys. Integ. a. s'ware/s'ware b. s'ware/h'ware	System system performance
Test requirement document	Programmers' notebook	Unit development folder	Build test plan	Software test plan	System test plan	System test
Test specification	Programmers' notebook	Unit development folder	Build test folder; pro-cedures, scenarios, data	Software test procedures, scenarios, data	Sys. test folder, procedures, scenarios, data	Sys. test procedures, scenarios, data

Figure 9.1 Test flow

193

The software test manager decided that in order to ensure that all groups involved with testing used the same terminology and had a common understanding of the requirements for each test level, a diagram, similar to Figure 9.1 would be developed and coordinated with the system test manager. This diagram proved invaluable in defining which testing was to be done by whom. It provided a common basis for all test planning, cleared up problems with terminology, and illustrated the flow of test activities to program, customer, and technical personnel. It served as the link between all organizations involved with testing at any level.

Redefining the Test Plan

The system and software test managers both agreed that because of the major changes in the program organization, the entire test planning structure should be at least reevaluated and, in some cases, redone. The previously defined workflow and responsibilities, the suite of tools and test cases, and the overall testing structure documented in the software development and test plans was invalid in light of the new split. Unfortunately, the rescheduled PDR was rapidly approaching and the demands on all project personnel, especially the managers, were significant. When the system and software test managers presented the replanning requirement to the software, system engineering, and program managers and suggested that the PDR schedule might be impacted, there was a hushed silence followed by an obvious feeling of disbelief. How could they consider impacting the first visible customer milestone after the problems that had gone on before? There would be plenty of time to fix the test planning after the PDR. The test plans were not a high-priority item just then since they were not needed until late in the project. If the test managers would just keep their priorities straight at the moment, a better world would be promised for the future.

The test managers discussed the effects of not straightening out the plans, evaluated the pros and cons, and decided that despite the PDR schedule the plans had to be fixed immediately since there would be no time later. The program manager was at first adamantly opposed, but when the software test manager threatened to leave the program, and perhaps the company, he folded.

As it turned out, the PDR schedule was delayed slightly. However, the customer felt that this was for the long-term benefit of the program and was certainly justified. By fixing the plans, the focus of the project testing requirements was retained.

Organizing the Work Force

Revision of the test plans was split into two segments. An initial release of the system and software test plans set out the requirements for each test level. This was to be followed by a second release to be developed later in order to detail the test case requirements for each of the test levels. It was felt that the previously defined suite of test cases, although reasonable, should be evaluated to ensure validity. The results of this analysis was to be included in the second release.

The schedule for the first release of the revised test plans was brought in line as closely as possible with the PDR. Both system and software test managers worked very hard to get the initial release of the test plans out on time. Simultaneously, the software project manager was reluctantly updating the software development plan. When completed, the plans were released for review but everyone was too busy to read them, much less comment on them. To elicit a response, the system test manager called a meeting of all plan recipients. Only half of those invited showed up. The general comment from those who attended was that, although the initial test plans and the software development plans appeared adequate, there were "bigger bears in the woods" than testing at that time. Until some agreement was received from the other areas of the project, concerning the implications of the test plans, it was difficult to commit any resources to the test approach or initiate any work. Because of the long lead times associated with the development of test materials, the system and software test managers were both concerned about these early delays.

Early Staff Motivation

As a result of early problems with the acceptance of the software test plans, the software test manager was sensitive to the reaction of personnel to the test issues. He felt a reluctance on the part of any program, customer, or project personnel to commit any time to testing. The problem came to a head when the software test manager was temporarily reassigned to another project. The system test manager was left with overall test responsibility. He was faced with inadequate resources, unrealistic schedules, and a general lack of support. Things were not looking good.

He went to the software project manager and found that many of the concerns were shared. The software project manager committed, to the best of his abilities, support and resources toward correcting the test problems. He provided budget, personnel, and authorization to bring in outside support to plan and develop test requirements. By going outside, the system test manager found a reservoir of available talent which could be immediately applied to supporting the test planning. He brought in a mixture of contractor and company personnel to plan the system and software testing. Immediately he was faced with significant motivational problems. He had brought in experienced individuals. However, the set of tasks which they were to do were poorly defined, resulting in poor initial effectiveness. The new staff appeared to be busy producing the system test plan, but without any understanding of the plan requirements or any guidance concerning the content, the efficiency of the team was not acceptable. The system test manager had fallen into the same trap as his predecessor; he was monitoring the planning effort, not managing it.

Recognizing the schedule slippage, the test manager took two actions. First, he developed a very detailed, annotated outline which defined what was to be included in each of the test plans and who was responsible for development of each section. Secondly, he generated and enforced a detailed section-by-section schedule for test plan development. The longest span on the schedule was four days and there were frequent scheduled reviews on the sections as they were being developed. Under this structure, both the software and system test plans were produced ahead of schedule and their quality surprised everyone. The success of the test planning seemed to buoy up the rest of the project. They seemed to have accomplished something tangible, on time, without visible strain.

Test Tool Selection

Shortly after completion of the test plans, the software test manager returned to the project. After meeting with the system test manager, he decided that the next logical planning step was to define the test tools and automated aids to be used by the project. As with the production of the test plans, there was a false start in identifying the tools. He went to the testing staff and asked what tools could be developed in order to expedite and control the test process. Many meetings were held, paper flew around the test organization describing tool requirements, and the emphasis of the project went from test planning to tool specification. After observing the problem for a short time, the software manager put a stop to the activities and gathered up the results. He found that the tools being evaluated did not correspond to the test requirements, nor was there a direct correlation to the requirements of each test level.

The software test manager, after reviewing the tool specification, had a flash of insight which ultimately proved the key to the success of the program. He realized that the inability to specify tools had a broader project significance. It indicated that the staff, which ultimately had to perform the testing tasks, had limited understanding of the testing methodologies to be used, the plans to be followed, the data products to result from testing, and the technical characteristics of the system. He decided that the tool definition effort could be redirected to address the more fundamental project problem. He assigned a team to review the test plans, summarize the testing approach, and define a set of technical requirements and characteristics which were essential "drivers" in defining the tools and test environment. This team was made up of senior personnel who were loaned to the software test manager. There was a dual benefit to the project: the senior personnel were forced to understand the project environment, test requirements, and technical environment, and the requirements for tools were on a firm basis.

As a result of this analysis, four tool categories were defined.

1. Configuration management and control tools developed specifically to support the test and integration phase of development.
2. Test tools developed specifically to support each test level. This category encompassed emulation instrumentation and analysis tools.
3. Simulation tools used to simulate the external system environment and input data to and received data from the test configuration.
4. Analytical tools which reduce the test data, analyze the integrity of the test, and report the results.

PROJECT CONTROLS DURING TESTING

The program was blessed with an extremely effective program support librarian. She was organized, knowledgeable and, most importantly, tough as nails. Shortly after the project redirection she had defined and documented a structure for controlling the data being developed or used by the project. The approach integrated manual, automated, procedural, and review requirements into an integrated "infrastructure." As the other parts of the program and software project took shape, and the Program Plans, Software Development Plan, and second-level planning documentation became available she diligently maintained and updated the plans for software configuration management. She felt that in order to ensure that controls were adequate for development, test, and integration and project support, early implementation of the controls was essential. She specified, by individual data product, the reviews and controls to be applied. She allocated a set of files and support tools to control the flow of data within the project. She also established a configuration management structure flexible enough to encompass system engineering control, program data, and whatever technical information was required to ensure the integrity of the software development.

The software configuration management responsibility was centralized in the Program Support Library (PSL). This group reported directly to the software manager and was responsible for all project support as well as software configuration management. A Software Configuration Review Board (SCRB) was established to review all proposed changes to data controlled by the PSL. All data approved by the software project through a walkthrough or project review was placed under software configuration management.

From the beginning, these controls proved effective. Requirements were controlled and specified in a consistent form. The changes to controlled project data were evaluated before the change was made and there was a full audit trail describing changes made to each controlled item. The flow of data and allocation of responsibility within the project was smooth, effective, and clearly specified. In short, the PSL proved to be an essential component of project success.

SCALING THE TEST EFFORT TO THE BUDGETS

The generation of test budgets and schedules was poorly done and proved to be a continuing critical problem. When the project was redirected the recosting and rescheduling of the software was hastily done and based on incomplete information. Because of project pressures these initial estimates were never updated. As the development moved into testing it became apparent that the budgets were not adequate. Unfortunately, in order to correct the problem several critical decisions were made which significantly affected project success.

The most serious problem which resulted from these decisions was a loss of discipline in the development of one of the software subsystems. As a result of earlier decisions, there was one faction in the project which felt that all this discipline and project control was unnecessary, expensive, and limited the technical and development prerogatives of the technical personnel. As money and schedule became tight, this group became increasingly vocal. Eventually they convinced the program and software managers that if the controls were removed from at least one of the subsystems the improvements in implementation efficiency would more than make up for the shortfalls. It was decided to conduct walkthroughs on a sample of the units within this subsystem rather than all of them. The integration disciplines and organizational responsibilities assigned to the requirements for this subsystem were short-circuited, at least through level 3, in an attempt to speed up the integration of the subsystem.

A second decision was made to strip out the "ramp" tests which had been defined to integrate the system and software. These tests were replaced by the test set being developed to demonstrate the system at level 6 and the software at level 4. The test configurations were modified to require instrumentation at the integration levels. The hope was that by monitoring the software execution parameters internally, the test set would do double duty: they would prove to be an effective integration environment since they monitored internal performance parameters and, with instrumentation out, would demonstrate performance and functional integrity. This did not prove to be the case.

The test cases had been designed to demonstrate externally visible performance parameters rather than internal execution characteristics. They proved to be a poor means to integrate. The tests executed certain segments of the software exhaustively, while not exercising other areas at all. Problems identified could not easily be isolated and, in too many instances, problems were nonreproduceable. The split between integration and functional test became unclear. Eventually a decision was made to merge level 3 and 4 into a single test level conducted parallel with the development tests. Much rationalization was done to justify the decision from a program and efficiency standpoint. The real reason for the decision was, however, that there would be less money required to develop the tests and that short-term budget performance would improve. This decision proved to have the desired effect in the near term; however, it was devastating to the long-term integrity of the project. The parallelism didn't work, the test structure was ineffective, and problems in the software which should have been caught early were not found until later when there were no resources to correct them.

DEVELOPMENT OF THE TEST REQUIREMENTS

The development of the test set was extremely difficult. Much time was spent attempting to define the optimum test set, reworking test specifications to fold in requirements which had been overlooked, and iteratively updating test cases to keep up with changing requirements. Schedules were being missed and, until the test cases were defined, progress in defining procedures, scenarios, data, and support tools couldn't be made. In frustration the system test manager issued an edict that there would be eight test cases for the program. They were:

1. **System Load.** Incorporate those functions which loaded the system from external media into to the various processors and initiate execution.

2. **System Initialization.** Includes the functions which initialize the system parameters, tailor it to the execution environment, and make the system ready for use.

3. **System Input.** Incorporates those functions which read data into the system and format it for use.

4. **Protocol Handling.** Incorporates the system functions which support the many layers of communications protocols required by the system application.

5. **System Output.** Incorporates those functions which format all output data and outputs it to external devices.

6. **Processing Support.** Incorporates those functions required by the specifications which process information in the system configuration.

7. **Security Functions.** Incorporates those functions which support the stringent system security requirements.

8. **System Error Recognition and Recovery.** Incorporates those functions which ensured the integrity of the system when components failed.

The system test manager's direction was to consider this test set inviolate, take all the system requirements—either provided by the customer or derived as part of the design process—and allocate them to the tests. The test definition bottleneck was solved. Test definition work took off. Very quickly a complete set of tests were defined to be used in this combined level 3–4 role, and the development of procedures was started. Not every segment of the project was elated by the breakthrough. The segment of the project developing the subsystem not using the project disciplines felt that the test allocation was, at best, naïve and would impact the reliability and acceptability of the end product. They felt that the only way to test a system like this was to use unstructured methods which corresponded to the unpredictable nature of the system execution. They continued to apply these techniques to the integration and test of the subsystem they were building. Payday was coming.

Test Scenarios—How They Helped

Once the test cases were defined the development of procedures went quickly. The time which had been lost on the schedule was quickly recovered and progress on the short-term milestones which were being used to schedule the program at this point was right on plan. As the development of the test cases moved from production of scenarios to actual development of test data, the effort again bogged down. It proved exceedingly difficult to identify what data would cause specific system conditions and to define at the data development level the interrelationships between test messages essential for testing effectiveness. A member of the staff suggested that they back up one level and look at the broader picture before the data was developed. The suggestion was to define on a large chart the requirements for all test messages first and what software was executed by each, then define the messages. This effort seemed like the only alternative. They certainly weren't getting anywhere the way they were headed.

The development of the scenarios was grueling. Thinking through which software was being executed by each data message took a long time and required project personnel who were busy on other things. Relating the test messages together to cause predictable internal system conditions and externally measurable results was almost impossible, but everyone stayed with it. When the scenarios were completed, all test schedules had been blown and both the system and software test managers were called on the carpet by the program manager. The latter pointed to the apparent progress being made by the test group not using this discipline. He suggested that time may be spent looking at what was being done there and hopefully, benefitting from their success. The system test manager warned the program manager that, despite the early success, the subsystem probably wouldn't work properly. The program manager said "nonsense" and ushered everyone out of his office.

Black Friday

The best day that the system and software test managers had on the project was the day that the three subsystems were brought together for the first time. There still were schedule problems; however, through judicious use of overtime they were rapidly improving. The development of the test data, once the scenarios had been completed, had gone well, and the test tools and support facilities had been completed early and were ready for use. The development tests and subsystem integration tests had been done according to the requirements and had been successfully completed. There had been an inordinate amount of difficulty integrating two of the subsystems because of the characteristics of the tests being used, but even these problems had been overcome. All software was controlled, walkthroughs had been uniformally applied, and the PSL and SCRB was working better than had been expected. The day the three subsystems were brought together for the first time everything worked perfectly. Three test cases were worked through fully, with problems in the third promptly corrected, and the testing proceeded without any loss of efficiency. The test managers, the software project manager, and the program managers were ecstatic.

The software project manager went to the group testing the other subsystem to get the software for integration and was astounded at the difference in attitudes. He hadn't been down there in a while because of the surly nature of the test leader. When he walked in, only half the staff was at their desks. The physical plant was a mess, and no one knew where the test leader was. He was finally found working on the hardware and when asked to build a system for test became very defensive. He pointed out that although the software appeared to be working well the hardware had been working so poorly it was impossible to accurately define its status. He also complained that there had been so many transient problems caused by poor hardware reliability that time had been wasted tracking nonreproduceable problems. After much pressing he agreed to have a subsystem configuration ready for test by the next Friday. Friday came and the software test manager sent the PSL librarian down to get the software, the configuration description, and the documentation relating to the subsystem and tests which had been run. She was given a tape and was told that the other things had not been required and therefore did not exist. They attempted to move the data into the PSL files and found that units were missing. The project standards had not been followed and, worst of all, the subsystem would not link edit. The subsystem test leader ran upstairs at that point, clutching another tape, saying that he thought this was the latest version. Sure enough, the configuration was complete; however, when it was link edited it was 50,000 bytes too large.

The software test manager got together with the project manager and they decided that they had better find out quickly what was going on. They assigned the best test person they had and the software system engineer who had designed the subsystem the task of quickly evaluating the software. They ran the subsystem tests developed for integrating the subsystem into the system configuration and found that not one would run. There were no records to go back to in order to evaluate the problems and, worst of all, the implementation did not match the design, nor was it traceable to requirements.

An emergency meeting was called where the subsystem test leader told a story of having to patch the software to get around hardware bugs, undocumented decisions and assumptions which were made and incorporated into the software without any technical or impact analysis, and a test structure which was not documented, understood, nor consistently applied. A decision was made to turn the two analysts loose with the subsystem for three weeks and to find out how bad the situation was. They ran the subsystem tests, reviewed whatever documentation was available, and interviewed the personnel who had performed the tests. Gradually a clear pattern emerged. There had been no organization to the earlier tests. No one knew what tests had run succesfully and, even worse, there was no understanding on anyone's part of what software had been tested or what problems existed in the subsystem. The subsystem testing had to be restarted. The impact of this on the program and software schedules was devastating. Even with good luck the subsystem could not be ready for system integration for six months. The problem was compounded by the earlier difficulties experienced by the program and the perceptions of the customer that this was a job in serious trouble. Unless this perception was changed, they could not sell the system and get paid.

What Was Done

The schedule slips were realized. In order to support the program budget pressures, the test staff had been cut by 25 percent and all integration testing, which was inadequate anyway because of previous decisions, was cut out entirely. The decision had been made to put the blinders on and go for level 6 success. There were 139 open problems which, after some analysis, appeared to be split as follows.

Twenty-seven critical problems which would preclude a start of testing.
Forty-nine problems which were serious but would not preclude test success.
Sixty-three problems which were noncritical and could be treated as latent defects.

After four weeks of testing, there were only three open critical problems, the rest having been resolved. A decision was made to schedule formal testing and invite the customer. The schedule called for formal dry runs to start in six weeks, followed by a three-day formal demonstration. Customer representatives were to fly in from around the country to witness the tests.

The period between the decision to start the test and the arrival of the customer was a whirlwind. The system ran twenty-four hours a day, with staff fighting for terminal access. The SCRB met three times a day to process problem reports and a new system was built daily to incorporate approved changes. Surprisingly, it began to appear that there was a shot at having a system configuration for test. One week before the start of test the system was still crashing; however, the crashes were no longer random and it was felt would not occur while the customer was there. The last week was spent documenting the test configuration and rehearsing the procedures. During the week the system only crashed once, although the crash was new, non-reproduceable, and in the subsystem which had experienced the development problems.

Monday came and the customer arrived. The week started well with the initial set of tests running well. In fact, the next several days went well and by Wednesday morning everyone was on Cloud Nine. They got into the section of test procedures that had not been previously executed and the system crashed. It crashed regularly from that point forward and the tests were finally abandoned.

Post-Mortem

The customer was extremely upset, threatening contract cancellation, loss of incentive fees, and any other actions that would force the contractor to complete the development in an orderly manner. The discipline which had held the development together earlier was reinforced and the program focused all energies toward completing the tests in a manner which would ensure success the second time the tests were run. Optimism was replaced by a clear perception of reality. The previous hope that everything would work out was replaced by a realization that it would not work out unless the system was brought to a level of reliability consistent with the requirements of the contract. It was clear also that this was going to take some time.

The program manager again went back to the customer to plead for schedule relief. Because of the recent debacle they were technically in default and, if the issue was pressed, the entire development could be canceled. The customer eventually agreed to give one more chance, cautioning the program manager that it was his last chance to succeed.

The program manager finally took an interest in the testing activities. The program system engineering staff, hardware engineering, and the support areas of the program organization were placed at the disposal of the system test manager. The program manager scheduled six months to complete the test preparation and made available adequate resources to ensure success. The short-term scheduling techniques which had proven so successful in supporting the software test activities were applied to the system test efforts. With proper support and program level emphasis the test efforts became extremely effective. The system came together in far less than the scheduled six months, and when they were run for the customer they ran perfectly. The system was sold, proved successful in the field, and was consistent with the expectations of the user.

LESSONS LEARNED

This development is representative of the problems which must be dealt with by a test manager if a system is to succeed. The software test manager was extremely effective early in the project. He defined a rigorous test environment, tailored to the characteristics of the program and software application. He planned a controlled testing structure, documented the structure, and ensured that the structure was integrated into the project. He ran into trouble translating the plans into a working project environment. In retrospect, the critical mistake he made was not dealing with the various factions of the project effectively. He only partially implemented the disciplines of testing, choosing to avoid personnel confrontations rather than uniformly enforcing the disciplines. He should have fought essential battles when needed, ensuring that all segments of the project followed the disciplines, not just those that didn't complain.

He should have understood the essential test relationships. A critical mistake was the merging of the test levels. By not understanding the test relationships and discarding the integration test cases for short-term schedule benefit, he affected the long-term success of the project. The test cases used for integration were ineffective and, until the scenarios were defined, did not exercise predetermined segments of the software.

Had the disciplines described in the previous chapters of the book been followed, the problems which almost brought the program to its demise would have been avoided. Seemingly overwhelming crises which occurred and destroyed productivity would have been avoided and any impacts would have been minimal. The environment would have been characterized by the smooth and controlled flow of data and responsibility rather than the uneven structure described in the example.

What held the project together during the periods of difficulty was the effectiveness of the data management and control. The librarian kept the project focused and ensured the integrity of the project structure and environment. Problems which could have destroyed the fiber of the organization were avoided through the actions of the librarian. By integrating the PSL actions with the review and walkthrough actions, all data controlled by the project was of uniform quality.

One critical problem which almost cost the project a successful conclusion could have easily been avoided. When dealing with customers, especially during periods of project stress and difficulty, forthrightness is essential. This particular project locked the customer out, surprising them at the end with an unreliable system. Had the customer been "clued in" early and provided accurate, albeit filtered data, the state of the system would not have been a surprise. Compromises could have been worked out, expectations could have been tailored to the state of the program, and the tests could have been properly scheduled.

What saved this project was the early planning and structure which was built into the testing. Even though the test program ran into difficulty, the early planning provided a structure which could be modified. Only when the structure was discarded did the test effort lose control. When it was reapplied to the subsystem which had not used it the testing proved effective.

The primary lesson learned through this test example is that without planning, structure, and order the testing of a system and the software components has little chance for success.

10 Summary

The previous chapters have described how to plan for, manage, and control the integration and test of a multi-subsystem system configuration.

Project testing requirements, relationships, and plans as described in the book will reduce the risks associated with integration and test of software subsystems.

They will not ensure success nor are they testing panaceas which negate the judicious application of effective testing technologies. The application of a well-planned test structure will reduce the risks of software testing to acceptable levels. Careful planning will reduce the number of unanticipated problems and productivity impacts to a level which can be managed and controlled. These advantages are only realized if the management and control processes used during testing are preplanned and the project structure is, especially during test, smooth, effective, and tailored to the project. Realization of these project characteristics are the responsibility of the test manager and staff and are measured by the cost, schedule, and technical project performance during integration and test.

Implementation of a test environment as described in the book places planning and testing development, implementation, and execution responsibility squarely where it belongs: with the software project and test managers.

Levels of bureaucracy, unnecessary administrative burdens, and management overhead is minimized at the technical levels. Management bureaucracy is replaced with planning, and administrative controls are only applied when they support the project infrastructure. Management overhead is offset by the effectiveness of the project data flow, project reviews, and management control options.

The process of software test management, as with any software management role, is demanding, rigorous, and requires a dedicated commitment for success. The test manager acts as the conduit through which design and code parameters are translated into operational and support capabilities.

Recent advances in software engineering, if judiciously applied to the problems of software development and test, will dramatically extend the range and effectiveness of the test manager. These increases will only be realized if available software engineers, tools, techniques, and methodologies are planned into the testing structure from the beginning, after definition of the goals, objectives, and project requirements. This definition should be the basis for all test planning and, before application to the project, should be agreed to by the layers of management above the test manager who are responsible for test performance and effectiveness and lower organizational levels responsible for implementation of the test program.

Selected testing tools, techniques, and methodologies should bear a clear relationship to these agreed-to needs and be tailored to the project data flow. They project technical, management, and support structure,the personnel needs and experience of the staff, and the project management and control infrastructure.

These parameters, the relationships between code, the support each provides to the phases of development and level of test, and the specific data products which are passed from each individual methodology, project phase, and area of the project must be planned into the project. This planning is hierarchical, starting with the needs and requirements of the program and treeing downwards through the various levels of test planning definition, implementation, execution, and test reporting. The planning should be complete. It should ensure:

1. **Testability and Traceability.** That all documented and approved program, software, design, and performance requirements are tested at some level of testing and that each test requirement is traceable to a basic system parameter.

2. **Success Measurements.** The foundations of the project testing environment are the criteria and techniques to be used for measuring and evaluating the success of test cases being executed. The rigorous testing described in the previous chapters forces the link between testing and the other project activities; requirements definition and analysis, functional and detailed design, code and performance analysis.

3. **Data and Responsibility Transition.** The determinant of productivity during testing is the smoothness of the "handoffs" between test organizational and project support elements and between the various technical areas of the project during test.

Early definition of the flow of work within the software project and early program and software project focus toward testing requirements is the means by which productive transitions are defined. Each project transition, the point at which the software product moves from one development or test activity, should be planned, documented in the Software Development Plan, PPS & C, and other secondary plans, project practices, and procedures. In these plans, project review requirements and acceptance criteria should be clearly specified, as should the steps in "handing off the product to the between organization." The data package requirements for each transition point should be identified, including acceptable content, format, and structure. Finally, the approval and update requirements for the transition package should be described, as should the management relationships.

4. **Resources.** Adequate resources should be planned into the test structure. Monitoring techniques should be used from the beginning to measure the expenditure and application effectiveness of resources. Project alternatives should be planned into the test structure. Monitoring techniques should be used from the beginning to measure the expenditure and effectiveness of resource application. Project alternatives should be considered to deal with anticipated contingencies and methods for avoiding project crises and productivity impacts should be identified.

Software test management requires a consistent, disciplined approach. The software test manager must work very hard, often being the visible center of the project during the latter stages of development. He or she must continually be willing to make decisions and take responsibility. The manager's effectiveness frequently paces the project and limits or enhances productivity.

If the software test manager fails, or the activities for which he or she is responsible bog down, the impact on the software project can be enormous. They include nonacceptable products, poor productivity or, in the worst case, premature project termination.

There is no easy road to effective test management or shortcut to success. There is, when managing the test phases of a project, continuous pressure to shorten schedules and cut budgets. On the surface these cuts often appear feasible by "building more parallel testing into the project" or skipping some levels of integration testing or functional demonstrations.

Long-term project success can only be ensured if the development and test disciplines implicit in the project structure are retained, even in times of stress. Temptations to shorten the development and test cycle by removing or reducing project rigor without restructuring the project environment provide short-term benefit at the expense of long-term development success. Often this leads to chaotic development and test, unacceptable productivity, and poor software quality and reliability.

The application of tools, techniques, technologies, methodologies, and management and technical controls as described in the previous chapters fit the specific project model used. They must be individually analyzed, evaluated, and tailored to the specific characteristics of the project to which they are to be applied. Each test level may not be required for every category of application. The test process used for small projects do not always work for large applications. The application of development and test methodologies may be limited by personnel experience. In short, the test manager must understand his or her project requirements, characteristics, and constraints and tailor a test structure and environment which is consistent with them.

He or she must think before acting. Test management development and implementation is a series of building blocks which must be carefully developed and linked if they are to prove effective. If the foundation is based on feeling rather than thought, or if the manager takes precipitous action without consideration of long-term project impacts or the effects on testing integrity, the entire structure may crumble.

The links between development and test may be lost and, if allowed to continue unchecked, the integrity of the test program may be affected. The test manager function can have a positive, often dramatic effect on the overall success of the project. If based on analysis and reason, the testing phases of the project can be the most productive period. The product has become tangible and observable, personnel on the project are motivated toward completing the project and observing the results of their labor, and all personnel associated with the project are buoyed up by the realization of project goals. Earlier pessimism turns to optimism, problems are solved and, as the system support becomes visible, customer-contractor interfaces improve. The challenge of the test manager is to cause this plan and manage toward this project culmination.

Bibliography

Amadio, M. A. "Breaking the Software Bottleneck," *INTERFACE* (Summer 1980), 27–33.

Baker, F. T. "Chief Programmer Team Management of Production Programming," *IBM Systems Journal,* No.1 (1972), 56–73.

Bersoff, E. H., V. D. Henderson, and S. G. Siegel. *Software Configuration Management—An Investment in Product Integrity.* Englewood Cliffs, N.J.: Prentice-Hall, 1980.

Block, A. *Murphy's Law.* Los Angeles: Price/Stern/Sloan, 1977.

Boehm, Barry W. "Software and Its Impact: A Quantitative Assessment," *Datamation* (May 1973), 48–59.

———, J. R. Brown, and M. Lipow. "Quantitative Evaluation of Software Quality," *Proceedings of the Second International Conference on Software Engineering* (October 1976), 592–605.

———, Charles L. Holmes, Gene R. Ratkus, James P. Ramanos, Robert C. McHenry, and E. Kent Gorden, "Structured Programming Quantitative Assessments," *Computer* (June 1975), 38–54.

Brandon, D. H. *Data Processing Organization and Manpower Planning.* New York: Petrocelli, 1974.

Brooks, Frederick P., Jr. *The Mythical Man-Month: Essays on Software Engineering.* Reading, Mass.: Addison-Wesley, 1974.

Brown, J. R., and M. Lipow. "Testing for Software Reliability," *Proceedings of 1975 International Conference on Reliable Software* (April 1975), 32–38.

Cartwright, D., and D. Zander, eds. *Group Dynamics: Research and Theory,* 3rd ed. New York: Harper & Row, 1968.

Cougar, J. D., and R. A. Zawacki, *Motivating and Managing Computer Personnel.* New York: Wiley-Interscience, 1980.

Daly, E. B. "Management of Software Development," *IEEE Transactions on Software Engineering* (May 1977), 230–42.

Dalkey, Norman, et al. "The Delphi Method IV: Effect of Percentile Feedback and Feeding of Relevant Facts," Rand Corporation (March 1970).

Donelson, William S. "Project Planning and Control," *Datamation* (June 1976), 62–65.

DeRose, B. C., and T. H. Nyman, "The Software Life Cycle: A Management Technological Challenge in the Department of Defense," *IEEE Transactions on Software Engineering* (July 1978), 309–18.

Drucker, P. F. *Management: Tasks, Responsibilities, and Practices.* New York: Harper & Row, 1974.

Evans M., P. Piazza, and J. Dolkas, *Principles of Productive Software Management.* New York: John Wiley and Sons, 1983.

Evans, M., P. Piazza, and P. Sonnenblick. "How to Salvage a Faltering Software Project," NSIA Conference, Washington, D.C. (October 1981).

French, N. "Programmer Productivity Rising Too Slowly: Tanaka," *Computerworld* (1977).

Gildersleeve, T. R. *Data Processing Project Management.* New York: Van Nostrand Reinhold, 1974.

Gunter, R. C. *Management Methodology for Software Product Engineering.* New York: Wiley, 1978.

Hinrichs, J. R. *Practical Management for Productivity.* New York: Van Nostrand Reinhold, 1978.

Hughes, Joan K., and Jay I. Mitchum. *A Structured Approach to Programming.* Englewood Cliffs, N.J.: Prentice-Hall, 1977 (reviewed in *Computer* [November 1977], 110).

"Improved Programming Technologies Management Overview," IBM Data Processing Division (August 1973).

Jeffrey, Seymour, and T. A. Linden. "Software Engineering Is Engineering," *IEEE Computer Society Software Engineering Technical Committee Newsletter* (September 1977), 5–6.

Jensen, R. W., and C. C. Tonies, eds. *Software Engineering* Englewood Cliffs, N.J.: Prentice-Hall, 1979.

Johnson, James R. "A Working Measure of Productivity," *Datamation* (February, 1977), 106–12.

Kernighan, B. W., and P. J. Plauger. *The Elements of Programming Style.* New York: McGraw-Hill, 1974.

Kieder, Stephen P. "Why Projects Fail," *Datamation* (December 1974), 35–37.

Koontz, H., and C. O'Donnell. *Principles of Management: An Analysis of Managerial Functions.* New York: McGraw-Hill, 1972.

McClure, C. L. *Managing Software Development and Maintenance.* New York: Van Nostrand Reinhold, 1981.

McGregor, D. *The Human Side of Enterprise.* New York: McGraw-Hill, 1960.

Metzger, P. W. *Managing a Programming Project,* 2nd ed. Englewood Cliffs, N.J.: Prentice-Hall, 1981.

Mills, Harlan D. "The Complexity of Programs." In *Program Test Methods,* W. C. Hetzel, ed., Englewood Cliffs, N.J.: Prentice-Hall, 1973.

———. "Chief Programmer Teams, Principles, and Procedures," IBM Federal Systems Division Report FSC 71–5108. Gaithersburg, Md., 1971.

———. "Software Development," *IEEE Transactions on Software Engineering* (December 1976), 265–73.

———. "Top-Down Programming in Large Systems." In *Debugging Techniques in Large Systems,* R. Rustin, ed., Englewood Cliffs, N.J.: Prentice-Hall, 1971, 41–55.

Myers, G. J. *Reliable Software through Composite Design.* New York: Petrocelli, 1975.

———. *Software Reliability.* New York: Wiley, 1976.

———. *The Art of Software Testing.* New York: Wiley, 1979.

Perlis, A., F. Sayward, and M. Shaw. *Software Metrics: An Analysis and Evaluation.* Cambridge, Mass.: The MIT Press, 1981.

Pooch, U. W., et al. "Computer Science and Computer Engineering Education in the 80's", *Computer,* **2**, No.9 (September 1978), 60–83.

Putnam, L. H. and A. Fitzsimmons. "Estimating Software Costs", *Datamation* (September 1979), 189–98.

Rogers, E. M., and R. Agarwala-Rogers. *Communication in Organizing.* New York: Free Press, 1976.

Semprevivo, P. C. *Teams in Information Systems Development.* New York: Yourdon Press, 1980.

Shneiderman, B. *Software Psychology.* New York: Winthrop, 1980.

Success of Management of Software Projects. Los Angeles: The MGI Management Institute, 1980.

Stevens, R. T. *Operational Test and Evaluation.* New York: Wiley, 1979. "Structured Walk Through A Project Management Tool," IBM Data Processing Division (August 1974).

Tharrington, J. M. "A Manager's Guide to Measuring Programmer Productivity," *Computerworld* (September 1, 1981), 55–66.

Thomsett, R. *People and Project Management.* New York: Yourdon Press, 1980.

Walston, C., and C. Felix. "A Method of Programming Measurement and Estimation," *IBM Systems Journal,* **16,** No.1 (1977).

Walton, R. E. "Improving the Quality of Work Life," *Harvard Business Review,* (May–June, 1974), 15–16.

Wasserman, Anthony I. "On the Meaning of Discipline in Software Design and Development." In *Software Engineering Techniques,* D. Bates, ed., San Francisco: Infotech International, 1976.

Weinberg, G. *The Psychology of Computer Programming.* New York: Van Nostrand Reinhold, 1971.

Yourdon, E. N. *Classics in Software Engineering.* New York: Yourdon Press, 1979.

———. *How to Manage Structured Programming.* New York: Yourdon Press, 1976.

———. *Managing the Structure Technique.* Englewood Cliffs, N.J.: Prentice-Hall, 1976.

———, and L. Constantine. *Structured Design.* Englewood Cliffs, N.J.: Prentice-Hall, 1977.

———. *Structured Walkthroughs.* Englewood Cliffs, N.J.: Prentice-Hall, 1979.

Index

Architecture, software, 40, 41, 80, 87,
    129, 134
Audit(s), 14, 31, 33, 68, 78, 79, 82, 105, 129
Automated Problem Reporting, 78

Baselines:
    allocated, 87, 88
    code, 7
    configuration management, 86–87, 97, 121
    document, 69, 87
    functional, 73, 87–88
    operations concept, 80
    product, 87–88
    project, 33, 82, 97
    test information, 7
    unit design, 7
    validating, 79
Bottom-up testing, 143, 148
Budgets:
    cost, 19–20, 26, 27, 32, 99, 105, 154, 180,
        181, 183–184, 189
    integration, 64–65
    memory, 40
    program, 30, 190
    timing, 40
    validation, 54
Build:
    allocation, 24, 127–133
    Build Test Folders (BTF), 8–9, 70, 81, 119,
        128, 134–136, 155, 158, 193
    Build Test Plan, 8, 11, 81, 118–119, 128,
        131, 133–134, 193
    certification, 8
    files, 71, 77
    integration, 7, 8, 42, 169–170

    parameters, 69
    planning, 8, 40, 60, 118, 127–134
    test philosophy, 33
    test review, 8
    walkthrough, 81, 132–133
Builds, library, 74, 169–170

Change control, 97–98, 121–122, 166–167
Code:
    development, 41
    evaluation, 126
    modularity, 41
    readability, 41
    requirements, 41
    review, 81
    traceability, 41
Communications protocol, 40, 157
Compatibility, 72
Completeness, 72
Configuration:
    control, *see* Configuration management
    description, 42
    identification, 42
    location, 42
    product approval, 43
    review, 80
    test, 33
Configuration Control Board (CCB), 68, 74–76,
    82
Configuration management:
    application of, 7, 9, 22, 25, 32, 33, 37, 61,
        69, 73, 78, 81, 82, 86–88, 93, 97–98,
        121–122, 124, 167, 190
    area of PSL, 68–70, 74, 167
    files, 69–70, 197